W0038006

Understanding Marriage

A Hong Kong Case Study

琴　棋　書　畫　酒　詩　花
當　丰　件　件　不　離　它
而　今　七　事　都　改　變
柴　米　油　鹽　醬　醋　茶

Music, chess, books, painting, wine, poems and flowers,

Over the years these memories we share;

Though the seven replaced have been

By wood, rice, oil, salt, sauce, vinegar and tea.

Understanding Marriage

A Hong Kong Case Study

Katherine P. H. Young

Hong Kong University Press
香港大學出版社

Hong Kong University Press
139 Pokfulam Road, Hong Kong

© Hong Kong University Press 1995

ISBN 962 209 366 3

All rights reserved. No portion of this
publication may be reproduced or
transmitted in any form or by any means,
electronic or mechanical, including
photocopy, recording, or any information
storage or retrieval system, without
permission in writing from the publisher.

Printed in Hong Kong by Nordica Printing Co., Ltd.

Contents

Preface

This book has been written for counsellors in training as well as for those in active practice who on a daily basis have to deal with real life marital issues, where the sound evaluation of a couple's relationship can greatly aid the spouses and the counsellor. Carefully selected marital assessment measures have been tested for their effectiveness and reliability in providing a way for spouses to describe their experiences. The structured format of the assessment measures enables the spouses to tap into the multi-facets of marital living and to provide the counsellor as an outsider as well as the spouses themselves with a basis on which the issues brought out in the interviewing sessions can be examined and understood.

The concept of interdependence in close relationships has guided the design of the study and, in turn, the central importance of this concept has been reaffirmed in the experiences of the married people involved. It would seem that married people develop mutual reliance and reciprocity in increasing interdependence through sharing the emotional and practical aspects of living together. If they experience their interdependence as adjusted and enjoyable, they move towards increasing attachment and commitment. If the interdependence is experienced as constricting, conflictual or stressful, a marriage may evolve with an exchange orientation, on a balance of equitable returns, or move towards dissolution. At these points spouses may seek counselling.

As counsellors endeavour to get in touch with the spouses' experiences within their marriage, they gradually begin to discern indicators of the nature of the interdependence between the spouses, the way in which these affect their interpretation of events, and their behaviour in response. This book is written from the perspective that as counsellors strive to evolve their developing understanding from what the spouses say during counselling sessions, self report assessment measures provide another valuable source of information.

Acknowledgements

During my work on this study on marriage in Hong Kong I have been impressed by the interest shown in this subject by the many social workers from various agencies. The extensive help that they have readily given me in the arduous work of data collection and the open way in which they have shared their experiences in counselling has made it clear that the condition of marriages in Hong Kong, and the need to understand what makes marriages strong and what can make them go wrong, are matters about which they feel deeply. This concern has led them to offer their help freely on many aspects of the work and to volunteer their expertise and their time.

I acknowledge with gratitude the help that I have received from the many front-line social workers from the Hong Kong Family Welfare Society, the Catholic Marriage Advisory Council, the Caritas Family Service, the Hong Kong Christian Service and the Boys and Girls Club Association, who did the hard work of data collection. I am also grateful to the directors and supervisors of the agencies who supported and encouraged their participation. In particular, I should mention Tom Mulvey, Lolita Wong, Justina Leung and Cheung Sui Kau, who offered helpful advice and critical commentary throughout the course of the research.

During a visit to the University of Minnesota, David Olson encouraged me to look more closely at the usefulness of assessment measures in understanding marriage, and he introduced me to a wide range of rigorously tested instruments. From this, the exciting prospect of adapting assessment scales across cultures evolved.

From a distance I have admired the work of Ronald Sabatelli of the University of Connecticut who has designed and tested assessment measures that seem to reflect the concerns of Chinese spouses seeking counselling. His very prompt response in sending his package of scales developed in association with Erin Cecil-Pigo demonstrated the generosity of fellow academics who unstintingly share their work.

The Dyadic Adjustment Scale was used at one of the largest family services in Hong Kong since it was introduced in training in 1989, and this agency now applies the scale systematically to all marriage counselling cases at the beginning and end of providing service. Gerald Spanier's readiness to allow the scale to be used for educational purposes greatly encourages cross cultural application and is much appreciated.

At a more personal level, my appreciation goes to my colleagues, Nancy Rhind, who meticulously read a raw manuscript and helped to make it more presentable with her many constructive comments, to Patricia Gray for her useful suggestions, and to Law Chi Kong for vetting the statistics. Similarly, I have valued the many personal exchanges with Phyllida Parsloe of the University of Bristol, who has stimulated and pushed my thinking and helped to crystallize my ideas. I appreciate her critical reading of the manuscript.

My reliance on Tam Kwok Kwan, my research worker, has been fully validated. He has organised a large volume of material and produced exciting research analyses that have enabled me to find the links between theory, empirical data and clinical experience. The fact that our normal means of communication was conducted by electronic mail did not appear to deter him and he made light of the distance between Toronto and Hong Kong. I greatly appreciate his persistence and enduring patience.

Finally, I should point out that the study would not have been possible without the cooperation of the one hundred and two couples who shared their experiences so freely and frankly. They offered their stories and the insights gleaned from the triumphs and the struggles of daily living, and their experiences have shaped my views. I am deeply grateful to them.

Katherine Young
3 January 1995

Prologue

When Mr and Mrs Lee walked through the door they were complete strangers to me. Mrs Lee said she did not know what was happening to them and to their relationship, but they seemed to be constantly bickering. She would like an outsider to sort things out with them. When asked what she thought was happening, Mrs Lee said it was all a matter of finances. Their incomes could not stretch to cover paying the mortgage and household expenses of two homes. Mr Lee countered by saying that the matter was his wife's attitude. He could not understand how it was that his wife who throughout the 18 years of their married life had been supportive and understanding, now would not share his joy at owning his own home, and his sense of achievement at the age of 42 of being at last able to provide for his family the way he would like to.

Mr and Mrs Lee are a dual income couple in their early forties with three teenage children. Throughout their married life they had lived in Mrs Lee's family house. Over the years, various members of the maternal family had emigrated and during the last ten years the Lee family had the house to themselves, except for a grandmother who had been left in their care. The maternal extended family had constantly encouraged the Lee family to join them overseas. With the political transition imminent, and with the children nearing the age for college entry, Mrs Lee had in the last two years been pursuing this possibility.

Mr Lee saw no place for himself in a non-Chinese speaking environment. He had come to Hong Kong from mainland China as a youth, engaged in a series of casual labouring jobs and become an overseer in a small, struggling factory. He liked his life here. He had a secure job, a diligent wife, healthy children, enjoyed leisure with his friends and felt that he was doing something worthwhile with his life. The talk of emigration in the family made him feel very insecure. He wanted to go to be with his wife and children, but he feared he would not fit in. In his middle age, he worried that he could not go through the hardships of his youth, or that he would become dependent on relatives. The talk of selling the family house prompted *him to put all his savings into buying a flat. He admitted that working overtime to increase their income meant he had less time with his wife and that his contribution to the overall family expenses was less.*

Running two households had caused havoc in their lives. To please him, Mrs Lee spent time at 'his' place, equipping, cleaning, cooking, and just being there with him. To please her, Mr Lee spent time at 'her' place. Mrs Lee felt very torn, she had been pleased to be the filial daughter looking after her mother. Until they emigrated, she felt she had to maintain the familial household. Increasingly, she heard her husband's clear message that he did not want to leave Hong Kong. She admitted her emotional ties with him to be very strong. She saw her place to be with her husband, and also with her children who wanted to emigrate. She called his purchase of the flat a declaration of intent to live a separate life. He considered the flat a symbol of his hard work and success. She was angry that he would not sacrifice for her and for the children. Buying the flat had used up all their savings, and reduced their means to make a new start elsewhere. She viewed this as selfishness on his part, showing that he was only looking after his own interests, not hers and the children's. More immediately, the two older children were spending more time at the new flat, and making it their base, leaving only the youngest child to keep her company. Mrs Lee felt they were all abandoning her and her old life style. Mr Lee was angry that she could not appreciate his position. He reminded her that he had long wanted to get a place of their own and had remained in her family home for her sake all these years, tolerating and supporting the stream of relatives who regularly returned to what they considered to be their rightful home.

Both wondered whether, despite all the years of sharing in the practical, social, familial, personal and emotional aspects of their lives, changing circumstances would now force them to live separate lives in the future, and that they would have to begin to look after their own interests.

In the short hour that we spent in our first meeting I was made privy to a vast amount of information regarding the Lees' life and marriage. They described in some detail their respective views on various events and issues, and what each considered to be the other's caring or non-caring responses. With a great deal of feeling, each repeatedly expressed the wish to make things work, interjected with expressions of anger and disappointment. 'Why are you doing this to me?' 'Why won't you do this for me?' 'Why must you always have things on your terms?' 'If you do not care enough for me to do what I am asking, is there any future for us together?'

In their bewilderment, they had turned to a counsellor for an impartial opinion, for assistance in reviewing their relationship and renegotiating a different balance. I had been drawn into the Lees' marriage.

In Hong Kong, almost every day husbands and wives seek help to sort out various aspects of living that affect their marriages. In a brief period of time, they pour out their feelings, aspirations and disappointments, the anger and pain that they feel, sometimes reaching back over the whole span of their relationship. Social workers as counsellors are faced with the complex task of immediately creating a safe climate for painful material to emerge and to develop a rapport with the spouses. At the same time, they have to organize the often confusing and partially given information in a form which makes sense to the clients and to themselves. To do this effectively they need a framework for assessing and understanding the multi-faceted and sometimes paradoxical aspects of this complex relationship.

The Hong Kong Marital Study seeks to provide a framework for understanding marriages, and assessment measures to aid the search for understanding.

Introduction

It has long been assumed that Asian marriages enjoy an intrinsic stability not to be found elsewhere and that an enduring quality is to be found in the relationship, based on tradition and family ties. This may once have been true. But to an increasing extent it is an assumption that cannot be supported by the evidence around us. Marital problems and dissolution are on the increase in Hong Kong, and this increase is exponential compared to the situation a generation ago.

This is not surprising. If it is true that the marital relationship can break down when inexorable external pressures bear on it, then many marriages in Hong Kong are at risk. Over the last decade our society has been presented with social and political problems of an unprecedented nature which have had an inevitable effect on our perception of personal ties, and on long-term marital and family stability. Global economists may be fond of pointing to Hong Kong in their search for an ideal example of free market enterprise, but marriage counsellors here have begun to count the cost of such frenetic activity in human terms.

In 1991, the Hong Kong Council of Social Services reported that out of an active counselling caseload of 9795, the main problem in 2284 or 23.3% of the cases was identified as some aspect of the marital relationship. Another cluster of 2576 (34.5%) cases, classified as parental-child, child care and child dispute cases, could be directly or indirectly associated with marital difficulties. The Social Welfare Department Annual Report (1990/1991) recorded for 1991, intakes of marital conflict cases to be 2854, as well as 198 cases of battered wives, 108 cases of child dispute, 374 in-law relationship difficulties, amongst a host of problems involving family relationships and children and young persons. The Department also carried a caseload of 1937 single parents though these included both widowed and separated parents. In 1981 the Judiciary reported that 2811 cases of divorce petitions were filed and 2060 decrees absolute granted. By 1991 this had risen to 7287 petitions and 6295 decrees absolute (Hong Kong Annual Report, 1992). The Hong Kong 1991 Population Census recorded that in the ten year span from 1981 to 1991, the percentage of divorced or separated men and women had doubled from 0.6% to 1.2% (Hong Kong Census and Statistics, 1991).

These figures may not compare with those of many other countries, in particular those of highly developed and industrialized countries such as the United States. However, in terms of the amount of distress and disruption to personal life, and in terms of the increasing number of spouses seeking help over tensions in their marriage, the indications are that marital issues in Hong Kong have begun to assume dimensions similar to those experienced elsewhere.

In Hong Kong, there is growing concern over threats to the stability of marriage as seen in the accelerating phenomenon of marital dissolution and the serious personal and social consequences that follow from this. The breakup of a marriage is an intensely personal experience which has widespread implications. Sustained efforts are now being made to promote a belief in the centrality of the family (Strachan, 1993) and in the marital relationship on which the family is based, and work is being done at the theoretical and clinical levels to understand the complexities which surround marital and family issues. The search for more effective practices in marriage counselling has focused attention on the need for assessment and intervention approaches culturally relevant for Chinese couples.

Concern over the quality and stability of marriage has been a central issue of research theorists for decades. Research in the 1960s in the United States focused on the relevance of various demographic characteristics, personality, and certain social variables as they affect marital happiness and permanence. Studies on the marital life cycle produced the surprising finding 'that children tend to detract from rather than contribute to marital happiness' (Hicks, and Platt, 1970). Reviews in the 1970s reported continued interest in the study of the effects of children on marriage, on marital quality over the life cycle and at transition points. New topics that emerged at this time reflected the social trends of the decade. These were cohabitation, student marriages, extramarital affairs, the impact of social networks, and the effects of wife employment (Spanier and Lewis, 1980). By the 1980s the scope of research had expanded to include feminist perspectives, new family forms in remarriage and stepfamilies, the marriages of older couples, marriages of different ethnic groups, and the effect of employment and family policy on marriage and the family (Berado, 1990).

We are now asking very similar questions to those raised by researchers on marriage in the 1960s in the West. In the face of accelerating change, and increasing demands on marriage to provide a quality relationship for spouses, a care giving foundation for the next generation, and a care taking resource for the older generation, what qualities are needed to enable couples to meet such expectations?

In 1991, a study on marriage in Hong Kong was conducted to gain some understanding of this pair relationship by asking husbands and wives to describe their experiences. Through this process, the aim was to experiment with certain assessment procedures in order to derive some meaningful patterns and classifications, from which a theoretical framework could be developed. The study tested a selection of self report instruments to determine their usefulness in understanding marriages. The aim was to derive assessment measures appropriate and meaningful for Hong Kong spouses. This book examines the findings of the Hong Kong marital study.

Some of the material presented may seem to be unnecessarily technical and at times the reader may be overwhelmed by the statistical data and tables that are presented. An attempt has been made to keep this material at a minimum, and the bulk of it has been relegated to the Appendices, where it may be referred to by practising counsellors. It has been necessary to include this material to demonstrate the reliability and validity of the self report measures that are used. This book has been written for practising counsellors who on a daily basis have to deal with real life issues where sound assessment could greatly aid both the spouses and the counsellor in their search for clarification and resolution.

Organization of the Chapters

This study on marriage in Hong Kong is written from the perspective that people enter into marriage to achieve an interdependent relationship where they can rely on each other for their happiness and well-being. The nature of this interdependence and the manner in which it affects the marital relationship and spousal transactions is analysed through the couples' experiences.

The book is divided into three parts. Part I presents the Hong Kong Marital study, and the spouses' descriptions of their marriages. In Chapter 1 the importance of assessment in understanding marriages is discussed. The development of technological innovations in the West for the analysis of personal relationships offers assessment instruments of proven reliability and validity. Three self report measures have been selected for use in the study, and these are tested for their effectiveness in examining marriages in Hong Kong and for their capacity in getting the spouses to open up and to participate actively in describing their experiences within their marriages. Chapter 2 presents the Hong Kong Marital Study, and examines the reliability and discriminant validity of the three self report measures, the Dyadic Adjustment Scale, ENRICH, and the Marital Comparison Level Index package of scales. Items from these scales with a high discriminant capacity for differentiating between adjusted and non-adjusted marriages are selected to develop a self report measure relevant for Hong Kong. Chapter 3 describes the couples' retrospective review of their relationship during the structured interviews. The couples' evaluation illustrates the unique aspects of what goes on between them as husband and wife, as seen through their feelings over the sense of 'fit' which greatly determines their perception and interpretation of what the other does or does not do.

The three chapters in Part II further analyse responses on the self report measures for variations in marital experiences. Besides differences between adjusted and non-adjusted spouses, other variations are to be found in the marital experience. Analysis to discover the nature of these diverse patterns of marital interaction has produced eight types. These are presented in Chapter 4, where case vignettes derived from cluster analysis of ENRICH scores are included to give the human picture of the unique experiences of the spouses in each marriage. The complex nature of marriage makes it inevitable that other variations will occur during the life cycle of any marriage. Moreover, in a Chinese society such as Hong Kong, gender differences and the nature of relationships between generations impact importantly on marriages. Data on these aspects will be analysed in Chapter 5 and Chapter 6.

The three chapters in Part III discuss the theoretical base which gradually crystallized as findings from the study confirmed or disproved observations of cultural propensities and observations from clinical experience. The spouses' views of what they value in their marriages indicate the emergence in contemporary Hong Kong of a shift in expectations in marriage. This transition from a pragmatic perspective of the institution of marriage to expectations of companionship in marriage is examined in Chapter 7. The spouses' description of their experience of relational interdependence is examined in Chapter 8. Marriage is perceived as a partnership in which a couple evolve interdependence within the emotional and physical space of the marital boundaries. The processes of developing interdependence, developing adjustment and developing means of coping with conflicts are closely interrelated and together they determine the spouses' experience within the relationship. To understand what goes on in the marriage requires tapping into these processes. Analysis of data from the study revealed refinements in the concept of interdependence. The interdependence which spouses evolve can be one with a commitment orientation, or an equity orientation, or an exchange orientation. Factor analysis indicates three distinct scales for measuring commitment, equity and exchange orientations. These combined with items reported in Chapter 2 are compiled to form a Marital Relationship Index particularly suitable for application in Hong Kong. Spouses with these different orientations negotiate and transact within their relationships differently. Chapter 9 suggests that an awareness of these differences enables the counsellor to assess whether the spouses are operating from a cooperative or a competitive stance and to utilize appropriate means to facilitate negotiations between the spouses. Spouses with a commitment orientation are likely to use more bonding processes and activities in their negotiations. Spouses who use more bargaining negotiations may be considered to be experiencing inequity and uncertainty as regards fair exchange for their efforts.

Each chapter focuses on an area of interest. The data is presented and discussed in the context of its relevance to the practising social worker. In order to assess the data and the issues involved in a wider perspective, reference will be made to the experience and research of others working in the same area, either in other communities or, when available, in Hong Kong. Each chapter is rounded off with a theoretical discussion on the implications of the findings for marriage work.

Part I

The Hong Kong Marital Study

Chapter One

Studying Marriages in Hong Kong

This chapter discusses the importance of assessment and the role of self report measures in this process. Self report measures provide a quick preliminary assessment of the spouses' evaluation of their marriage. This enables an outsider such as a marriage counsellor, and the spouses as participants of the relationship, some understanding of the background against which issues and events past and present can be considered in context.

In the study and conceptualization of marriage three major approaches have been used to address and analyse the many dimensions of this dyadic relationship.

The psychodynamic tradition views marriage as a relationship most similar in nature to the early caring experience of the parent child bond. The spouse is expected to be a caring person who meets affectional and dependency needs, offers comfort and reaffirms the partner's sense of worth. The partners choose each other to complement and supplement themselves as they mutually support each other in the next phase of their development as adults. Marriage creates a safe setting to promote further growth and to rework unresolved issues of the past. Marital distress occurs when these expectations of mutual gratification are unfulfilled. From the psychodynamic perspective, assessment focuses on intrapsychic conflicts and also interpersonal conflicts from unmet needs arising from both outside and within the spouses' awareness (Meissner, 1978; Nadelson, 1978).

The systemic perspective focuses on the feedback transactions between spouses within the marital boundaries, as they negotiate to meet their own and their partner's needs for affectional and power sharing. Marital distress stems from tensions in the system as it adjusts to the changing needs and requirements of each spouse, from the relationship and from the impact of life circumstances. Assessment is an integral part of therapy on this approach, and tends to focus on specific themes, dimensions and sequences of behaviour, which reflect particular tensions in the system (Guerin, 1987; Gurman, 1978)

The behavioral perspective sees spouses as engaging in a reciprocal exchange of reinforcing behaviour. Cognitive and affective aspects affect the interaction, influencing the partners' views of each other, their feelings and their behavioral transactions. Marital distress results from disturbance in the balance of rewarding and non-rewarding experiences. Assessment is essential to this conceptualization. In fact, many of the standardized and most rigorously tested assessment measures are derived from this theoretical framework (Jacobson and Margolin, 1979; Weiss, 1978).

Marriage counsellors have usually been trained in one or the other of these or associated approaches and generally their working experience has been influenced by that particular perspective. Although their theoretical conceptualizations of marriage may differ, each approach has made important contributions to the understanding of marriage, and each offers a rich array of innovative interventions to guide therapeutic endeavours.

The Assessment and Evaluation of Marriage

It should be noted that all three approaches emphasize the importance of assessment (Gurman, 1978:541). Assessments made from the different perspectives may address different dimensions, but they all share a common viewpoint regarding the purposes of assessment. Assessment which is the gathering and organizing of information serves to enable the outsider as well as the spouses as insiders to evaluate their experiences within the relationship, to identify those aspects which are fulfilling and those that lead to distress. The understanding which emerges from a thorough assessment often suggests directions for changes that are needed for the maintenance and continuation of the marriage.

Each of the various approaches to studying close relationships, through observation, interviewing, diaries and log books, have their particular advantages and disadvantages. The study of marriage deals with many of the intangible and non-observable aspects of human relationships, such as feelings, expectations, thoughts and personal attributions, as well as private events, intimate only to the spouses, such as kissing, sexual activities and conflict (Harvey, Christensen and McClintock, 1983). Such information is only available through the reports of the participants themselves.

Since the Hong Kong Marital Study seeks to draw out this form of personal and private information, self report measures have been selected as the most appropriate method to permit the spouses themselves to describe their experiences as participants of the relationship.

Self Report Measures

It could be said that self report measures first found their place in the assessment procedures of marital work when Hamilton applied his 13-item measure to assess marriage in 1929. Since then there has been steady progress in the development of marital scales. Initially, many of these were too lengthy to be suitable for widespread use, including Terman's scales which appeared in 1938. However, in the 1960s the 15-item Locke-Wallace Marital Adjustment Test gained in popularity and began to be applied extensively (1959). It served as the yardstick for testing the validity of many subsequent marital inventories. In 1976, after conducting a critical and extensive review of research, theoretical propositions, and the measurement scales then being used, Spanier presented the Dyadic Adjustment Scale (Spanier, 1976; Spanier, and Cole, 1976). This has since become one of the most frequently cited and utilized scales by both clinicians and researchers.

The use of computer technology over the last two decades has led to a tremendous growth in the development and refinement of measurement format and methodology. Some of these measurement instruments are designed as multi-dimensional assessments of marital quality or stability. Marital quality is variously defined by different researchers as satisfaction, adjustment, happiness or success (Lewis and Spanier, 1979). Some instruments are specifically focused on assessing instability; and concern over marital breakdown has led to the identification of variables associated with marital dissolution (Booth and Edwards, 1987; Weiss and Cerreto, 1980). Some instruments examine various aspects of a marital dimension, such as intimacy (Miller and Lefcourt, 1982), conflict (Strauss, 1979) and communication (Fitzpatrick, 1988). A number of these self report measures have been extensively tested in research and clinical usage (Fowers and Olson, 1989; Norton, 1983; Synder, 1979; Taylor and Morrison, 1984). Some have been translated and used across cultures. Critical analysis of these measures in a variety of studies has led to regular revision and helped to disseminate information on them and on the findings they provide (Fredman and Sherman, 1987; Sabatelli, 1988).

Self report measures can help to expedite information gathering as they tap basic aspects of the marital relationship systematically and efficiently. The precise format of these measures helps to structure the responses of both husbands and wives. A carefully designed scale can comprehensively survey relevant areas and specify aspects which are fulfilling as well as aspects which are disturbing. Moreover, the matter of fact format in which these scales are worded helps the spouses to reduce reactivity and emotionality in describing their marriage.

In the design and application of self report scales, some of their limitations have been identified and attempts have been made to build in means to address these (Galligan, 1982). Of particular concern is the possibility of bias arising from the respondents' tendency to answer according to conventional norms or according to what they consider to be socially desirable. Some marital inventories, such as ENRICH, have built in idealistic distortion items and statistically readjusted scores to take account of conventionality and social desirability. A more serious bias actually arises from the very nature of self reports, which require retrospective recall and memory retrieval. This could be distorted over time, by the interference of other events, by selective attention to particular features and neglect of other salient aspects. Moreover, the current state of the relationship may affect the interpretation of past events. Such possibilities must be taken into account in reading the responses in self rating measures.

Over the years there has been active debate over the application of self report assessment measures in clinical settings. Advocates for tapping the spouses' perspective through self report measures argue that the specific items on these scales stimulate and activate the respondents' evaluation of particular aspects of the relationship. They also provide a structured format for the precise expression of an insider view which serves to supplement the professional outsiders' view which can be impressionistic and unstandardized. Opponents of structured assessment procedures feel that the scales restrict spontaneous and idiosyncratic responses, and reduce dynamic processes to static statistics (Schwartz and Breulin, 1983). However, the one particular treatment setting where self reports have increasingly been used to contribute to treatment decision has been in marital work (Baucom and Epstein, 1990; Crowe and Ridley, 1990; Weeks and Hof, 1989).

The design and development of self report measures is a rigorous process requiring multi-disciplinary contribution, extensive testing to ensure their validity and reliability and careful revision and refinement. Hong Kong has yet to develop assessment instruments that comprehensively measure the multiple dimensions of family and marital relationships. Until it does it will need to borrow and modify instrumemts from other cultures and to test these out for their relevance in the Chinese context.

The Choice of Self Report Measures for the Hong Kong Marital Study

When instruments derived from and designed for a different culture are used, their cross-cultural relevance and potential for transfer is necessarily a prime consideration. The measures selected should focus on essential issues relevant to spouses in societies at the same level of social and economic development. In addition, the theoretical orientation on which the instrument is based has to complement the research framework of the study to ensure that the information sought effectively pinpoints and draws out the empirical data needed for analysis.

The Measuring Instruments

The three measures selected for use in the Hong Kong study are:
— Spanier's Dyadic Adjustment Scale, the DAS (Spanier, 1976);
— Olson's Evaluating Relationship Issues Communication & Happiness inventory, the ENRICH (Olson, Fournier & Druckman, 1987);
— Sabatelli and Cecil-Pigo's Marital Comparison Level Index, and related scales on equity, commitment, and barriers to dissolution, the MCLI package (Sabatelli, 1984; Sabatelli & Cecil-Pigo, 1985).

A particular strength of the Spanier's Dyadic Adjustment Scale is that it addresses adjustment processes in close relationships. In an extensive review of conceptual and methodological issues to determine a precise definition, Spanier and Cole (1976) selected adjustment as the most appropriate variable to reflect the quality of a relationship. They defined adjustment as an ever changing on-going interactional process in a relationship. The intention of the Hong Kong Marital Study is to examine the processes adopted by spouses as they accommodate to each other in mutual adjustment. The Dyadic Adjustment Scale (DAS) was selected as the most suitable instrument to provide information on interpersonal *processes* within the marital boundaries.

The adjustment processes of spouses focus on many aspects of living. Spouses are responding and adjusting to each other constantly in their daily transactions. They adjust their communication and conflict coping patterns, their personal propensities, ethical and equalitarian stances, their sexual and affectional relations to accommodate the other. They adjust to each other over the practical issues of arranging finance, leisure activities, and over family issues of relationship with their children, family and friends. An inventory which comprehensively covers these issues, thus ensuring that information from these areas is included in the assessment, is to be found in ENRICH, the inventory for Evaluating Nurturing Relationship Issues Communication and Happiness developed by David Olson and his associates (Olson, Fournier, and Druckman, 1987). ENRICH is a multi-dimensional inventory which addresses the entire spectrum of essential concerns of married people, incorporating processes as well as aspects of content. For this study, ENRICH has been specifically selected to provide information on the content of marital transactions.

In the process of adjusting to each other over the myriad aspects of daily living married people become increasingly interdependent on each other to meet their expectations of a secure relationship in which needs are met. To assess the *outcome* in interdependency of couples, this study has applied a package of scales from the Marital Comparison Level Index, or MCLI, which includes scales on expectation, commitment, equity, and barriers to dissolution. These factors, according to Sabatelli and Cecil-Pigo (1985) the originators of this package, contribute to the experience of interdependence in relationships.

These three marital inventories tap different aspects of marriage in a complementary manner. Each provides extensive information on overall marital functioning. However, in this study each has been especially selected for its specific focus.

For ———> Assessing	Process of adjusting	Content of spousal transactions	Outcome in interdependence
The Instrument Selected ———>	DAS	ENRICH	MCLI package

In combination, these measures provide a rich and comprehensive volume of data. Each addresses a number of marital dimensions. Nevertheless, before using them for an understanding of marriages in Hong

Kong a careful review of their relevance for Chinese couples was made. The scales were translated into Chinese, then back to English independently by another group, and were further refined after pilot tests. The translation team debated extensively the modifications required in the cross-cultural transfer and in the translation into another language. These will be alluded to in the discussion on each of the three scales.

In summary, the Hong Kong Marital Study has selected these three inventories to assess marriages of Chinese spouses for the following reasons. First, in the translation and testing of the translation, these assessment measures have been found to contain items meaningful to the Hong Kong respondents. Second, the dimensions addressed by these measures are compatible with the conceptual framework of the study. Third, their psychometric properties have been proven in rigorous research testing and in clinical usage. Fourth, they can be efficiently administered and accurately scored in clinical settings. Further details of DAS, ENRICH and the MCLI package in Chinese and English are presented in Appendix 1.

The Dyadic Adjustment Scale

The Dyadic Adjustment Scale, DAS, is a 32-item marital inventory with four subscales on affectional expression, consensus, cohesion and satisfaction. Spanier and his associates consider that these subscales adequately demonstrate the levels of adjustment in pair relationships. The more positive the subjective experience of each spouse in these aspects the happier the relationship. **Affectional expression** taps the nature of sexual and loving interactions in the relationship. **Dyadic consensus** refers to the spouses' agreement or disagreement in a number of areas of living, finance, recreation, religion, friends, conventional behaviour, philosophy of life and goals, relationship with parents, time together, decision making, household tasks, leisure and career concerns. **Dyadic cohesion** relates to shared activities, discussing ideas, laughing and working together. **Dyadic satisfaction** reflects the general sense of happiness and confidence in the future of the relationship, as seen in confiding, kissing, no regrets, frequency levels of fights, quarrels and irritations in spousal transactions.

The range of scores on the DAS is 0-151. Each of the subscales is made up of a different number of items, and the various items are weighted differently. The scores for affectional expression range from 0-12; consensus from 0-65; cohesion from 0-24; and satisfaction from 0-50. In Spanier's study (1976), the mean score for married and divorced spouses was 114.8 and 70.7. In a recently completed study on active marriage counselling cases in Hong Kong, the mean score for husbands and wives

in committed marriages was 116.4 and 101.1; and in conflictual marriages, the mean score was 74.3 and 66.1 (Young, 1993: 17).

Tests by Spanier and his associates on a purposive sample of married
and divorced respondents in 1976 showed coefficient alphas of overall
dyadic adjustment at .96, for affectional expression at .73, for consensus
at .90, for cohesion at .86, and for satisfaction at .94 (Spanier, 1976). A
confirmatory analysis of the DAS has demonstrated that subscale factors
account for 94% of the co-variance among the items (Spanier and
Thompson, 1982). Tests with other populations in Australia (Sharpley
and Cross, 1982), Canada (Sabournin, Laporte and Wright, 1990), with
Mexican Americans (Casas and Ortiz, 1985) confirm the validity and
reliability of the DAS when applied across cultures. By 1988, Spanier
reported that more than a thousand studies have applied the scale. While
clinicans adopt the scale to provide a measure of adjustment in a marriage, marital researchers have continued to use and to cite the DAS as
the measure to determine criterion groups. Many of these studies adopt
the 200 couple score to differentiate between marriages.

The DAS is the most frequently cited, utilized and criticized marital
scale. Some researchers have criticized the instrument for including both
descriptive and evaluative items. They point out that specific reports of
behaviour can be confounded by attitudinal inferences, making precise
interpretation uncertain. An example of this is the statement on agreement or disagreement over sexual relations. From the wording, it is unclear
whether the referent point addresses the degree of agreement, or the
degree of sexual exchange (Fincham and Bradbury, 1987; Huston and
Robins, 1982; Norton, 1983). The uneven weighting of the subscales has
also been criticized by other researchers on the ground that the contribution of each of the four dimensions to overall adjustment is not balanced
or explained (Fincham and Bradbury, 1987; Norton, 1983). In clinical
practice this unbalanced weighting tends to make feedback to clients
cumbersome.

The 32 items in the DAS address essential concerns basic to most
marriages. These items refer to the ordinary aspects of daily life and they
are relevant to married people in Hong Kong. The DAS has already been
tested in clinical practice in Hong Kong and has been well received by
clients (Young, 1993). Translation into Chinese has been a straightfor-
ward matter as the precise wording and the specific focus of each item is
meaningful to Chinese spouses. The DAS is regarded as being biased
towards traditional assumptions (Fitzpatrick, 1988). This actually makes it
more appropriate for Hong Kong marriages. Scores from the DAS give a
preliminary indication of adjustment within the marital boundaries. When
it is administered at the beginning and at the end of therapy it offers a
measure of changes in the relationship.

The ENRICH marital inventory

In 1981 David Olson and his associates devised ENRICH, the Evaluating Nurturing Relationship Issues Communication and Happiness inventory, as a measuring instrument to assist clinical and educational activities in marriage counselling and enrichment programmes. ENRICH was a logical development of an earlier inventory, PREPARE, or the Premarital Personal and Relationship Evaluation inventory, a measure which assesses premarital attitudes of couples participating in marriage preparation programmes. Since the 1970s, Olson and his team reviewed and evaluated a large number of instruments prior to designing, testing and refining PREPARE and ENRICH. The two instruments have the same design format, and have been put through equally rigorous testing procedures for their psychometric aspects and applicability (Fournier, Olson and Druckman, 1983).

ENRICH is a 125-item multi-dimensional inventory which provides a framework for analysing relationship issues such as **communication, conflict resolution** and **sexual relations;** spousal issues such as **personality, equalitarian roles** and **ethical orientation**; couple issues such as **satisfaction, adaptability, cohesion** and **idealistic distortion**; family issues such as **children and parenting, relationships with family and friends**; and life style issues of **financial management** and **leisure.** The inventory is organized into 14 subscales or categories. Of these, eleven categories contain 10 items, and three 5 items. The shorter subscales are idealistic distortion, adaptability and cohesion. Spouses are asked to respond to each item on a 5 point range of strongly agree or disagree or undecided.

Both the husband and the wife are required to complete answer sheets which are sent to PREPARE-ENRICH Incorporated for computer analysis. The ENRICH Couple Profile which is returned contains individual scores for the husband and the wife, and a couple score, the Positive Couple Agreement, PCA. The profile also includes a chart on the husband's and wife's type of marriage according to the Circumplex model. Individual scores are computed and adjusted for social desirability according to their entries on idealistic distortion. Couples scores (PCA -Positive Couple Agreement) are arrived at by organizing each spouse's responses into four types: positive agreement (both agree, a strength in the relationship); disagreement (each recording opposing views, therefore a work area); special focus (negative agreement, both agree the issue is a problem, an area for special focus for marriage enrichment or counselling); and indecision (one or both undecided, hence requiring attention and discussion). These procedures help to identify each scale as either a relationship strength or a work area for the couple.

Tests by Olson's team report that the ENRICH inventory was able to discriminate happily from unhappily married couples with 85-95% accuracy (Fowers and Olson, 1989). The alpha coefficient of the scales ranged from .86 for marital satisfaction to .68 for equalitarian roles, testifying to the reliability of the ENRICH scales (Olson, Fournier and Druckman, 1987: 67).

The ENRICH inventory is often referred to in research and clinical literature. Critical review of the instrument itself has come mainly from Olson and his associates in their attempts to ensure its validity and clinical utility. However, the Circumplex model of which ENRICH constitutes one of a package of measures has come under careful scrutiny. Much of the criticism focuses on the conceptualization of the curvilinear nature of cohesion and adaptability (Beavers and Voeller, 1984; Epstein, Bishop, and Baldwin, 1984). According to the Circumplex model, balanced levels of separateness and connections in cohesion, and balanced levels of flexibility and structure in adaptability, are functional. Extremes in disengagement and enmeshment, or extreme adaptability in constant change can be chaotic, while displays of extreme rigidity are problematic for the relationship. Critics argue that high levels of adaptability, that is high ability to change can be functional, and that absence of pathology in the balanced range does not necessarily imply optimal health.

In translating ENRICH into Chinese, the scale on **religious orientation** presented some difficulties. The original sponsor of PREPARE/ENRICH was a Church organization, and the inventory was devised for people with Christian beliefs. While some spouses in the Hong Kong sample were Christians, others were Buddhist, Taoist, or subscribed to ancestral worship or folk beliefs. The translation team decided to interpret religious orientation as ethical orientation, encompassing a philosophy of living that guides behaviour in Chinese people without emphasizing any formal religious association. In this regard, the most difficult item to translate was 'praying together' — item 65. This could refer to communication with a higher being, a shared spiritual experience, or possibly both. The translation team had to decide what could be an equivalent experience for people who may not believe in a higher being. The difficulty lay not in finding the right form of words but in transmitting the essence of what praying together contributes to a marriage. The translators settled on shared spiritual communion (對我來說，與我的配偶心靈相通是十分重要的。). Two other items required some modification. Item 76 'I believe that our marriage should include active religious involvement' was translated as 'I believe that our marriage should include actively practising our ethical values.' (我相信我們的婚姻應該包括積極的道德/文化實踐。) Item 89 'In loving my partner, I feel that I am able to better understand the concept that God is love,' was rendered as 'In loving my partner, I feel that I am able to better understand the concept of love.' (在愛我的配偶

之時，我感到更能深入了解愛的真諦。) In application, as demonstrated by the findings, the Ethical Orientation scale which addressed abstract issues was of importance in drawing out the essence of intimate sharing in marriage.

The theoretical position adopted by ENRICH is that marriage incorporates multiple facets of living. The combined experience of the partners in all these areas determines their sense of satisfaction and general well-being.

The advantage of using ENRICH in the Hong Kong Marital Study is that it comprehensively covers most areas of marital transactions. It is designed to enable each spouse to note specific details of the relationship, and thus it readily provides a more accurate record than could be tediously obtained through verbal responses in an interview. Most importantly, ENRICH provides dyadic measurement in the form of a positive couple agreement score — a joint assessment which emphasizes the collaborative nature of marital interdependence.

The Marital Comparison Level Index package

The Marital Comparison Level Index package comprises four scales on expectation, equity, commitment, and barriers to dissolution. These scales in combination constitute the third instrument that has been selected for use in the Hong Kong study.

The scales of the Marital Comparision Level Index have been designed on the basis that the spouses' experience of interdependence in their daily transactions contributes to their overall sense of satisfaction and to the maintainance of the relationship. Couples who experience high levels of interdependence as reflected in their evaluation that expectations are met, that they are committed to each other, that constraints against dissolution are strong, are likely to consider their marriage as fulfilling and stable. Couples who experience a lower level of interdependence may be more concerned with fair exchange and an equitable balance as the possibility of dissolution increases, since they perceive their marriage as lacking in fulfilment and face uncertainty as regards the continued stability of the relationship.

Many of the spouses in the study described their marriages in terms of expectations fulfilled or otherwise, with their sense of stability being determined by their partner's commitment, or by the achievement of equity or fair balance in reciprocity. In some vulnerable marriages, some spouses referred to constraints against dissolution even as they discussed the difficulties of remaining in the relationship. The Marital Comparison Level Index package of scales (Sabatelli, 1984; Sabatelli, and Cecil-Pigo,

1985)) tap into these dimensions on the assumption that where benefits from a marriage are equal or better than expected, then the spouses will consider their relationship as rewarding. Conversely, where benefits are less than expected, the spouses would have more complaints against the relationship.

The Marital Comparison Index and the related scales on commitment, equity and barriers to dissolution were developed by Sabatelli and Cecil-Pigo from a perspective of interpersonal processes based on social exchange theory. The scales are designed with a comparative stance and with a consideration of alternatives available.

The **Marital Comparison Index** in particular focuses on the comparative process by which spouses evaluate their marital experience in contrast to their expectations. Respondents are asked to rate if their experience in the relationship on each item is better than expected, about what they expected, or worse than expected. This comparative stance recognises that each person's expectations from marriage varies, so that a similiar amount of time together may be defined by one spouse as acceptable and as expected, or defined as inadequate and less than expected by another. The comparision level against which a person measures his experience is a standard that he/she has internalized from past and present experiences and observation in interpersonal relationships. Sabatelli proposed a 32-item unidimensional index on a seven-point scale. Cronbach alpha of the scale was .93. Factor loading for the 32 items ranged from .77 to .38 (Sabatelli and Cecil-Pigo, 1985).

In the Hong Kong Marital Study, 20 items were extracted from the MCLI. These included five items on general expectations of marriage in commitment, compatibility, mutual respect and physical attractiveness; five items to cover affectional and sexual expectations; five items dealing with coping with conflict; and five items on sharing equally , in confiding, time together, life style, and household tasks. These items are rated on a five-point scale.

Relational commitment reflects stability and cohesion in a relationship, balanced against the alternatives available. This scale defines commitment as the tendency to remain in the relationship, and not consider alternatives as viable. The scale consists of six items, on a five-point liker-type scale. It has an alpha reliability of .82 (Sabatelli and Cecil-Pigo, 1985).

In applying these measures, the Hong Kong study has also been influenced by Murstein and McDonald (1983), who include permanency in the relationship and attachment to spouse in their definition of commitment. On this basis, commitment in the relationship can in itself be rewarding, and the partners function to provide rewards for each other without consideration of returns. Accordingly, the commitment scale was modified: two items from Sabatelli and Cecil-Pigo have been included and four questions on commitment, couched to reflect investment in the spouse and the relationship beyond reciprocal considerations, were added.

The scale on **relational equity** developed by Cecil-Pigo and Sabatelli to accompany the commitment scale, puts into operation Homans' proposition (1974) that, to be equitable, distributive justice requires that rewards in relationship exchanges should be proportionate to investment. This scale contains items which reflect an equity orientation by tapping into the respondents' perception as to whether the relationship they experience is fair in the way they contribute and share equally, are equally dependent, and share power equally. Some items manifest more of an exchange orientation, a perception that they put in more than they get out, and that they feel taken advantage of, cheated, or manipulated. From a review of the 10 items on this scale it is possible to measure two different orientations, an equity and an exchange orientation. All the items on this scale have been adopted in the Hong Kong study. The Cronbach alpha of this scale is .85.

Sabatelli and Cecil-Pigo's scale on **barriers to dissolution** has been influenced by Levinger's research (1965) which proposed that deterrents against separation can come from both internal and external constraints. Internal constraints refer to moral prescriptions against marital dissolution, and external constraints refer to obligations of family and social restraints. This 11 item scale has a reliability alpha of .74 (Sabatelli, and Cecil-Pigo, 1985).

One item, that 'marriage is forever', from the barriers scale has been included in the Hong Kong study. Other items were added to reflect cultural restraints against marital separation. For Hong Kong spouses, internal barriers are likely to be a sense of loss over leaving a marriage, and a fear of the future; while concern over the impact of dissolution on significant people in their lives, particularly children and the spouses' parents, could constitute external barriers.

The Marital Comparision Level Index assesses the outcome of relationships, in terms of whether they are fulfilling or otherwise. These scales provide spouses with a conceptual framework to express their experience of interdependence in terms of expectations met or unmet, and whether this interdependence is high at a commitment level or lower at a equitable or exchange level. They provide the data that reflects the quality and stability of the marriage. High quality and high stability is likely to be related to high interdependence and commitment. Lower quality and lower stability is likely to be related with a lower level of interdependence, and an equitable or an exchange orientation in the relationship.

Assessment Measures for Understanding Marriage

These three self report measures, together with the information obtained from the spouses' structured interviews which will be discussed in a later chapter, enabled the spouses to structure and to express their experiences within their marriage as presented diagrammatically in Figure 1.1.

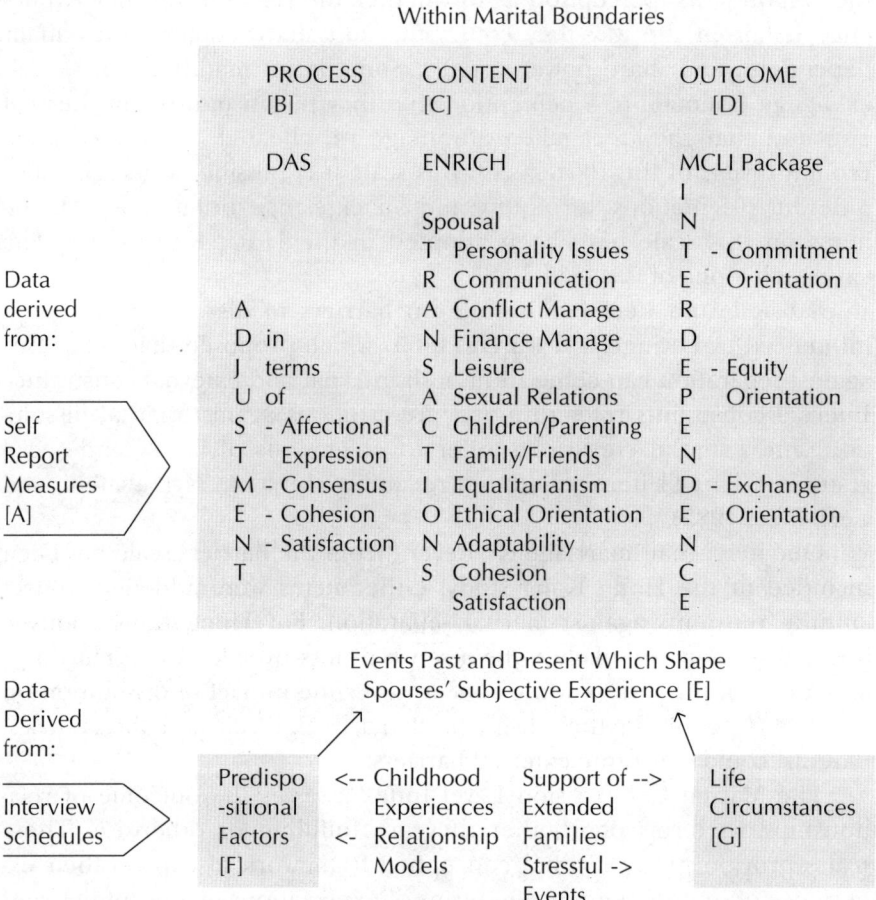

Within Marital Boundaries

	PROCESS [B]	CONTENT [C]	OUTCOME [D]
	DAS	ENRICH	MCLI Package
			I
		Spousal	N
		T Personality Issues	T - Commitment
Data		R Communication	E Orientation
derived	A	A Conflict Manage	R
from:	D in	N Finance Manage	D
	J terms	S Leisure	E - Equity
	U of	A Sexual Relations	P Orientation
Self	S - Affectional	C Children/Parenting	E
Report	T Expression	T Family/Friends	N
Measures	M - Consensus	I Equalitarianism	D - Exchange
[A]	E - Cohesion	O Ethical Orientation	E Orientation
	N - Satisfaction	N Adaptability	N
	T	S Cohesion	C
		Satisfaction	E

Events Past and Present Which Shape
Data
Derived
Spouses' Subjective Experience [E]
from:

Interview	Predispo	<-- Childhood	Support of -->	Life
Schedules	-sitional	Experiences	Extended	Circumstances
	Factors	<- Relationship	Families	[G]
	[F]	Models	Stressful ->	
			Events	

**Figure 1.1   Assessment Measures for Understanding Marriages
in the Hong Kong Study**

When spouses seek an understanding of or help over their relationship, the marriage counsellor as an outsider needs to get in touch with what is going on currently within the marriage. This requires the counsellor together with the spouses to explore on-going transactions within the marital boundaries. The self report measures [A] allow quick entry to the many spheres of shared living between the spouses, providing specific information on the adjustment process according to DAS [B], the nature of spousal transactions as provided by ENRICH [C], and the outcome in terms of the interdependence evolved by the spouses' MCLI [D].

The spouses enjoyment and memory of shared experiences provides a sense of interdependence which colours their subjective evaluation of the relationship [E].

Interview schedules record information on predispositional factors that may affect the relationship [F]. In particular this study focuses on childhood experiences and relational models derived from the couple's parents' marriages. According to Lewis and Spanier (1979:274) the quality of the parents' marriage, and happiness in childhood, can be predictive of subsequent marital quality. Whether this is so for Hong Kong couples has yet to be examined. Support from significant others can contribute to strengthening a marriage, just as adverse life circumstances can undermine the relationship [G]. These issues are examined to assess their impact on each spouse's experience of the marriage.

Among other things, this study examines the notion that carefully selected assessment measures enable the spouses as well as the marriage counsellor to understand their marriage. A thorough assessment of marriage requires the assessment to be made across the whole spectrum of the relationship, back into the past as well as the present and also expectations into the future. In addition, the relationship has to be seen in the context of other systems, the children and the extended family, for these also affect the total sense of marital well-being. Figure 1.1 specifies some of the multiple dimensions that need to be taken into account in the search for understanding.

Chapter Two

The Hong Kong Marital Study

This chapter presents the Hong Kong Marital Study, and assesses the reliability, validity and discriminant capacity of the three self report measures adopted in the study. These are the Dyadic Adjustment Scale, ENRICH, and the Marital Comparison Level Index package of scales. The findings which differentiate adjusted and non-adjusted spouses are analysed to identify subscales or scale items with high discriminant capacity and therefore of particular relevance to Chinese couples in the sample. These are highlighted as they constitute the basis for the development of assessment measures for application in Hong Kong.

Deriving Assessment Measures for Hong Kong

The main focus of the Hong Kong Marital Study is to identify and describe patterns of marital transactions in Hong Kong marriages. These patterns are drawn from the accounts provided by the husbands and wives through the use of self report measures and in their responses during interviews. This material has been organized and analysed to reflect the couple's evaluation of the relationship. The study presents the couple's own definition of what constitutes a happy *mei mun* marriage.

The study tests the discriminant capacity, reliability and validity of the DAS, ENRICH and MCLI Packages, the three assessment measures selected for use in the Hong Kong Marital Study. The aim is to apply well-tested Western marital inventories to Asian marriages to determine their applicability and relevance in cross-cultural transfer. Through this exercise, the intention is to derive assessment measures suitable for clinical practice in Hong Kong. Secondly, the information acquired has been analysed to differentiate various patterns of marital interaction that reflect the experiences of spouses in contemporary Hong Kong. Third, the empirical data is further analysed to examine the implications of adopting an interdependence framework for understanding marriage in Hong Kong.

The sample of the Hong Kong marital study

Research on intimate pair relationships such as marriage requires the particpation of both partners. In developing the sample, it was essential to obtain the willing cooperation of both husband and wife in a review of their marriage. The criteria for inclusion in the sample was that both husband and wife agreed to attend two interviewing sessions and to complete a package of self-rating measures. The sample was formed from couples who were currently undergoing marriage counselling at the Hong Kong Family Society, the Catholic Marriage Advisory Council, the Caritas Family Service and the Hong Kong Christian Service, who were invited to participate in an in-depth review of their marriages. Fifty-two couples from these agencies agreed to participate. To ensure that the sample comprised not only couples who had sought help over their marriages but also those who had not, married people from other community agencies were also invited to assist in the research, and another 50 volunteers were recruited from community groups. These included parents whose children were members of the Boys and Girls Clubs Association, participants from Family Life Education groups conducted by the Family Welfare Society, Caritas, and the Christian Service. This method of recruitment resulted in a non-probability purposive sample of 102 couples.

Demographic characteristics of the couples

The 102 couples in the Hong Kong sample had been married a mean of 9.13 years. The husbands' mean age was 37.4 years; the wives' mean age, 34 years. The mean household monthly income was $9461. Of the 204 spouses, 11.8% had been educated to university level, 63.3% to the level of secondary school or technical training, and 25% had primary school education or no education. The Hong Kong 1991 Population Census (Hong Kong Government, 1991) gives percentage figures of 11.3% with university education, 50.7% secondary school to matriculation, and 38% primary school. The couples in the sample thus had higher educational attainment. Employment-wise, a larger proportion were in the professional and skilled occupations, with 33.5% of the sample in professional, business or managerial occupations; 40.3% were in clerical, sales, services and production occupations; 25% were homemakers; and 1.5% were unemployed (one for health reasons; one retired; one an ivory carver in transition to alternative employment).

A large percentage, 81.4% of the couples were at the stage of having school age children. The mean number of children was 2 per couple.

The mean number of months that the couples knew each other before getting married was 25 months. The choice of mate arising from mutual attraction was indicated by 42.6% of the spouses, while 26.7% married for life style choice having reached marriageable age, and another 26.7% due to forced circumstances such as unplanned pregnancies, arranged marriages, or marrying to get away from difficulties in their families of origin.

While 39.2% recorded no religious affiliations, 19.7% subscribed to either Buddhism, Taoism or ancestor worship; 18.1% were Protestants and 23% were Catholics.

Data collection procedures

Data collection was conducted through two interviews. At the first session, the couples were guided through a structured interview to explore aspects of their current marital situation, their developmental experience, relationships models, and relationship with their families of origin. They also completed ENRICH. The DAS was given to them to complete and return by post before the next session, if this had not been attended to before the interview.

The second session commenced with feedback from their ENRICH Computer Report. This 12-page document was the product of a computer analysis of the couple's completed ENRICH inventory which had been mailed to ENRICH-Canada. Each spouse's responses to the 125 items in 14 subscales were computerized to provide an individual score. The responses were also synchronized on each item and scale to provide couple scores. The feedback exchange over the ENRICH report then initiated another structured interview which explored the type of marriage according to the Circumplex model associated with ENRICH, their perception of their marriage, changes desired by each spouse, the couple's satisfactions and frustrations, and their sexual exchange at the beginning of the marriage and currently. This session ended with each spouse completing the MCLI expectation, equity, commitment, and barriers to dissolution scales. Scoring was done on the spot. Feedback on these dimensions was given to the couple and further discussion encouraged. This concluded the very arduous process which the couples engaged in to examine their relationship.

As the couple reviewed their experiences they were in effect evaluating their marriage and gaining an understanding of the nature of the interdependence they had built up together.

Determining Criterion Groups

Various factors needed to be taken into account in determining criterion groups within the sample. One possibility was to accept the spouses' own perception of their marital experience, as given verbally in interview. On this basis, 113 of the spouses could be considered to be 'happy-satisfied' in that they reported that they were happy, satisfied, enjoyed the relationship, were getting love, had a life companion and mutual support from being married. Thirty-six spouses seem to have had mixed feelings. This was expressed in terms of having to learn to adjust, and finding marriage constricting and not quite what they had expected. These spouses could be considered to feel 'mixed, experiencing a bit of both satisfaction and frustration'. The 33 spouses who referred to conflict, tensions, avoidance, distance, could be regarded to have a 'tense, difficult' marriage. The remaining responses were marked under 'others' without specifying what these were. The limiting factor against accepting such verbal statements was that they could have been affected by the presence of the other spouse at the interview, with possible distortion.

Another alternative was to determine criterion groups from the one-item global statement on satisfaction in the ENRICH inventory. Overall, 131 reported they were 'satisfied' to 'extremely satisfied', and 73 replied they were 'somewhat dissatisfied' to 'dissatisfied'. The limitation on this one item global statement of satisfaction was that it did not take account of social desirability.

Another approach was to apply the mean score of adjustment on the DAS which came to 103.1 with a standard deviation of 23.7.

All these were individual evaluations; however, the assessment of marriage needs to incorporate a joint evaluation with the marriage as the unit for measurement (Thompson and Walker, 1982). Thus a measure which takes account of both spouses' experience within the marriage had to be selected to determine criterion groups.

The DAS is a multi-dimensional measure which balances responses over a number of areas of spousal concern thus reducing bias in any one area. The DAS has already been proven to be helpful in practice to differentiate the degree of adjustment in marriages. A combination of the DAS scores of the responses of the husbands and wives offered the surest form of joint assessment in evaluating marriage.

A review of other research studies showed that a total couple score of 200 was frequently adopted to differentiate between adjusted and non-adjusted groups (Davidson, Balswick and Halverson, 1983; Floyd and Markman, 1983; Sabournin, Laporte and Wright, 1990). In keeping with this practice, the Hong Kong study also selected the DAS couple score of 200 to determine criterion groups. Univariate analysis of the DAS for discriminating perceived marital quality, global marital satisfaction and the spouses' consideration of divorce, has confirmed the appropriateness of the DAS to determine criterion groups. See Appendix 2, Table A2.1.

With a 200 DAS couple score as the cut-off point to differentiate between adjusted and non-adjusted marriages, the sample of 102 marriages divides into two groups:

(1) 55.8% , that is 57 couples or 114 spouses, with combined DAS scores of 200 or more, experienced their marriage as **adjusted**
(2) 44.1% , that is 45 couples or 90 spouses, with combined DAS scores of below 200, experienced their marriage as **non-adjusted**

On this basis, spouses, couples, and marriages are designated as adjusted if the DAS scores of the husband and the wife in combination is 200 or over, whatever the individual scores may be. And, spouses, couples and marriages are designated as non-adjusted if the DAS scores of the husband and the wife in combination is under 200, whatever the individual scores. Statistical analysis of DAS scores, showed that the mean individual spouse DAS scores in the adjusted group was 119.7 with a standard deviation of 11.71. The mean individual spouse DAS score in the non-adjusted group was 82.1 with a standard deviation of 17.44.

The data from the assessment measures and from the interview schedules will be analysed to differentiate and to describe these adjusted and non-adjusted marriages.

The DAS, ENRICH, and the MCLI package will also be examined for reliability and validity in application to the sample. Items with discriminant capacity will be identified to develop assessment measures appropriate for application in Hong Kong.

The Adjusting Process

The information collected through the Dyadic Adjustment Scale helps to promote an understanding of the adjusting processes between the spouses in terms of their affectional and sexual exchange, the degree of consensus between them and the cohesion and satisfaction in their relationship. This information is designed to discriminate between the responses of spouses in adjusted and non-adjusted marriages.

The mean scores of adjusted and non-adjusted spouses are presented in Table A2.2 in Appendix 2. The mean score of the DAS for the total sample of 204 was 103.1, with a standard deviation of 23.7. The median score was 107.5, with a range from a minimum of 31 to a maximum of 146.

Internal consistency for the scale assessed using Cronbach's coefficient alpha was .95, indicating that the DAS is a very promising measurement instrument for Chinese couples in Hong Kong. The coefficient alpha of the four subscales ranged from .73 to .90. (See Table A2.3.)

The use of DAS subscales has been found to be very helpful in organizing feedback exchange with spouses in research and in clinical work. Consequently, special care was taken in the study to analyze the subscales for their appropriateness in this task. Each of the subscales was able to differentiate adjusted and non-adjusted spouses at the significant level of $p<.001$. **Inter-correlation matrix analysis** showed that the satisfaction subscale correlated with the affection subscale at $r = .72$, and with consensus at $r = .71$. This means that the higher the affection or the consensus, the higher the satisfaction. The consensus scale correlated moderately with the cohesion scale, $r = .54$, and higher with affection $r = .69$. (See Table A2.4.)

Logistic regression analysis shows that three subscales — satisfaction, cohesion and consensus — were able correctly to predict 93.14% of group membership. (See Table A2.5.) The affectional expression scale seems to be less sensitive in its discriminant capacity.

Since DAS subscales are differently weighted, they have been translated to percentage scores to facilitate comparison, and are presented in bar charts in Figure 2.1.

In all four dimensions of adjustment, the difference between adjusted and non-adjusted spouses is significant. Adjusted spouses rated their adjustment in the four dimensions at 75.8% of total score for cohesion, to 78% for affectional expression, 78.6% for consensus, and 79.4% for satisfaction. Non-adjusted spouses, rated their adjustment in cohesion at 39.2%, reflecting the low level of sharing in these marriages. Scores of satisfaction at 52.4% and affectional expression at 57.5% signal the vulnerable state of these marriages. The slightly higher rating on consensus at 60.5% demonstrates that even in troubled marriages the value that Chinese place on maintaining harmony is upheld, even when other areas of spousal transactions in affectional behaviour, cohesion in sharing life concerns, and satisfaction in the relationship, are unfulfilling.

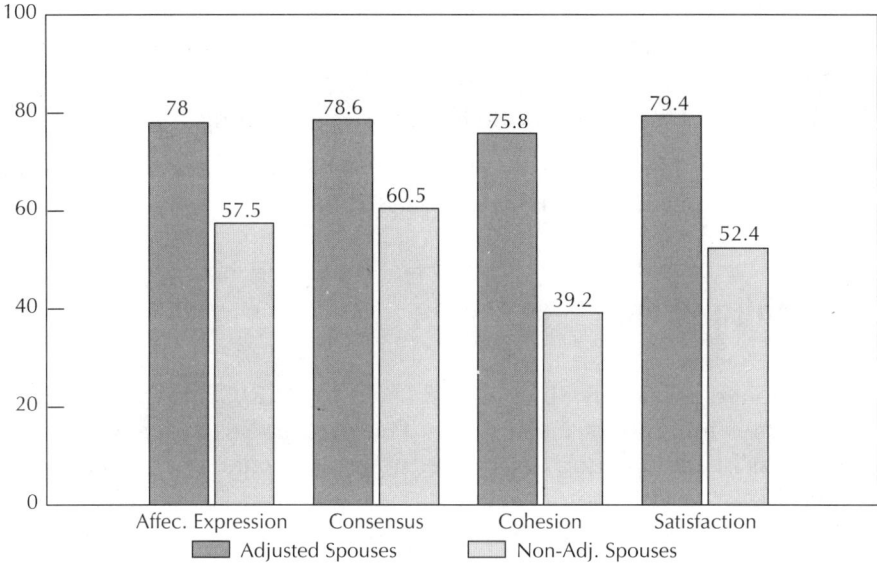

Figure 2.1   Affectional Expression, Consensus, Cohesion, and Satisfaction of Adjusted and Non-Adjusted Spouses

One-way analysis of variance of each of the 32 DAS items indicates significant differences between adjusted and non-adjusted spouses on all items at p<.001 level. Discriminant analysis through logistic regression identified eight items as significant predictors of adjustment.

DAS 31 — Degree of happiness in the relationship.
DAS 16 — Discussed/considered terminating relationship.
DAS 26 — Laughed together.
DAS 1 — Agree on handling finances.
DAS 14 — Agree on leisure interest and activities.
DAS 17 — Leave house after fight.
DAS 19 — Confide in mate.
DAS 28 — Work together on something.

These eight items correctly classified 96.08% of the adjusted and non-adjusted group membership. (See Table A2.6.)

In the sample, 69.6% (142) spouses responded that they had not considered separation or divorce; 30.4% (62) responded that they had considered separation or divorce. Logistic regression analysis identified four DAS items as being able to predict 82.27% of those spouses who have or have not considered separation or divorce. These were:

DAS 8 — Consensus on philosophy of life.
DAS 16 — Discussed/considered terminating relationship.
DAS 20 — Regret getting married.
DAS 27 — Frequency of calmly discussed something.

These four items correctly classified 82.27% of those spouses who have or have not considered divorce. (See Table A2.7.)

The Multiple Facets of Living

As mentioned previously, the position taken by ENRICH is that marriage incorporates multiple facets of living. The partners' experience in all of these areas in combination determines their satisfaction and general well-being.

ENRICH provides individual scores for each of the 14 subscales but no total score. The individual percentage scores for each husband and wife are revised according to responses on idealistic distortion to account for answers influenced by social conventions. The differences in individual mean scores for adjusted and non-adjusted spouses on twelve of the ENRICH categories are all statistically significant at $p<.001$ level; for equalitarian roles the significance was at $p<.05$ and adaptability was not significant. (See Table A2.8.)

ENRICH also provides a couples score, PCA for positive couple agreement, derived from pairing the husband's and wife's individual responses to arrive at a joint assessment which emphasizes the collaborative set of marital transactions. The mean positive couple agreement scores for ENRICH categories are presented in bar charts in Figure 2.2 to provide a visual image of the difference between adjusted and non-adjusted marriages.

Anova results show significance at $p<.001$ in ten subscales; at $p<.01$ for equalitarian roles, and no significance for adaptability and cohesion.

The greatest differences between PCA mean scores of adjusted and non-adjusted marriages were in satisfaction, communication, ethical orientation and sexual relations. This shows that transactions in these areas significantly shape the different experiences of couples in their marriage. (See Table A2.9.)

Logistic regression analysis to test the discriminate capacity of the PCA scores indicates that two scales — communication and ethical orientation — are able to predict 84.31% of adjusted and non-adjusted group memberships. (See Table A2.12.)

ENRICH applied in Hong Kong showed a Cronbach coefficient alpha of .84 for the marital satisfaction scale. Scales with coefficient alpha

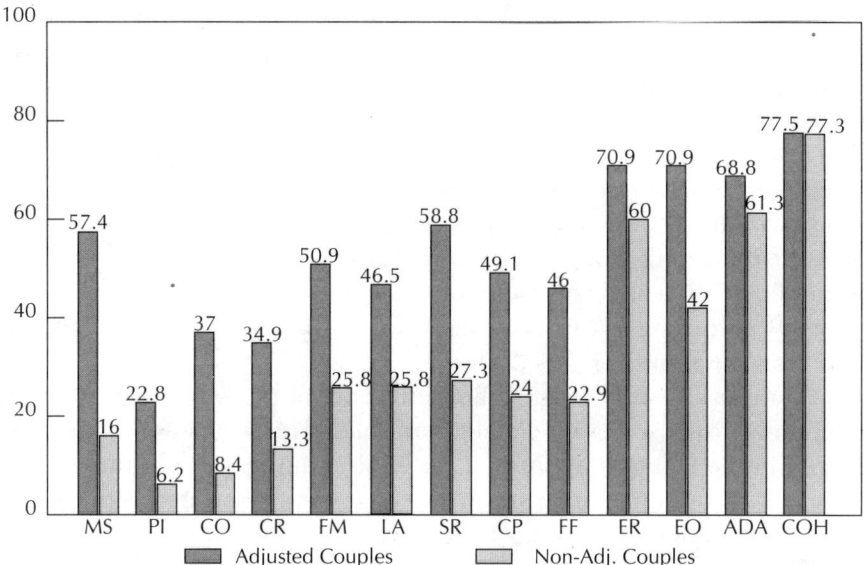

MS - Marital Satisfaction, PI - Personality Issues, CO - Communication, CR - Conflict Resolution, FM - Financial Management, LA - Leisure Activities, SR - Sexual Relations, CP - Children & Parenting, FF - Family & Friends, ER - Equalitarian Roles, EO - Ethical Orientation, ADA - Adaptability, COH - Cohesion

Figure 2.2   ENRICH Categories - PCA Scores for Adjusted and Non-Adjusted Couples

in the 70 range were personality issues (.76), financial management (.76), children and parenting (.76), sexual relations (.75), and communication (.72). Scales with coefficient alpha in the 60 range were conflict management (.68), ethical orientation (.67), family and friends (.64). The scales on leisure activities (.50) and equalitarian roles (.32) raise questions about their appropriateness for use in Hong Kong marriages, as reliability below .60 is not acceptable. (See Table A2.10.) These two scales — leisure activities and equalitarian roles — also carried the lowest alpha in Olson, Fournier and Druckman's study (reported in Fowers and Olson,1989) although their alpha of .71 and .68 are respectable.

Inter-correlation matrix analysis shows the extent of the association between the scales. The highest correlation is found in communication and conflict resolution at r = .77. Fowers and Olson's study (1987) also reported similar findings of the highest correlation between communication and conflict resolution, and the lowest correlation between equalitarian roles and the other scales. In the Hong Kong study, it is interesting to note that the sexual relations scale correlates highly with marital satisfaction at r = .68 and with the communication scale at r = .60, and is moderately correlated with the conflict resolution scale r = .57 and the ethical orientation scale r = .55. (See Table A2.11.)

Four scales — sexual relations, children and parenting, equalitarian roles, and ethical orientation — can correctly predict 82.84% of group membership of spouses who considered separation or divorce (See Table A2.13.)

Eleven of the ENRICH scales were able to discriminate between adjusted from non-adjusted marriages significantly at p<.001. Three scales — adaptability, cohesion and equalitarian roles — presented some problems. In the Hong Kong sample the marital adaptability scale had no discriminant capacity. The cohesion scale showed significant difference at p<.001 according to the individual scores, while analysis of PCA couple scores was not significant.

Anova results show a significant difference at p<.05 between adjusted and non-adjusted scores on equalitarian roles. This scale was of particular interest in the Hong Kong study as the clinical impression was that higher expectations of equalitarianism in marriages was associated with higher degrees of friction. The mean PCA score of 70.9 for adjusted marriages and 60 for non-adjusted marriages confirms that generally there was high consensus between husbands and wives over equalitarian roles. However, the individual mean score for adjusted spouses at 41.1 and for non-adjusted spouses at 47.8 demonstrates the preference for higher equalitarianism in non-adjusted spouses. Scores in the 40 range for equalitarian roles indicate the ambivalence of Hong Kong spouses who value traditional husband-wife roles and responsibilities, and at the same time wish for more equal sharing in their marriages.

Relationship Outcomes

Sabatelli and Cecil-Pigo propose that the experience of interdependence in a marriage affects and is affected by the level to which expectations are met, by the couple's sense of commitment and equity in the relationship, and by their perception of alternatives available. They designed and tested four uni-dimensional scales to examine these aspects in marriage. The Marital Comparison Level Index — MCLI — evaluates whether expectations are met at a level equal to, better or worse than is anticipated. The commitment scale assesses the degree of cohesion felt and therefore indicates the tendency towards stability or instability in the relationship. The equity scale examines the degree to which spouses consider that what they receive from their investment reflects a fair balance from what they put into the exchange. The barriers to dissolution scale refers to constraints against separation arising from personal anxiety and a sense of obligation towards children or parents.

The total scores for the MCLI expectation scale is 100, for the equity scale, 50; for the commitment and barriers scales, 30. The mean scores of the scales are converted to percentage scores and presented in bar charts in Figure 2.3. so that comparisons can be made between adjusted and non-adjusted spouses.

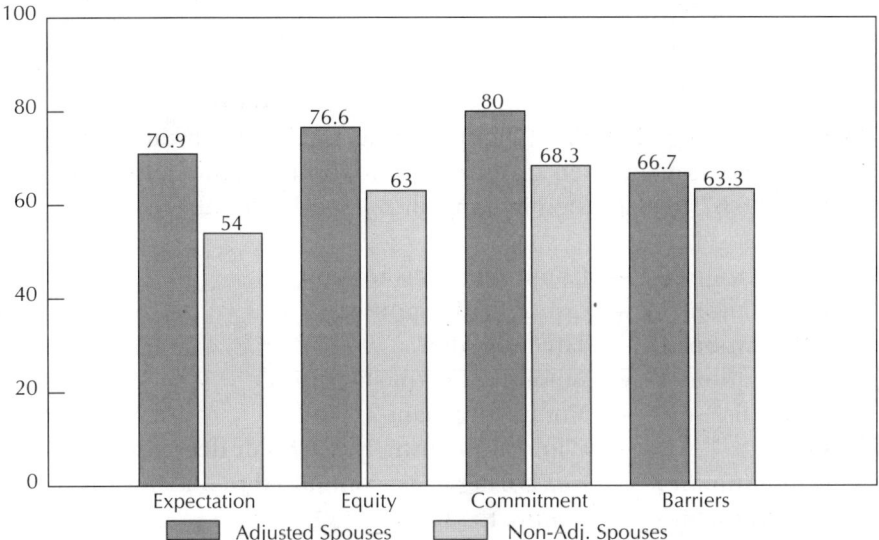

Figure 2.3   Expectation, Equity, Commitment, and Barriers of Adjusted and Non-Adjusted Spouses

The mean scores for adjusted and non-adjusted spouses on expectations, equity and commitment scales are significantly different at p<.001; while for the barriers scale the significance was at p<.05. The difference in the mean scores between the two groups for expectations was high. It is interesting to note that non-adjusted spouses feel that about half their expectations have been met. Scores reflecting constraints against dissolution are not greatly different between adjusted and non-adjusted spouses. (See Table A2.14.)

The reliability according to Cronbach alpha for the expectation scale is .95; the equity scale .75; the commitment scale .67; and the barriers scale .33. The low reliability of the barriers scale indicates low internal consistency. In the Hong Kong study this six-item scale has been revised so that two items refer to the spouse's personal concerns about dissolution, two other items to concerns over significant others, namely the children and their parents and the remaining two to societal constraints.

Since these refer to different aspects of barriers against dissolution, and are not homogenous, it is not surprising that the internal consistency is low. Although this scale has low internal consistency, it was able to differentiate adjusted and non-adjusted spouses. (See Table A2.15.)

Inter-correlation matrix analysis of the MCLI Package of scales shows very high correlation at $r = .84$ between the commitment and the equity scales. This reflects some overlap between these two scales. The correlation between expectation and equity is $r = .78$, between expectation and commitment $r = .74$, and between expectation and barriers $r = .62$. (See Table A2.16.)

Discriminant analysis through logistic regression of the 42 items in the MCLI package identified eight items as significant in differentiating adjusted and non-adjusted groups. The following eight items correctly classified 86.67% of adjusted membership. (See Table A2.17.)

> Expectations 6　—　Commitment from spouse.
> Expectations 11 — 'Confiding in spouse.
> Expectations 12 — Time together.
> Expectations 15 — Amount of sexual activities.
> Equity 6　　　　— Not feeling manipulated.
> Equity 8　　　　— When argue usually reach fair decision.
> Commitment 2 — Not boring to be committed to one person.
> Commitment 4 — Willing to sacrifice.

Logistic regression of items in the MCLI package was carried out to discover their capacity in discriminating instability, as seen in spouses who have considered divorce. Five items were significant predictors of instability, being able to discriminate 82.05% group membership. (See Table A2.18.) The five items with the highest discriminant capacity for predicting spouses who have considered separation or divorce are:

> Expectations 4　—　Commitment of spouse.
> Equity 4　　　　— Feeling taken advantage of.
> Commitment 3 — Probably marry someone else.
> Barriers 3　　　— If leave marriage, lose a great deal.
> Barriers 6　　　— Children needs deter.

These items were particularly meaningful to spouses in the sample, and were sensitive in indicating adjustment and instability in the relationships.

The MCLI package reflected the experience of spouses in terms of their sense of expectation, commitment, equity and security in the marital exchange. The detailed specification of the spouses' hopes and wishes in the expectations scale allow them to show their disappointment at what did not materialize. However, this also leads them to recognize areas where expectations are met. This holds true even for non-adjusted spouses with a mean score of 54 whose expectations are fulfilled about half the time. However, it serves to counter-balance their general feeling that 'all expectations have been unmet'. While some items in the equity, commitment and the barriers scales facilitated the spouses' expression of negative sentiments, permitting the discharge of anger at being let down, other items helped to identify and recognize areas of fulfilment and areas of value in the relationship.

Assessment Measures for Hong Kong

Self-rating scales were used in this study to enable spouses to convey their subjective feelings on specific concerns and to make precise evaluations of aspects of their relationship in a clear and focused way.

Measuring marital quality

The eight single items from DAS and the eight from the MCLI Package which had the highest discriminant capacity for determining criterion groups in the sample could be combined in a package, as a possible measuring scale appropriate for Hong Kong marriages. The item 'confiding in spouse' was identified through logistic regression analysis on both the DAS and the MCLI package but to avoid double weighting only the DAS item on confiding was included in the final 15 item scale derived from this study.

These 15 items can be used to derive a scale to gauge marital quality for Hong Kong couples:

Confide in mate   DAS 19
Agree on handling finance   DAS 1
Laugh together   DAS 26
Work together on something   DAS 28
Degree of happiness in marriage   DAS 31
Agree on leisure interests   DAS 14
Leave after a fight   DAS 7
Discussed/considered leaving   DAS 16
Expectations of sexual activities   Exp 15
Expectations of time together   Exp 12

Expectations of commitment from spouse   Exp 6
Willing to sacrifice   Commit 4
When argue usually reach fair solution   Equity 8
Boring to be committed to one person   Commit 2
Often feel manipulated by partner   Equity 6

The internal consistency reliability of these 15 items in combination, using Cronbach coefficient alpha is .89. Principal component analysis with varimax rotation of the items, produced a three factor solution which explained 54.5% of the total variance.

A review of the content of all these items shows that the first six refer to adjusting processes of sharing and enjoyment of interdependent activities, the next two to the consequences of conflict. Five items address expectations from an affectionate, caring, committed and equitable relationship. The last two specify negative sentiments to be avoided in a happy marriage. These items generally concentrate on the more personally valued aspects of the spouse and the relationship.

Measuring marital instability

Nine items which significantly discriminate those who considered divorce in the Hong Kong sample, could be adopted to measure marital instability. These are:

Regret marriage   DAS 20
Discussed/considered divorce   DAS 16
Expectation of commitment of spouse   Exp 4
Disagree on philosophy of life   DAS 8
Feel taken advantage of   Equity 4
Calmly discussed something   DAS 27
Probably marry someone else   Commit 3
Children needs deter   Barriers 6
If leave, lose a great deal   Barriers 3

The internal consistency reliability of these nine items using Cronbach coefficient alpha is .76. Principal component analysis with varimax rotation for nine items, which significantly discriminates those who considered divorce, produced two factors which explained 51.5% of the total variance.

These items clearly reflect unhappiness, tension, and a lack of fit and confidence in the relationship. The first seven items reveal tensions in the attitudinal sphere in disagreement over the philosophy of life, in feelings of regret and wishing to marry someone else, being taken advantage of, lacking in commitment, and in considering terminating the relationship. The last two items indicate the sense of personal loss. This nine-item scale can be used to assess marital instability for Hong Kong couples.

The application of assessment measures in marriage counselling

This chapter has dwelt extensively on an examination of the statistical properties of the assessment measures selected. The detailed presentation of the discriminant capacity of the scales has been necessary to evaluate their applicability for Chinese couples since self rating scales are untried and unfamiliar in marriage counselling settings in Hong Kong. If the service agencies are to apply them, evidence that they are reliable and valid needs to be supplied. Statistical analysis confirms the reliability, validity and discriminant capacity of the DAS, ENRICH, and the MCLI package.

The research findings of the self report measures give trends and patterns of the total sample under study. These need to be translated to be relevant for application in case-by-case clinical settings. If assessment procedures are adopted, they have to be acceptable to both the respondent clients and to the social workers. For the respondents, the measures have to be relevant because they tap issues of concern in the day-to-day transactions of the spouses. These have to be clearly defined, meaningful and answerable in the help-seeking context. For the professionals who administer the measures, they have to be easily manageable with clear instructions for coding, scoring, interpretation and feedback to the clients.

The scales for differentiating marital adjustment and instability distilled through a research process meets both these criteria. The scales derived are reliable and able to discriminate between types of marital relationships. The items of these scales are immediately relevant to married people who, in responding to them, are already initiating the process of a more structured and systematic review of their relationship. The adjustment and expectations items, combined with the interdependence scale to be discussed in Chapter 8, provide an assessment framework which offers the spouses as well as the counsellors a perspective to view on-going issues and events in the context of their overall marital experience.

Chapter Three

The Couple's Descriptions of Their Relationship

This chapter analyses the spouses' descriptions and evaluations of various aspects of their relationship, derived from their retrospective review in two structured interviews.

Some spouses suggested during the interviews that the subjective evaluation of 'fit' in these various aspects coloured their experience of the relationship. This viewpoint is critically examined.

The couples interviews commenced with compliments to the spouses for investing time and effort in a review of their relationship, and with an introduction to self report questionaires as providing the structure to enable a comprehensive overview of the multiple facets of married living. After completing ENRICH, the spouses then participated in their first joint session to review various aspects of their relationship. This information was recorded in schedules which had been drawn up as an integral part of the research process.

After the computer analysis of the ENRICH package had been returned from ENRICH-Canada by post the couple were invited for a feedback session in a second interview. The information provided by the inventories was openly discussed with the spouses. It was clearly understood that these interviews were confidential and that all material used in the survey would be analysed in a generalized way. The spouses were thoughtfully reminiscent and participated actively at these interviews.

The research interviewers who conducted these sessions noted the very positive interest of the couple in understanding more about their relationship. This may have been due to the fact that the spouses were aware that they were participating in a project and their personal reservations were alleviated by a feeling of joint activity. The fact that they had specific tasks to perform at these interviews was also an important factor in overcoming reservations. The matter-of-fact way in which the inventories were presented, as well as the structure of the proceedings, allowed searching emotional questions to be asked in an neutral way. More importantly, it enabled the spouses to respond with an openness that may not have been possible in an emotionally charged situation. The act of filling out the inventories and of checking the meaning and accuracy of particular details became a shared activity which encouraged communication between the spouses, and with the counsellor.

The Structured Interviews

The interview schedules were designed to obtain information on the unique aspects and special events of married living as experienced by the spouses. The areas focused on were:

Aspects of Shared Living, incorporating
- The spouses' descriptions and feelings about their expectations, goals, sharing in parenting, homemaking, leisure and work concerns.
- A review of the development of their relationship from the wedding, and a discussion of the development of their sexual relations.
- Their recall of joyful and sad memories.
- Stressful events and problems experienced in the course of their marriage.
- Life circumstances which affected the marriage.

Aspects of Early Life Experiences, including
- The spouses' descriptions of their parents' marriage; and the perceived effects of the parents' marriage subsequently on their own marriage.
- The spouses' descriptions of their childhood experiences; and the perceived effects of these experiences on them.

Contact with Paternal and Maternal Extended Families which touched on the reciprocity between generations in terms of exchange of advice, finance, time, affection, support and practical care.

The spouses' reminiscences on aspects of shared living will be discussed in this chapter. Their descriptions of early life experiences and relationships with the extended families will be examined in Chapter 6.

In the interviews, the spouses' descriptions and evaluation of various aspects of their relationship were encouraged. Their feelings on the extent to which they shared similar or different characteristics, preferences and interests were explored, as were their experiences of shared activities in various aspects of daily life, including affectional and sexual sharing. Problems which were affecting their relationship were identified. The couple also reviewed together their experience of stress in the marriage, as manifested in events such as periods of separation due to marital tension, suicide threats or attempts, spouse abuse, extramarital affairs, and considerations of divorce.

Some spouses suggested during the interviews that a feeling of 'fit' 夾 in these various aspects of interdependent living tended to influence their experience of the relationship. This concept of 'fit' figured prominently in the discussions during the interviews. It was a simple term which expressed their feeling of achieving a close matching of needs and interests with their partners.

The Couple's Reports on Shared Living

The structured interviews were designed to elicit a description of the interdependence that had been built up between the spouses. The couples were encouraged to review the ups and downs in the history of their marriage, identifying joyful and sad events. The most frequently cited joyful event was the birth of a child (38.7%); enjoying family time (20.1%); and the wedding/honeymoon period (11.3%). No pattern in sad events is discernible, though 25.5% considered quarrelling and conflict as the most memorable negative events. It is interesting to note that children (46.1%) and in-laws (46.1%) were considered the most problematic issues in married life. This was followed by finance (34.3%), which was identified not just as a shortage of money but also tense negotiations over spending and budgeting.

Between husbands and wives

Some couples prefaced their joint review by explaining that their marriage was adjusted because they were well matched. Some explained that their marriage was strained because they did not match, and were therefore incompatible. In this regard they were mainly referring to the matching ·of personal styles and preferences. Of the adjusted couples 82% considered they had arrived at some 'fit' because they had similar characteristics, styles and preferences, or because they were different but complementary, or that they were different but adjusting and slowly evolving compatibility. On the other hand, 75% of the non-adjusted couples were convinced that differences between them was the reason for their lack of fit and adjustment would not work as the other could not change.

Overall, there was consensus regarding the sharing of common goals, with 99% of the husbands and wives in adjusted marriages and 61% from non-adjusted marriages identifying similar sets of goals for themselves as a unit. The goals selected were first to raise children to be healthy and happy, then to cooperate to improve the family's standard of living, and build a stable family life for the whole family. All of these were family oriented objectives.

Where the matching of leisure interests and activities were concerned there was little difference between types of marriage. About two-fifths of the sample felt that they shared similar interests, and engaged in some mutual and some separate activities. About just over a quarter reported they had different interests, with one spouse wishing to do things together, the other independently, or the two partners reported that each was not able to appreciate the other's hobbies or pastimes. Another one-fifth agreed they had different interests but were compromising and learning to develop an interest in each other's pursuits. Just over one-tenth of the couples said they had no leisure activities together. This was explained as due to high conflict making time together uncomfortable, or the husband had outside activities of his own so the wife felt deprived, or it was due to a lack of time because of other life demands, or it was admitted that this was a neglected dimension in their lives.

Affectional and sexual sharing

In the sharing of love, affection, companionship and sexual interests and activities, there were significant differences between the adjusted and non-adjusted groups. The spouses were able to describe this aspect of their relationship more precisely through self report items. Of the adjusted spouses, 91.2% noted that their *experience of love* in the marriage was better or equal to their expectations. On the other hand, 41% of the non-adjusted spouses recorded that their experience of love was worse than expected. Very similar percentages were reported when the issue of companionship was raised.

The difference in sexual activities between adjusted and non-adjusted marriages was manifested not only in the current context, but also at the commencement of the marriage. The couples were asked about the frequency of sexual activities over one month in the first year of the marriage, and the frequency in one month currently. Adjusted couples recalled a mean of 11.6 sexual contacts in one month in the first year, and a mean of 6.6 in the current year (t=8.06, df52, p<.001). Non-adjusted couples recalled a mean of 8.6 sexual contacts in one month in the first year, and a mean of 3.4 in the current year (t=4.88, df 38, p<.001). The difference of frequency in the first month between adjusted couples and non-adjusted was significant (F=6.31, p<.05), as was difference of frequency in one month currently for adjusted and non-adjusted couples (F=20.28, p<.001).

Both adjusted and non-adjusted couples reported a decline in frequency of sexual intercourse over time, though some reported an increase. Increase in frequency was reported by ten couples; the reasons given being the opportunities presented by the privacy of one's own home, better adjustment over time, increased frequency to show affection, greater feelings of intimacy, increasing need, or the desire for pregnancy. Decrease in frequency was reported by 82 couples; the reasons given being physical tiredness 19 (16.1%); that attention had shifted to other concerns, such as children 18 (15.3%); the relationship was not satisfactory 17 (14.4%); work conditions such as shift and night work 15 (12.7%); and housing conditions which lacked privacy 13 (11%). Where interest in sex displayed by partner was concerned, 50% of the adjusted spouses evaluated this to be better than expected, while 44.6% of the non-adjusted spouses found this to be worse than expected. Where the amount of sexual activity was concerned 57% of the adjusted spouses rated this to be better than expected, and 39.8% of the non-adjusted spouses rated this as worse than expected.

Attitudes over marital exclusivity were conventional. Of the adjusted spouses 82.5% and 73.2% of the non-adjusted spouses took the view that sexual activities should be confined to marriage (F=4.84, p<.05).

Joint concerns

Of the adjusted couples 56% said they *shared household chores* and mutually supported each other in the daily tasks of family living; 32% said they held different opinions on the proper extent of each spouse's contribution; 12% of the sample believed that this was the responsibility of the wife. Among the non-adjusted couples, similar views were held, although percentages were in reverse. In this group, 61% held the opinion that domestic concerns were the responsibility of the wife; 26% reported some sharing; and 13% reported different perspectives on household tasks, making this an area of disagreement and argument for them.

In the *care and discipline of children*, adjusted couples showed high to moderate degrees of sharing, while non-adjusted couples reported little or no sharing. A large percentage of the adjusted couples (74%) reported joint collaboration over matters regarding the children; 24% had different opinions; only 2% considered this to be the responsibility of the wife. In non-adjusted marriages, a large proportion (54%) of the group said that they had different opinions about what was appropriate in the care of children, and about discipline. This disagreement often led to conflict, or the withdrawal of one partner. However, 31% of the non-adjusted spouses said they shared in the upbringing of their children.

Of the adjusted couples, 86% of working husbands and wives brought home *work concerns* to sort out with their spouses. In comparison, 40% of the non-adjusted couples separated these spheres of activities, reporting no sharing in work concerns, as they perceived that their partners would not understand their work demands, or that their different and conflicting opinions could only lead to argument.

Budgeting and disagreements over the level of contribution from each partner caused tension in some marriages, with 28.1% of adjusted couples identifying finance as an issue in their relationship. In comparision, close on half of the non-adjusted couples (48.9%) talked about *tensions over finances*. For these couples, this was a conflict area which attracted discontent from other areas of living. The contribution or withholding of money was sometimes used as a means to gain compliance. Some marriages were affected by debts, gambling, and loan sharks threats. The decision over the choice and purchase of a flat, and the financial responsibility of the mortgage payments, was humorously referred to by a number of couples as the most serious financial issue between them. Eight couples referred to high mortgage payments as their greatest financial difficulty.

Life Circumstances External to the Marriage

External life stresses came from work pressures, from different values over financial expenditure, from extended family relationship demands, and for a few from ill health. Two ordinary life issues considered by the couples to be particularly difficult to manage were demands related to work and to relationships with the extended family.

In Hong Kong it is commonly assumed that there is *stress from work* and from over-working. It is interesting to note that 61.6% of adjusted spouses reported stress from work, while about the same percentage (63.3%) of the non-adjusted spouses felt that work circumstances were manageable. Work pressures were related to long work hours, shift duties, and disagreements about taking on overtime work. Some working wives complained of tiredness leading to increased irritability. Some conflict arose over wives working outside the home against their husbands' wishes.

Where *extended family* relationships were concerned adjusted spouses reported a more positive exchange with 67.3% evaluating relations as supportive, and 23.5% as stressful. Of the non-adjusted spouses, 46.2% considered the exchanges to be stressful, and 42.3% gauged these to be supportive. Supportive exchanges referred to the reciprocation of feelings, goods and services. Stressful exchanges mainly centered on unwelcome advice and interference. Some spouses said that extended family relations were stressful, as they felt themselves to be looked down upon by their in-laws because of their lower education and poorer social backgrounds or prospects.

Problems of Living and Stressful Events

Stress in this area came from problems of daily living and from particularly memorable events such as one spouse walking out after an argument, involving separation for one or more nights. Stress also came from and resulted in suicide threats or attempts, violence, threatening actions, or extramarital affairs.

An overall view of the problems which constituted areas of tension in marriage is presented in rank order of highest incidence in Table 3.1.

Table 3.1   Problems Identified

Overall Sample N=204		Nature of problem	Adjusted spouses N = 114		Non-adjusted spouses N = 90		Chi-square
%	Rank		%	Rank	%	Rank	
46.1	1	Parenting	47.4	1	44.4	3	ns
46.1	1	In-Laws	36.8	2	57.8	1	8.05 df1**
34.3	2	Finance	22.8	5	48.9	2	14.04 df1***
30.4	3	Work	28.1	3	33.3	5	ns
24.5	4	Health	24.6	4	24.4	6	ns
22.5	5	Value Diff.	8.8	8	40.0	4	26.32 df1***
19.6	6	Leisure	15.8	6	24.4	6	ns
12.7	7	Friends	10.5	7	15.6	8	ns
8.8	8	Gambling	1.8		17.8	7	14.12 df1***
7.8	9	Drinking	1.8		15.6	8	11.41 df1***

** p<.01   *** p<.001   Highlights 40% and over

Their importance in affecting adjusted and non-adjusted marriages is also noted.

The major difficulties perceived by the adjusted group were associated with joint efforts in dealing with other relationships important to the marriage, such as bringing up children and coping with in-laws. The next set of difficulties reflect circumstances in health and work. These could be external to the marital exchange. About half of the non-adjusted spouses were experiencing difficulties over in-laws, parenting, and finance. It was interesting to note that fully 40% referred to differences in values as giving rise to conflict. Responses to the self report measures also identified the scale on ethical orientation as having a high discriminant capacity in predicting marital adjustment and in predicting the potential for divorce. Although complaints of gambling and drinking were brought up by non-adjusted spouses, these activities did not affect adjusted spouses to the same extent.

On average, adjusted couples identified 2.1 difficulties; the non-adjusted couples 3.3. The difference in the experiencing of problems was significant for the different types of marriage, $F = 13.39$, $p<.001$.

Marriage counsellors in Hong Kong, as elsewhere, are concerned over the rising rate of divorce, separation, spouse abuse and extramarital affairs. These stressful events can occur in adjusted as well as non-adjusted marriages and impact on the relationship, as demonstrated by the figures in the following table. However, the rate at which they occur varies.

The indications are that adjusted marriages can be affected by stressful events, while non-adjusted marriages are highly implicated by their occurrence. The 61% of spouses from the non-adjusted group who considered divorce, and the 40% who reported leaving home overnight due to marital tensions, testify to the vulnerability and instability of non-ad-

Table 3.2   Stressful Events Reported

Stressful event	Adjusted spouse N = 114 %	Non-adjusted spouse N = 90 %	Chi-square
– Considered Divorce	6.0	61.0	55.33 df2***
– Separation due to Mar.Tensions	8.8	40.0	26.32 df1***
– Extramarital Affairs	1.8	10.0	5.18 df1*
– Spouse Abuse	2.6	11.1	8.41 df1**
– Suicide Threats	4.4	15.6	6.65 df1**
– Suicide Attempts	1.8	8.9	4.07 df1*

* p<.05   ** p<.01   *** p<.001

justed marriages. It is often the occurrence of these events that leads to help seeking decisions. Discussions on separation, spouse abuse, suicidal attempts, and extramarital affairs were raised during the interviews with both spouses present and some under reporting is possible.

The Couple's Review of Satisfaction and Frustrations

In their reminiscences over their experiences, the couples in both adjusted and non-adjusted marriages referred to the different levels of fulfillment at various stages in their relationship, from the time of first being married through the family years of raising children. Those who experienced an increase in satisfaction explained this as due to being deeper in love and in being happier than they had expected, joy over the birth of a child, better adjustment, or having their own home. The explanation for maintaining the same level of fulfillment was that satisfaction continued with little fluctuations. Decrease in satisfaction was related to marital adjustment problems, conflicts, in-law difficulties, pressure from child rearing, lack of time for the spouse because of the children, lack of understanding from one's spouse, and financial stress.

While recalling the *satisfactory aspects* of their marriage some of the spouses complimented and showed appreciation of each other. The reasons most frequently given for satisfaction were appreciation of the spouse's care and concern, appreciation of the characteristics of the spouse, confidence in the partner's reliability, and enjoyment in loving the partner. Some found self esteem and satisfaction in the life style provided by marriage. Others found satisfaction in marriage as a relationship in which one could enjoy the experience of shared living whilst maintaining a degree of individualism. Some couples talked about the happiness of having their own family and home, and of their enjoyment of a family life style.

About one-fifth of the group said they could not think of any frustrations arising from their relationship. Those who admitted *frustrations* tended to identify these as coming from conflict over the many major and minor issues in their lives. Their explanation was that the high level of disagreement between them was due to their being too dissimilar and to having too many differences to be able to understand each other.

Frustrations were expressed in terms of complaints against the spouse which generally were focused on behavior, such as being too demanding, inflexible, non expressive, or having a hot temper. Discontented spouses tended to emphasize the negative effect that the marital situation had on them personally, in making them carry responsibilities that were too heavy, in having to surrender independence, and in making them give up their own self development. Some also admitted to frustration because of unhappy past events, ill health, interference from in-laws, and children.

In determining the sort of marriage they would like, about half of the spouses decided that they would like more closeness and intimacy in their relationship. About one-quarter opted for more independence. Another quarter were of the opinion that they could not expect any changes in their relationship.

Negotiating 'Fit' and Struggling With Differences

As the spouses evaluated their marriage with each other and with the interviewer, a theme that came up again and again was their perception of 'fit'. It would seem that they intuitively perceived accommodating to each other as searching for a 'fit'. If the couple considered there to be a 'fit' between them, then they happily commented on how well their differences complemented each other. If they did not perceive a 'fit', they complained of incompatibility because of their differences. The areas of difference or similarity that seemed important was the matching of their personalities.

The non-adjusted spouses tended to describe each other as opposites. She is an extrovert; he is an introvert. She likes to play mahjong; he likes outdoor sports. She worries; he is carefree. She uses reason to discipline the children; he punishes. They explained that because of these differences they clashed and had constant disagreements, leaving a prevailing sense of incompatibility in their daily transactions. However, similarity in temperament was also perceived as a source of tension. 'We are both fiery' therefore incompatible; or 'we are both strong willed, so we argue'.

Generally, adjusted spouses saw themselves as well matched. They were able to find the reason for this match in either their similarities or their differences. When they perceived they were different, their comment was that they appreciated their dissimiliarities, as they could then complement each other. Some adjusted spouses admitted to having divergent views, dissimilar styles and preferences, but then added they would try to compromise to accommodate the partner.

It would seem that a feeling of compatibility is not just a matter of difference or similarity; it is the interpretation that the couple place on these. Drawing on empirical data from his classic study of 1935 which was repeated in 1938, Terman, who produced the Stanford Binet Test, referred to the 'aptitude for compatibility' which spouses bring to their marriage. In this study which may seem dated, but is still cited, Terman documented the effects of personality characteristics on the marital relationship. Some of the self descriptions given by spouses who considered they were compatible or not compatible in his study reflect similar sentiments expressed by spouses who considered they have achieved a fit or not in the Hong Kong study.

The process of achieving fit in marriage is described by Prosky and Prosky (1980) in terms of a process of dyadic adjustment in their developmental model of intimate relationships. It would seem that progression towards achieving 'fit' would require undergoing the same process. Like the spouses in the Hong Kong study, they see the struggle with differences as the crucial issue in the development of a marriage. They propose the first developmental stage of intimate relations as the *fusion* of two people who choose each other to 'complete' and 'complement' what they are and who they are. Complementing is defined as the process of mutually making up what is lacking. Differences thus both attract and detract, contributing both to a sense of fulfillment and to instances of actual conflict in their interaction. The second stage is one of *struggling with differences*. If differences overwhelm them at stage two, they may separate. Or they may institutionalize their differences by each becoming fixed in their particular ways, the introvert and the extrovert each remaining so. Such relationships are vulnerable to stress and difficulties when confronted by change. Spouses able to integrate the strengths and weaknesses in themselves and in their partners emerge into the third stage as *self-directed* persons. They can be sensitive to their own and their spouses propensities, value their differences and are able to shift their stances in order to negotiate a different 'fit' according to changing circumstances.

Analysis of the responses of the sample according to the Proskys' model of development in intimate relationships seems to indicate that some of the younger married couples of this study, with the type of 'romantic marriage' described in Chapter 4, were working from a position of fusion to accommodate themselves to each other to achieve a mutually gratifying 'fit' and to blend as a couple. Those who achieve a match are reassured in their choice of partners. Those who are still not matched, explain this away by saying that they are working on adjusting to each other and that they are gradually improving. Couples who are overwhelmed by the differences and similarities in each other begin to describe these in polarized terms, and with increasing rigidity they tend to label each other in ways that leave little room for manoeuver in the relationship.

In an account of progression toward mutuality in married people, Wynne (1988) describes a development that bears a similarity to 'fit'. He refers to the 'step-by-step growth of relatedness' in the interdependence of a couple built on affectional bonding and shared commitment. 'Fit' develops through transactional processes in which each partner in the pair undergoes internal change and experiences change in the relationship with the other. 'Fit' between the spouses forms the basis for continuing growth in relatedness towards mutuality.

In the interviews, when the adjusted spouses reviewed their experiences and shared their satisfaction with each other they seemed to be talking about a harmonizing level of fit in a number of areas of marital life which strengthened their sense of compatibility in the relationship, contributing to their overall sense of subjective well being.

Supplementing Clinical Interviews With Self Report Measures

Self report measures and guided interviews enable the spouses to review and to evaluate their marriage. The skill of the counsellor in interviewing the spouses and in developing a rapport with them to create a safe climate for the sharing of personal and private information is of basic importance in all marriage counselling. The material from the self report measures is used to supplement the clinical observations of the counsellor, as he or she works with the spouses to evaluate, redefine and renegotiate issues and events affecting their relationship.

Many people in Hong Kong who may be reticent to open up in unfamiliar therapy sessions and who may be reluctant to talk freely about personal and relational issues may respond more readily to self-rating inventories which are short and to the point. The practical procedure of completing the self-rating inventories initiates the reflective process and encourages them to participate in a joint activity of retrospective review. The carefully selected items in self report measures enable them to examine various aspects of their marriage in a detailed and in-depth manner, and offer alternative perspectives to see issues in a different light and from a different point of view. The activity itself initiates the essential process of the spouses cooperating in a shared endeavour with each other and with the counsellor to promote collaboration in their transactions.

In clinical application, self reports provide vital information to the counsellor in the initial phase of counselling. Administered at the beginning and at the completion of counselling they provide a precise means of monitoring change and therapeutic progress during counselling. They constitute an accountability system for marriage counsellors to evaluate the effectiveness and outcome of intervention. The spouses' experiences as participants of their marriage, expressed through self reports, serves to supplement the counsellor's on-going assessment. Information from self report measures and from clinical exploration, can enlighten, confirm or disconfirm each other, contributing to increasing understanding. Above that, self reports encourage the active participation of the spouses in reviewing their relationship.

Part II

Variations in Marriage

Chapter Four

Classification of Types of Marriage

The process of organizing data into meaningful patterns is one of the exciting challenges of research work. This chapter analyses scores from the ENRICH inventory to identify patterns of the varieties in types of marriages. One classification is based on types of marriages as proposed in the Circumplex model. Another is derived from cluster analysis of the ENRICH Couple Positive Agreement Scores.

Case studies will be used to illustrate each type.

Types of Marriage According to the Circumplex Model

The ENRICH marital inventory is one of the scales associated with the Circumplex model which proposes a typology of 16 types of marriage. The ENRICH computer report includes a map showing the spouses' type of marriage according to their responses on the cohesion and adaptability subscales. Scores on cohesion reflects the balance of separate-togetherness in the marriage which can range from being enmeshed, connected, separated, disengaged. Scores on adaptability reflects the stability-change balance and can range from being rigid, structured, flexible, to chaotic.

The mid-range levels, connected and separated for cohesion and flexible and structured for adaptability, are considered to be the functional levels. Levels of extreme cohesion and extreme adaptability are considered to be dysfunctional (Olson, Fournier, and Druckman, 1987).

Spouses in the same marriage may not experience or view their relationship in the same way. One spouse may consider the marriage to be flexible with each spouse taking responsibility or assuming the leadership role according to the situation. The other spouse may be of the opinion that the manner in which they deal with decisions and tasks is quite fixed. One may regard the amount of togetherness and closeness which they share to be adequate, and the other may feel this to be too much or too little. In determining the type of marriage as perceived by each spouse, the Circumplex model takes account of each partner's perspective, and adopts individual scores on cohesion and adaptability to plot their position on a topology of sixteen types of marriage.

On this basis, the 204 spouses in the Hong Kong sample have been plotted on the Circumplex model as presented in Figure 4.1.

Analysis of the types of marriage according to the Circumplex model showed no significant difference between adjusted and non-adjusted spouses; or between husbands and wives.

Types of Marriages Through Cluster Analysis

In organizing types of marriage, it is also possible to statistically cluster groups with similar characteristics. Synder and Smith (1986) utilized entire scores from one inventory, the Marital Satisfaction Index (MSI), to derive five types. Filsinger, McAvoy, and Lewis (1984) used four scales to make up a Pair Formation Inventory. Cluster analysis of this combination produced seven types which they considered represent pathways along which marriages can develop.

The Hong Kong study adopted Ward's (1963) technique in cluster hierarchial agglomerative analysis to sort out the sample according to their scores on 13 ENRICH scales. In this analysis couples most similar are grouped together to form a type. A type consists of members that are more similar to each other than members of other types. The grouping is determined by the smallest increase in the Errors Sum of Squares, ESS, to the centroid (means of the dimensions) of the parent cluster.

Cluster Analysis — ENRICH Scales

While the Circumplex model registers the spouses' types of marriage on the basis of individual scores, cluster analysis will determine the type of marital relationship according to the Positive Couple Agreement scores,

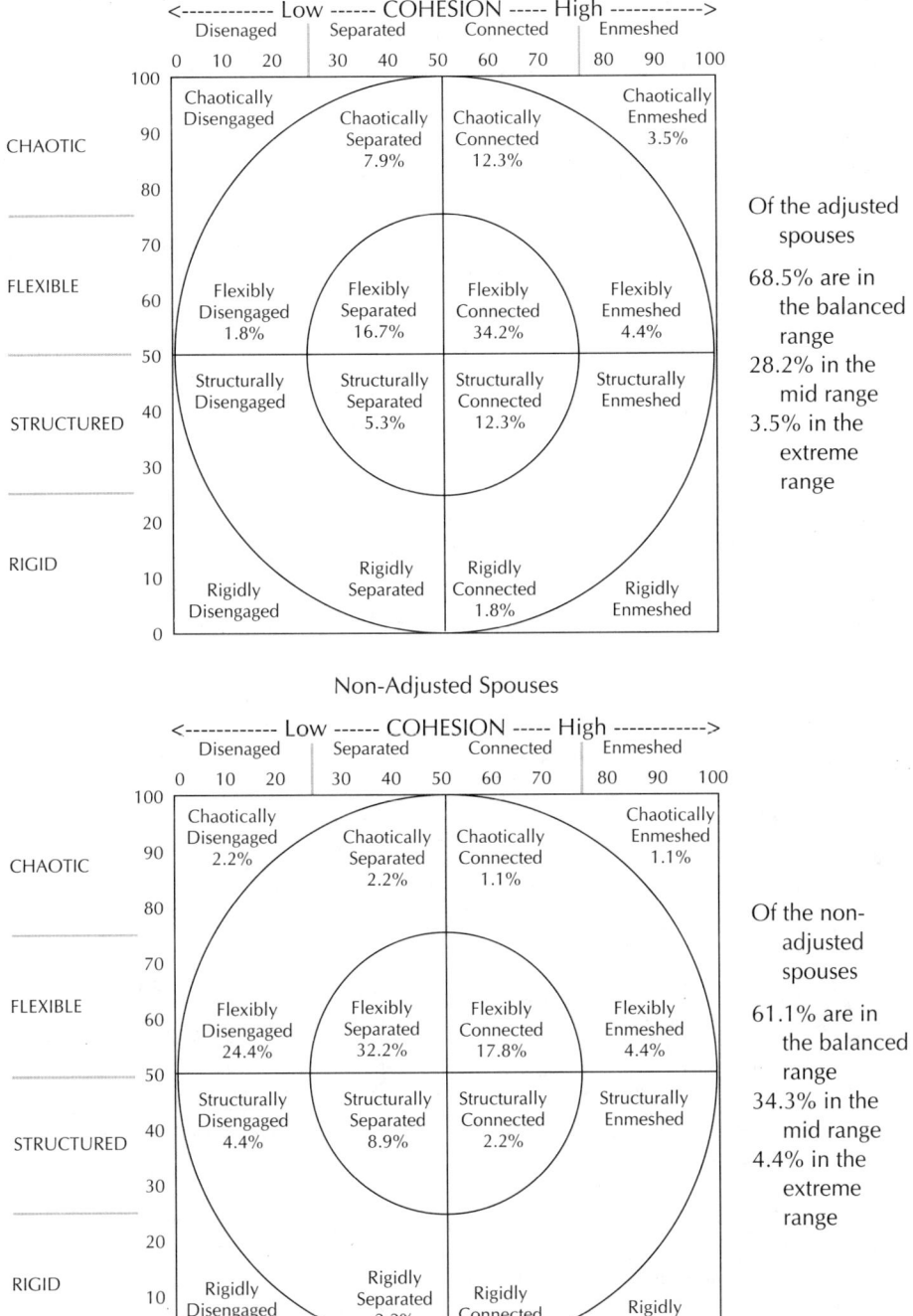

Figure 4.1   Type of marriage based on the Circumplex model

the PCA. This couple score is obtained by synchronizing the spouses' responses according to whether they agree or disagree with each other.

In the Hong Kong study, preliminary cluster analysis of the 102 marriages produced two clusters, 59 in one and 43 in the other. The DAS, applied to determine criterion groups, classified the marriages into 57 couples in the adjusted group and 45 in the non-adjusted group. Thus, ENRICH and DAS applied to the same sample of married people produced very similar results.

Further cluster analysis to derive six groups produced four groups with scores indicating positive marriages and two groups with scores indicating difficult marriages. This is diagrammatically presented in Table 4.1.

Computer analysis to the seventh cluster permitted further refinement, differentiating the **harmonious marriages** group into two clusters: one **harmonious marriages** and another group consisting of a few outstandingly *mei mun* happy marriages. These marriages reflect high levels of personal fulfillment in general satisfaction, in liking the person of the spouse, in spousal transactions over a number of areas and particularly high scores in relationships with children, family and friends. They have been designated as **familial marriages**. When DAS scores were examined, familial marriages revealed a mean of 132.9, while the DAS mean of

Table 4.1 Types of Marriages from Cluster Analysis

	Positive marriages cluster	*Difficult marriages cluster*
Two Clusters	59	43
Three Clusters	31 28	43
Four –	8 23 28	43
Five –	8 23 16 12	43
Six –	8 23 16 12	36 7
	Romantic Harmonious Tested Life Style	Conflictual Confrontive
Seven Clusters	5 18 Familial Harmonious	
Eight Clusters		16 20 Struggling Conflictual

harmonious marriages stood at 120.2. Couples in familial and harmonious marriages have different experiences, though both types of marriage offer high levels of gratification.

Further distillation to an eighth cluster divided the **conflictual marriages** into two groups and generated a group of **struggling marriages**. Review of the content of these cases showed the struggling marriages to be appreciably different from conflictual marriages. The ENRICH marital satisfaction scale shows a mean of 21.88 for struggling marriages and 4.5 for conflictual marriages (Table 4.2). When adjustment scores were taken into account, the DAS mean of struggling marriages was borderline at 94.5, the DAS mean of conflictual marriages was 76.6 indicating relationships at risk.

Cluster analysis of the ENRICH scales differentiates eight types of marital relationships that may epitomize marriages observed in Hong Kong. **Familial marriages** portray many of the qualities of what would be considered *mei mun* marriages for the Chinese. Conjugal concerns are central, but family relationships are also fostered. **Romantic marriages** are the young marriages when the spouses are still very much concentrated on each other, and on delineating their positions regarding values and a philosophy of life. These marriages present a picture of two young people striving for convergence through getting acquainted with each other's ethical orientation, and each other's adaptive ability in order to build up a degree of mutuality. **Harmonious marriages** represent the Chinese stereotype of a complementary marriage where husbands and wives compromise to achieve cohesion in the relationship. It was not felt to be important that each spouse may not like certain personality traits or behavioral patterns in the other . What was important is that they shared a common set of values and ethics, had a high level of general satisfaction, sex relations that were enjoyable, and that they cooperated in the care and discipline of the children. **Tested marriages** are very high in cohesion and adaptability, record the highest equalitarian scores, and rate moderately high in satisfaction despite low levels in a number of marital processes such as communication and conflict management. These are nevertheless adjusted marriages which have undergone and survived some serious crises.

Cluster analysis identified four types of vulnerable marriages; one with borderline adjustment, one struggling, one tense, and one seriously stressed. **Life style marriages** highlight duty and the preservation of the institution of marriage. When both spouses share this perspective, these marriages offer security and a sense of comfort. **Struggling marriages** have high cohesion. However, there is tension in most areas of living. **Confrontive marriages** have the lowest cohesion, poor communication and great difficulties in resolving arguments or avoiding disagreements.

Conflictual marriages are very distressing for both spouses, who are actively dissatisfied, do not like each other, cannot communicate or resolve
their differences. For some, the history of their relationship has been
marked by a series of separations and reconciliations. These spouses have
difficulties living together and difficulties living apart.

A fuller description of each of these types of marriage is presented in
case profiles. The PCA scores of the 13 ENRICH scales used to produce
the types of marriages are presented in Table 4.2. This table also contains
other factual information including the spouses' statements of levels of
satisfaction and the mean DAS scores. The number of years married is
presented to show the length of time which the couple have had to build
up an enjoyable interdependence, or frustrations and disappointments.

Table 4.2   Eight Types of Marriages Cluster Analysis of ENRICH PCA Scores

ENRICH PCA Mean	Famil N=5	Romant N=8	Harmoni N=18	Tested N=16	LifeSt N=12	Strugg N=16	Confron N=7	Confl N=20
MS	82	75.8	67.2	53.1	28.3	21.9	15.7	4.5
PI	44.	32.5	26.7	13.1	12.5	6.3	12.8	3.5
CO	60.	57.5	41.7	28.1	15.8	13.8	4.3	4.5
CR	64.	53.8	38.3	25.0	21.7	16.9	8.6	8.0
FM	70.	80.0	52.2	40.6	45.0	23.1	42.9	13.5
LA	58.	63.8	47.2	50.6	27.5	28.1	34.3	16.5
SR	76.	82.5	68.9	38.8	57.5	26.9	35.7	15.5
CP	80.	-	68.9	62.5	22.5	25.0	32.9	16.5
FF	88.	61.3	47.8	36.3	21.7	27.5	38.6	15.5
ER	62.	70.0	75.6	77.5	63.3	68.8	45.7	54.5
EO	76.	83.8	77.2	67.5	53.3	50.0	45.7	32.5
ADA	52.	80.0	55.6	83.8	90.0	53.8	45.7	59.0
COH	84.	80.0	81.1	83.8	90.0	73.8	34.3	84.0
Glob. Satis	70.	64.5	65.7	59.9	44.0	36.5	35.4	26.8
DAS Mean	132.9	125.4	120.2	110.0	98.6	94.5	99.0	76.6
Years Married	12	1.6	11.3	11.8	7.8	7.8	8.9	9.6
Monthly Income	$8611	$8167	$10521	$10326	$9211	$9397	$7000	$9609

| Total | 102 |

ENRICH Scales:	MS	-	marital satisfaction	CP	-	children & parenting
	PI	-	personality issues	FF	-	family & friends
	CO	-	communication	ER	-	equalitarian roles
	CR	-	conflict management	EO	-	ethical orientation
	FM	-	financial management	ADA	-	marital adaptability
	LA	-	leisure activities	COH	-	marital cohesion
	SR	-	sexual relations			

The romantic marriages were all young marriages experiencing the initial glow of a promising union. The mean income of this group is fairly low, though as a two-person unit their expenses may also be low. It is interesting to note that the happiest marriages do not have the highest income.

Profiles of Eight Marriages

Cluster analysis produces some very revealing patterns of marriage. In order to appreciate the experience of a couple within each type of marriage, the following section will present personal profiles of each type through case studies. The case studies will focus on the events and transactions between the spouses that influenced their subjective experiences within the marriage relationship. Adjustment processes and ways of coping with conflict will be highlighted. The descriptions will also refer to the nature of the interdependence evolved by the couple and whether this mutual reliance is enjoyable, qualified, partial, or a focus of contention.

The term used to describe happy marriages among the Chinese is *mei mun*, which literally means beautiful and full. A happy marriage therefore is beautifully full. When Spanier developed his topology of marriage using the dimensions of satisfaction and stability he considered a marriage with high satisfaction and high stability to be a full shell marriage. The title 'ENRICH' which Olson and his associates gave to the inventory also emphasizes plentifulness. The Chinese translation of ENRICH replicates this emphasis on the fullness of good things. This representation of the fulsomeness of happy marriages, and the contrasting emptiness of unhappy marriages is graphically illustrated by including a box with bar charts for each profile. The range of eight types of marriages starts with the familial marriage where the box presented on p. 68 is almost full, and concludes with the conflictual marriage where the box given on p. 79 is painfully bare.

Type 1 Familial marriages

As the bar charts in the box show, these marriages are full and fulfilling. Transactions between the spouses are varied and active, and involve not only the couple, their children and their extended families; they spread into the community as they participate in public and voluntary projects. These couples talk about trips at weekends and school holidays, plan family projects, attend community functions, night classes, dine with old school friends and work colleagues. Some of these activities are under-taken together, some separately according to each person's interests. In the interviews they were lively as they poked fun and teased each other for being inconsistent or quick tempered, but each was generally sup-portive of the other. All these couples volunteered to participate in the research as they were interested to find out how ENRICH would evaluate their relationship. They had many of the problems usual to family living, including difficulties with children and in-laws, financial and work pres-sures, which they expected to sort out between themselves.

These marriages record high scores in most of the scales, with the highest in the areas of family and friends. The strengths in these mar-riages (80+ scores according to ENRICH) are in marital satisfaction, children and parenting, family and friends, and cohesion.

Possible strengths (70+ on ENRICH) are in financial management, sexual relationships, ethical orientation.

These couples had marginal scores which could indicate areas to work on, in personality issues and adaptability (50%).

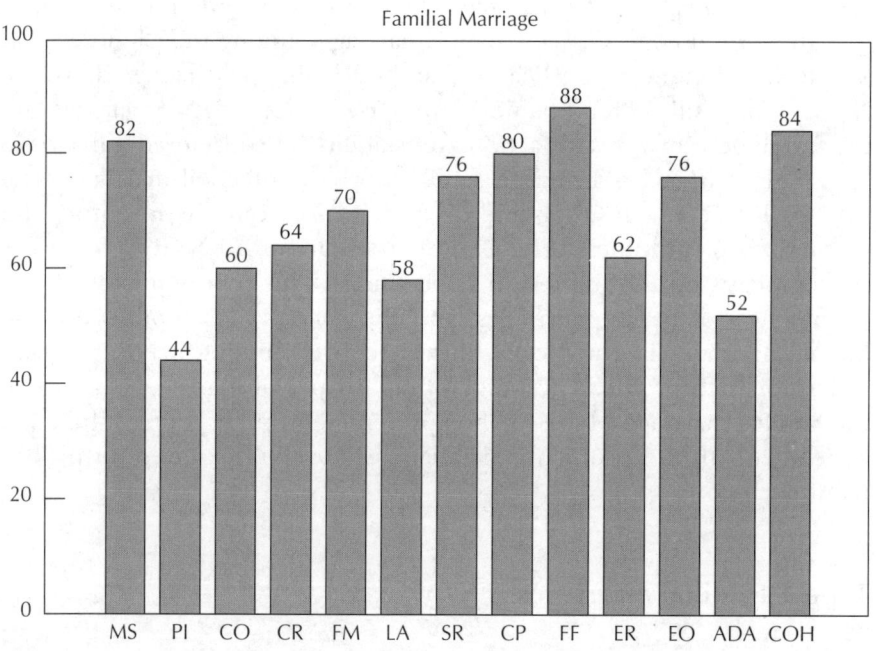

Personal Profile: Mr and Mrs Au

When talking about what is good about being married, Mr Au said he just likes to go home. He enjoyed the welcome, comfort and the order of his home. He enjoys reviewing with his wife and children the happenings of the day. Mrs Au, when recalling what her husband does which pleases her, referred to his ingenuity in thinking up surprises that makes her so happy. Mr Au in describing what his wife does which pleases him, cites the times she does things for him which he does not like doing, without being asked.

This empathy between the spouses can also be seen in the way they have merged their lives, each acquiring the interests of the other and making these their own, as with their love of music. They intermittently devise common interests that energize the relationship. These include viewing new flats together, looking at household equipment, renting videos, making home movies, and annual family trips to other places. They sometimes meet for yum cha *and for lunch. Apart from their time together and with the family, both maintain active social lives with their own friends, or attend evening classes, sometimes inviting, sometimes refusing the request of the other to join particular events.*

The children, who are their pride and joy, take an active part in the exchange of gifts and in planning surprises within the family and between the parents. When disagreement arises over the children's discipline, the parents support each other in front of the children, then later share their opinions in private. They have evolved very similar ways of dealing with tensions between themselves. When differences arise, one or the other does not push the point and waits until they have cooled off, then brings the matter up for renegotiation. They do not recall leaving any issue unattended.

Both Mr and Mrs Au subscribe to the view that in a marriage each should try the utmost to do what the other would like. They feel it is not possible and not important to compare whether one does more or gives more than the other. In pleasing the spouse, one pleases the self.

Type 2 Romantic marriages

These are all young marriages. The couples had been married a mean of 1.6 years. These spouses felt very secure in their financial situation, scoring the highest on financial management, even though their income was not high. The strengths and possible strengths in their marriage are in overall satisfaction, financial management, sexual relationships, equalitarian roles, ethical orientation, and adaptability and cohesion.

The 50+ to 60+ on communication, leisure activities, and family and friends may indicate that they are still in the process of negotiating these aspects of their marriage.

These couples were very absorbed in each other. They were using different means to get to know each other, to get closer, to learn new experiences together. Many had already participated in marriage preparation classes. Volunteering to join the research project was another means to explore themselves and their relationship.

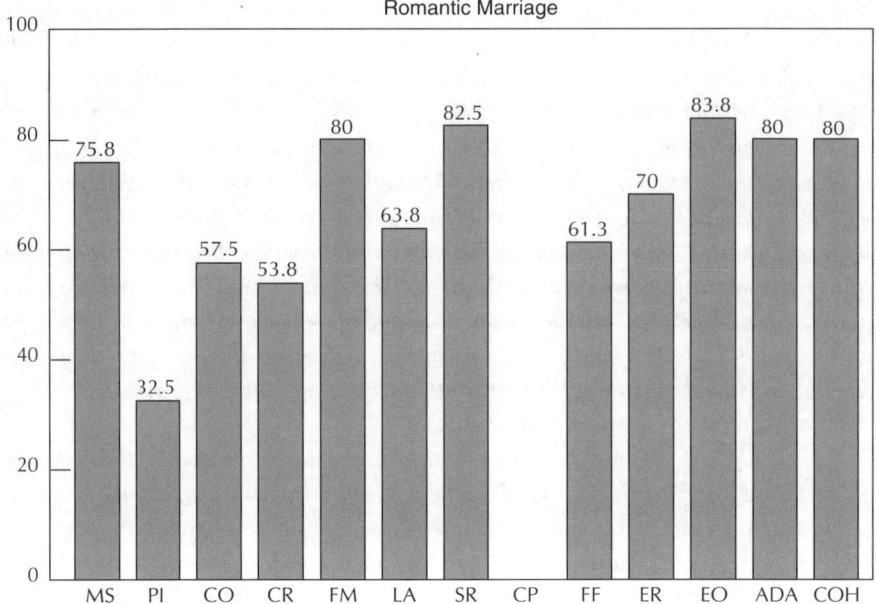

Personal Profile: Mr and Mrs Bao

Since making a home of their own a year ago after getting married, Mr and Mrs Bao have made a point of going out to work and travelling part of their route together. Mr Bao feels proud to have a wife who is both able and nurturing. Mrs Bao is happy to have a husband who is family orientated, responsible and reliable.

The couple came from similar social, educational and religious backgrounds. Consensus between them over most areas of living is high, and they find they reaffirm each other in various ways. They plan and participate together in many joint activities, but also have their own set of friends. Equality is an ideal with both. They believe each of them should contribute to making the marriage work, whether in balancing finances, in doing housework, or in resolving conflict. When differences arise between them Mrs Bao tends to keep quiet. Mr Bao is more verbally expressive, he explains and clarifies to persuade his wife. He feels he works harder at this, and would like his wife to take the initiative sometimes. When they reach deadlock, they do not allow it to continue overnight, praying aloud and conversing through prayer to reach an understanding.

The couple engage in a great many bonding behaviours, writing little notes if the other is not around when they have something to communicate, leaving cards with loving messages for the other, supporting each other in their relationship with the extended family. Though Mr Bao is a filial son who phones home every evening, he nevertheless protects his wife from expectations which are intrusive. On her part, Mrs Bao accompanies her husband to dinner at his parents' home, though this is more frequently than she likes.

Type 3 Harmonious marriages

Spouses in harmonious marriages feel secure and comfortable in their relationship. They share similar ethical and value systems, are content over the division of roles and responsibilities, and are committed to maintaining the cohesion of the family. They enjoy fulfilling sexual relations and shared parenting. Their responses indicate that they are only moderately successful over financial management, also leisure activities together could be better; and their communication and conflict management could be more effective. However, in general their overall marital satisfaction is high.

The harmonious marriages in the study which encountered crisis were able to meet the challenge of demands made on them. When crises occur they serve as an opportunity for enrichment and sometimes lead to an increased appreciation of the partner.

A review of the research records revealed that many of these couples were recruited from parents' training classes and other community groups. One-sixth of the spouses in harmonious marriages were undergoing the final stages of counselling. Two of these marriages had been working out what Guerin (1987) referred to as purser-distancer tensions with the wives reaching out to their husbands for greater emotional connections. In one marriage of this type, the wife was under treatment for depression and the family required help to reorganize and to deal with this.

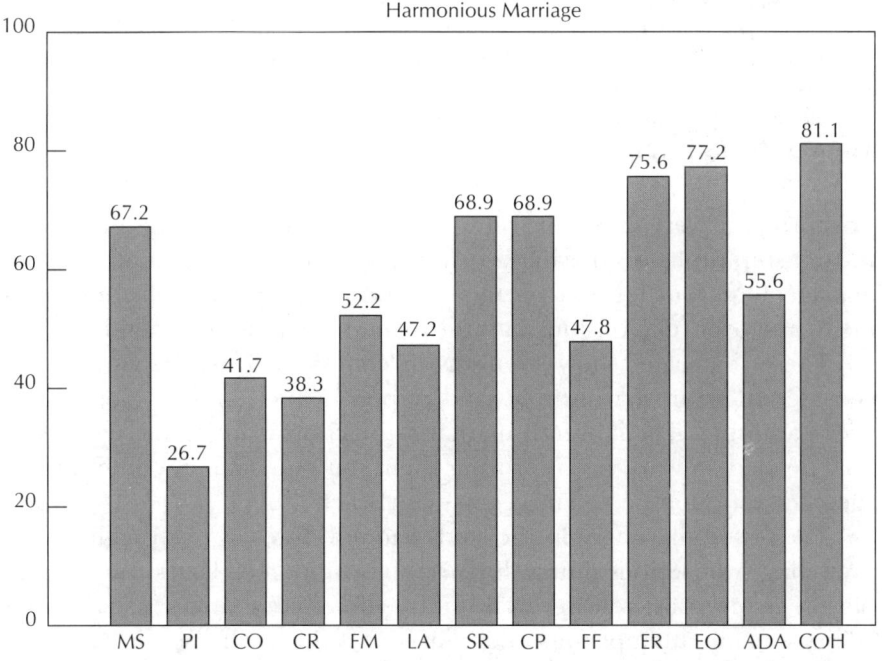

Personal Profile: Mr and Mrs Chan

Mr and Mrs Chan recall their wedding day as important and happy. Both report the birth of the children to be the second most happy and memorable event in their lives, though the children do detract attention from each other.

The couple consider themselves to be well matched. Their development of interdependence has been facilitated by the way they are able to complement each other. Mr Chan hands over his wages to Mrs Chan whom he feels manages their finances fairly, and in ways beneficial to the family. Mrs Chan sometimes accompanies her husband to dinner with his employer and his work mates, and helps out in little ways. Mr Chan generally helps out with housework, but prefers to be involved in doing things with and for the children. They agree with and support each other in their belief that children need a balance of nurturing and discipline.

The couple live with the husband's parents. They are very traditional, and the role and behaviour of each person in the household is clearly defined and therefore manageable. Mr Chan feels dutifully bound to continue this living arrangement. Mrs Chan's one aim in life is to buy their own flat. She brings this matter up frequently, sometimes as a joke, at other times coyly, placating or provocative in turn. However, the bottom line seems to be that she respects Mr Chan's decision not to act on this.

In general, consensus and compromise between the couple is high. These actually constitute values in their philosophy regarding family relationships. Thus conflict is contained. Because of their attitudinal perspectives emphasizing cooperation and support, there is little room for bargaining. One spouse having stated his or her preference, accepts that when able to do so the other would respond. In the meantime, the bond between them and the bonding behaviours make any differences tolerable.

Type 4 Tested marriages

This profile is very different from the previous three in areas of spousal relationship processes, having very low scores in communication, conflict management, and tensions in their sexual exchange, financial management, and over relationships with the extended family and friends.

These marriages show strengths in cohesion, flexibility and ethical considerations; in sharing roles and responsibilities; and in cooperation over parenting. Their overall marital satisfaction is moderate. However, they needed to work on improving their communication, conflict management and their personal acceptance of each other.

The tested marriages in the study showed histories of struggling and prevailing over serious illness, financial hardship, loan shark threats, employment reversals, role reversal due to life circumstances, extramarital affairs, suicide attempts, and devitalization, with each spouse having to work through tremendous pain, distress and ambivalence in the relationship. For some of these marriages, testing events had been adverse for the marriage, leaving them highly vulnerable and stressed. For some, crises had shaken the relationship, but they also served to stimulate a greater appreciation and awareness of the spouse as a person, leading to more sharing and investment in the relationship. Professional help and support had been important in sustaining some of these marriage over particularly demanding periods.

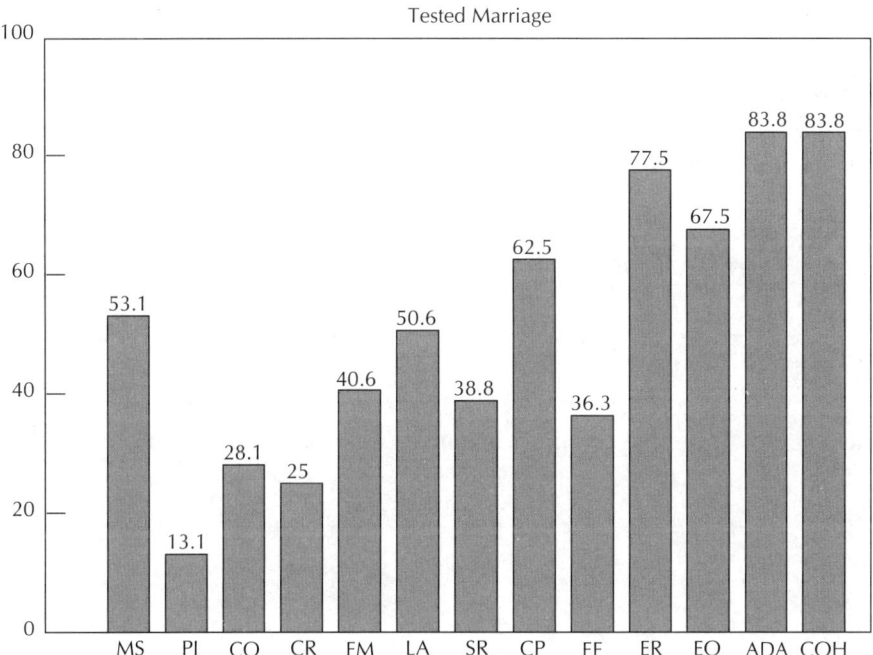

Tested Marriage

Personal Profile: Mr and Mrs Deng

Mr and Mrs Deng married young. He was 21 and she 19. Their relationship was not too secure due to practical reasons related to work, housing and finance, but they were in love. The birth of their first daughter consolidated the relationship. Then, in the struggle of making a living and bringing up a young family, the relationship became devitalized.

Mr Deng's work in restaurants exposed him to gambling between shifts and casual relationships with other women. The marriage went through turmoil for a few years. When Mr Deng had to hide from loan sharks, Mrs Deng was protective and helpful, working part-time and taking care of the children on her own. When Mr Deng engaged in affairs, there were fights. Mrs Deng made a suicide attempt, and threatened divorce. The couple had not built up interdependence in the practi-

cal aspects of living, the wife having to function much on her own. However, the emotional interdependence continued to be important to both. Throughout his period in hiding, the wife kept the husband informed and connected to family events, and he admired the manner she was able to evade the loan sharks. Despite the struggles and the many ups and downs of their relationship, Mrs Deng felt that she could find satisfaction in the marriage. She was willing to put up with financial difficulties, irregular support, long hours away from home due to her husband's work and leisure priorities, but she was not willing to put up with an affair. She demanded his involvement in the daily life of the family and regular financial contributions to the family. The marriage went through an intense period of bonding and bargaining exchanges. Mr Deng finds certain irritations in married life. However he respects his wife's competence in managing family living. He is touched by her constancy and her loyal support of him during difficult times. He finds he enjoys family activities. As his work became more stable and their financial situation improving, the marriage was being re-established and becoming more fulfilling.

Type 5 Life style marriages

These marriages provide the spouses with the domestic and sexual benefits of the married life style.

Compared to tested marriages, life style marriages experienced lower satisfaction, poorer communication, more disagreement, more tension

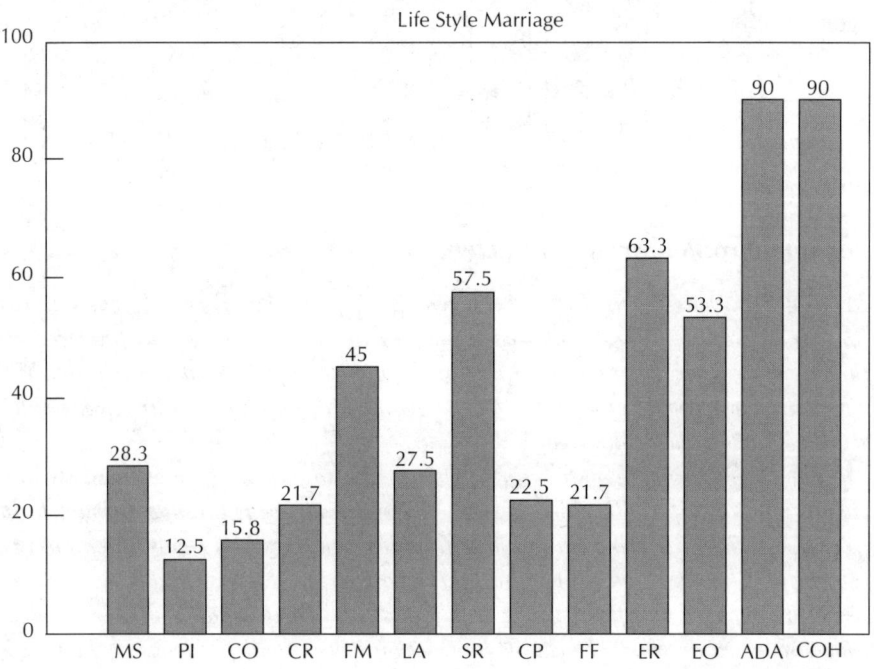

over parenting and extended family relationships. However, they recorded better sexual relations, and high degrees of cohesion and flexibility. The couples are moderately effective in sharing ethical ideas and roles and responsibilities. Overall marital satisfaction is very low, as is spousal transaction in communication, and conflict management.

Most of these marriages were undergoing counselling. The few who had volunteered from community groups complained of somatic conditions, minor health concerns and difficulties in the care and discipline of their children.

Personal Profile: Mr and Mrs Eu

Mr and Mrs Eu feel that they share a similar sense of duty and responsibility in their marital and parental roles. In their marriage, they have evolved interdependence in certain aspects of living, while maintaining separateness in others. As they do not expect or demand too much from each other, their relationship adjustment has been steady, without much fluctuation and with no particular highs or lows.

Both see the married life style, with its security and regularity, a steady sexual partner, and continuity in raising healthy children, to be important. Mr Eu is clear about the division of labour and responsibility, the separation of work and home concerns, and the naturalness of having a life of his own. Mrs Eu prefers more sharing, but she does not voice this strongly. Instead, she attempts to get the attention of her husband by complaining of her ill health and by involving him over the children.

Both believe that for a peaceful life, each must make some compromise. Where relationship with in-laws are concerned, this poses a problem. Mrs Eu finds the in-laws demanding, difficult and fault finding. Mr Eu subscribes to a great many 'shoulds' where filial obligations are concerned. When he feels his wife does not understand his position or does not do as he asks, he loses his temper. Mrs Eu generally gives way and has headaches. Certain issues remain unresolved. Disagreements may flare up but are pushed aside, and a false sense of harmony prevails. Family cohesion is highly valued by both.

In the agreed shared areas of living, there is bonding and support of each other's endeavour. Outside these areas, the other spouse is not supposed to interfere. There is a carefully balanced reciprocity so that any bargaining between the spouses is subtle and indirect.

Type 6 Struggling marriages

The common feature of these marriages was that they were all in the process of coping with difficult and painful negotiations. Some, like the couple described below, were negotiating basic marital expectations of who does what, and the regulation of the degree of mutual control, closeness and distance, but had not yet arrived at a level agreeable to both. Others were in the midst of sorting past unresolved issues, an unwilling abortion, the feeling of having been pushed into the marriage when not ready, and lack of support when this was needed. Some were in the aftermath of dealing with stressful events such as separation, abuse, affairs, and serious illness. These couples had decided to rebuild their marriage and were still seeking ways to redefine the relationship. However, their efforts were still blocked by resentment and disappointment, and this is reflected in their ENRICH responses.

These are distressed marriages. Eight areas of marital transactions need working on (ENRICH scores below 30). These areas cover the entire range of marital interaction from processes of communication, conflict management, sexual relations, to practical issues of financial management and leisure activities, and tensions in relationships with children, parents and friends. These marriages record strengths in high levels of cohesion and in sharing roles and responsibilities. This seems to be the profile of couples who are tied into their marriages, though in negative and painful ways.

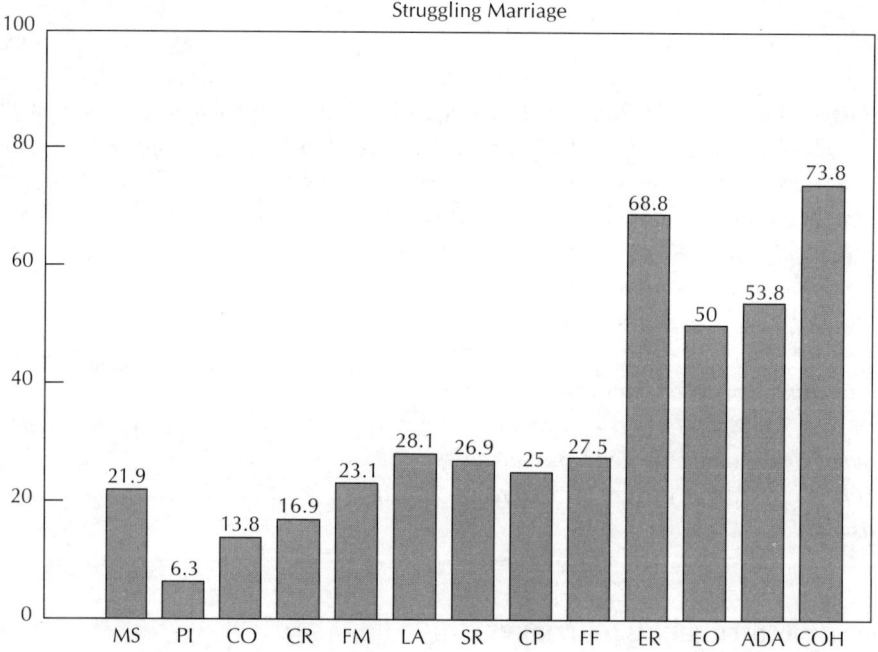

Personal Profile: Mr and Mrs Fung

Mr and Mrs Fung have been married for seven years and have two sons in primary school. Mr Fung is in a high risk occupation, works shifts and is on call.

Their relationship is intense with a great deal of interaction laced with agitation and mutual blaming. Mr Fung complains that Mrs Fung is too dependent and demands too much from him. He considers himself a responsible provider, a loving father though strict in discipline. He even helps in housework, complaining of his wife's neglect of this due to her part-time work which earns so little. Mrs Fung complains that her husband does not respect her, spends little time at home, has leisure with friends, thus depriving her and their sons of family time together. She disagrees with her husband's belief in corporal punishment in disciplining the children and claims she has to work to supplement her husband's inadequate financial contribution.

This couple's daily life is intricately inter-twined. However, this very interdependence is a matter of contention, with one spouse wanting more involvement and the other withdrawing. When tension builds up, he goes off to work, and she to her parents. When distance becomes too threatening, they come together and reassume an exchange of concern, control and criticism. Insecurity arising from the tension in the relationship every now and then triggers Mrs Fung to reach out for reassurance from her husband in the form of more togetherness. This he interprets as his wife demanding compliance from him. He is willing to spend more time at home if she makes sure the cubicle is well kept and tidy. She agrees to stay home to attend to household chores and not to work if he would contribute more for housekeeping. However, she feels anxious that if she does more housework it would leave him with nothing to do when at home, therefore she should leave something for him to do to keep him engaged with the family. She tells him that she needs him, and she sometimes demonstrates this behaviorally and verbally, and he does feel needed and important to his wife and the boys.

Type 7 Confrontive marriages

The clinical impression is that these couples were undergoing intense and contentious negotiations to achieve changes in the marriage. They were all undergoing counselling. Their records note comments such as 'wife hot tempered; husband indecisive'; 'wife wants to go to work, husband dislikes'; husband or wife 'beat child, wants attention from other parent'; 'wife strong, husband not fulfilled at home'.

This group has the lowest score on consensus over equalitarian roles, on cohesion in the relationship, and in communication. Their overall marital satisfaction is very low; however, the spouses seem invested in, though sometimes ambivalent about the marriage. They required a great deal of support and counselling input.

These marriages form a sizeable portion of counselling caseloads. A part of their conflict arises from one spouse holding onto traditional gender role stereotypes, unrealistic expectations, or inconsistent parenting practices, exacerbated by provocative communication styles, financial pressures, in-law interference, and other problems such as drinking and gambling.

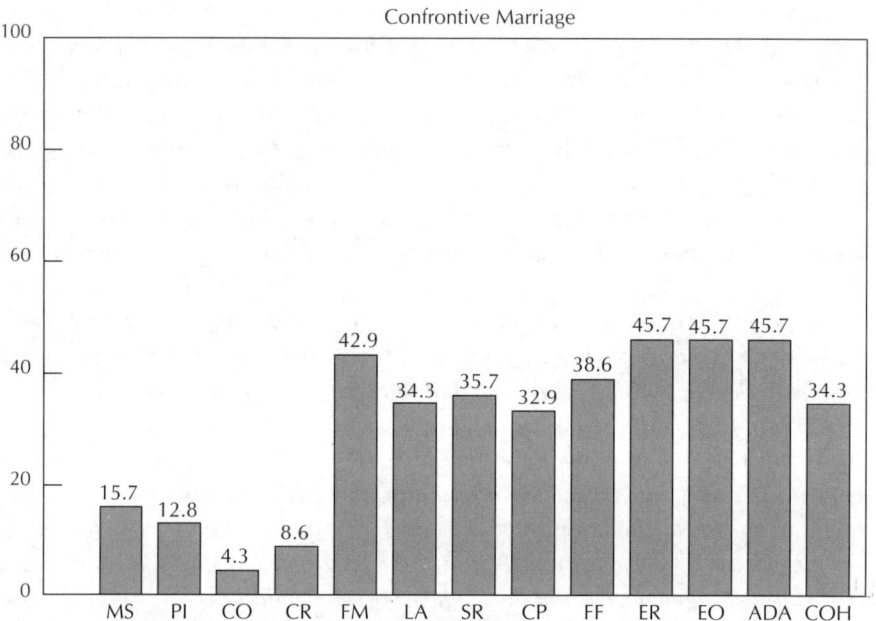

Personal Profile: Mr and Mrs Goh

In the practical aspects of everyday life, Mr and Mrs Goh each attend to their own spheres of concern. However, in the spousal relationship they are sensitive and reactive to each other. This reactive responsiveness is tinged with competitiveness, with the more competent Mrs Goh attempting to encourage her husband to be more assertive, more achieving. She uses confrontive means to do so, sometimes supportively confrontive, sometimes critically so.

Mr Goh is a self employed artisan; much of his work is related to his wife's family firm. He finds work stressful and feels that his wife does not understand the difficulties of his work position. He does not have a very active role at home; he does not feel fulfilled at work and he does not have many friends. His main enjoyment is gambling — not excessively, but enough to get him into debt every now and then. When this happens his wife has been active and helpful in seeking out ways to cover what is owed.

Mr Goh both relies on and resents his wife's assistance and concern. He acknowledges his wife is a better financial manager, and that she is resourceful in repaying his debts and in covering up for him before other people, but he regrets his need to be dependent on her. They have few common interests or mutual friends, so sharing leisure time together seems irrelevant to Mr Goh. Mrs Goh would like more time together as a family for the sake of the growing children. Mr Goh compliments his wife on being a good mother. However, he resists her attempts to make him more active as a parent. They both agree to work together to present a united front to family and friends. They are only able to maintain these attitudes by denying and avoiding conflict. When this surfaces, their tension blocks transactions. When things are going well, life is routine as expected; when things are not going well, both become quickly flustered.

The practical interdependence between the spouses is acknowledged by them. However, one spouse is active and seems to do more for the relationship. Both are concerned about making some effort to reach a more comfortable balance, but the going is hard, and they are not sure if they can make it. Every now and then, one of them feels like giving up.

Type 8 Conflictual marriages

These are actively conflictual marriages. Twelve have been classified by their marriage counsellors as habitually conflictual marriages. Four are serious abuse cases; four have psychiatric labels. Most have records of multiple separations, seriously disturbed personal histories, and histories of gambling and drinking.

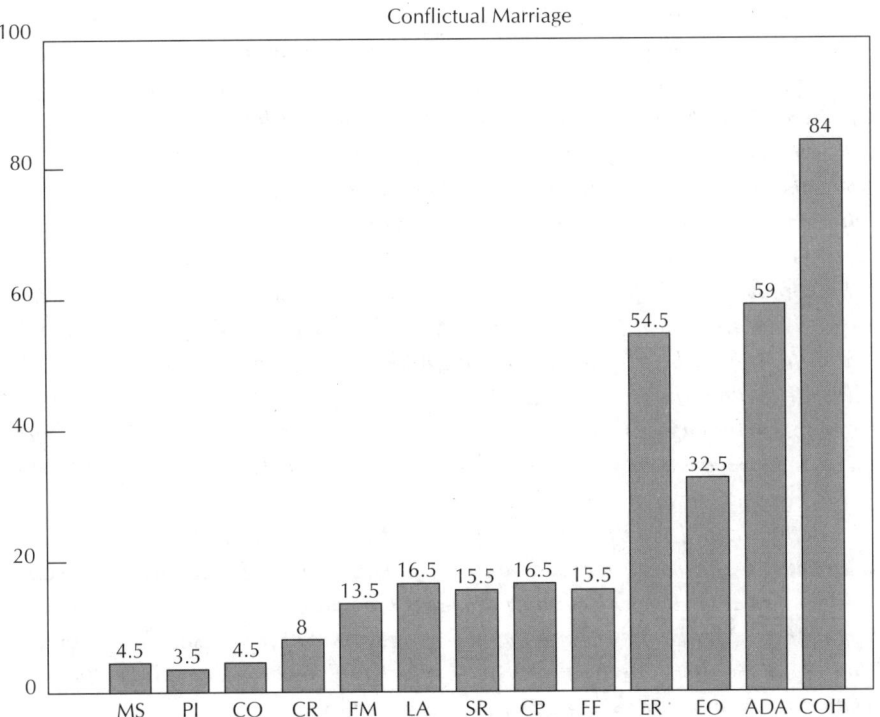

Conflictual Marriage

The emptiness of these marriages is clearly illustrated by the emptiness of the box with the bar chart. That these relationships share very little is confirmed by frequent separations over the course of their married life. These couples experience hardly any satisfaction from the relationship, do not seem to like their partners, have little communication, feel misunderstood, and feel unable to do anything to change their spouses.

It is interesting to note the high cohesion score. The items on emotional bonding are couched in positive terms. The question arises as to whether the couple responded from the point of view of social desirability. To these couples, cohesion may be a value they hope for, but the underpinnings of this are not present in their marriage.

Personal Profile: Mr and Mrs Ho

Though Mr and Mrs Ho claim that they chose each other because of mutual attraction, their marriage had been conflictual from the beginning of the wedding, when the two in-law families could not agree over the wedding arrangements. The marriage was not consummated for another half a year, with Mrs Ho insisting that she was not going to be dominated by a husband who showed her little care and concern.

In ten years of married life, Mrs Ho had returned to her parent's home three times for periods of up to three months, and had walked out of the marriage many other times. In the last episode, she took her son with her to a shelter and filed for divorce, which she later withdrew. The repetitive sequence of tension, release of tension by fighting, time away, reconciliation and truce till the next build-up of tension, has not allowed them to develop an interdependent life style. Mr Ho wants to be with his wife and son, to care for them and to have a home together. When negotiating for reconciliation, he is full of good intentions. He is a direct man of few words, with a quick temper. When things upset him, he communicates the only way he knows how, behaviorally. Mrs Ho feels very alone and expects care and concern; when she fails to get it, she asks for it provocatively. Neither feels that there is equity in their relationship, thus each feels the need to look after his or her own interests or be taken advantage of by the other party. Their many reconciliations have been arranged through mediation by either family members or marriage counsellors, and their agreements have always been contingent on certain conditions. This approach marks most of the transactions of their married life.

Both extended families are active in the marriage. Mr Ho's father tells him a man must be authoritative and control what goes on in his family. His mother died while he was a young child and he was brought up by sisters who continue to mother him. Mrs Ho has been brought up to expect that a wife should be protected and cared for. Both husband and wife expect and yearn for care and attention; neither seems able to provide this for the other.

Their one area of common concern is their son who is beginning to manifest behavioral problems. This has drawn them together.

Analysis of Types of Marriages in the Hong Kong Sample

Analysis of ENRICH clusters offers some very interesting patterns which confirm and help to organize the clinical observations. The various types which emerge from this exercise may be illustrative of marital relationships among Chinese people. From our Hong Kong experience in applying ENRICH we have found the instrument very helpful in enabling couples to gain comprehensive and comprehensible perspectives of their marriages. This assessment measure seems particularly sensitive to the better types of marriage. The ENRICH scores provide an informative reading for the patterns of the familial, the romantic, the harmonious, the tested, and the life style marriages. The very low scores for the struggling, the confrontive and the conflictual marriages were not in themselves adequately informative. For a more comprehensive understanding of these three clusters it was necessary to use the clinical material to explain the patterns produced by Ward's analysis.

However, the organization of the sample into these clusters revealed types of marriages which do represent certain marriage patterns observed in Hong Kong.

Comparison Between a Hong Kong and an American Sample

The distribution of types of marriage in Hong Kong that are fulfilling or troubled according to ENRICH scores compares interestingly with Synder and Smith's study of an American sample, published in 1986. They present a classification of five types of marriage from cluster analysis of the scores of 178 couples drawn from the Marital Satisfaction Inventory (MSI). Their sample is made up of clinical and non-clinical cases similar to those of the Hong Kong sample. The MSI is a 280-item self-rating inventory with 11 sub-scales on social desirability, global distress, affective and problem solving communication, quality and quantity of leisure time together, finances, sexual dissatisfaction, role orientation, distress with family of origin, children, and conflict over child rearing.

These two samples reflect somewhat different patterns. For the Hong Kong sample, about one-third are happy marriages, about one-quarter are congenial marriages, and under half are troubled marriages.

Table 4.3   Comparison Between the Hong Kong Marital Study by ENRICH Scores and Synder's Study by MSI Scores

Hong Kong Types of Marriages			American Types of Marriage		
Famil/Romantic	13	} = 30.4%	Non-distressed Type I		} 35.4%
Harmonious	18		Type II		
Tested	16	} = 27.5%	Moderately distressed Type III		} 9.6%
Life Style	12		Extensively distressed Type IV		} 55.1%
Struggling	16		Type V		
Confrontive	7	} = 42.2%			
Conflictual	20				

Issues Relating to Classification

It may be that these eight types do not cover the whole spectrum of possible types of marriage. The differentiation into diverse types serves to remind us that in seeking to understand marriages we are examining the entire range of possible types, where spouses communicate, fight, love and share in different ways towards many different end points.

The eight types that have been described have been derived through statistical analysis, a procedure not appropriate in practice situations. It must also be added that these eight statistical clusters of figures produced through computer analysis were not meaningful until they were reviewed in the light of what had been recorded from the couple's interviews.

The classifications of marriages proposed from clinical experience have either focused on individual characteristics, relationship processes, or on overall marital transactions (Barker, 1988). Sager's (1977) classification presents seven individual partner's profiles, the equal, romantic, parental, childlike, rational, companionate, and parallel partners. He suggests that these in complementary combinations result in workable, satisfactory partnerships. Lederer and Jackson (1968) use colourful, graphic language to dramatize a topology based on control and collaboration in power exchange, to derive eight types from stable-satisfactory to unstable-unsatisfactory marriages. Cuber and Harroff (1974) have produced a frequently cited classification which refers to five marital life styles. These are the total, the vital, the devitalized, the congenial, and the conflict habituated marriage. They consider all five types to be satisfactory, and that the different types basically reflect differences in preference and personal styles in the conception of marriage held by the spouses.

Many clinical classifications have been criticized for being intuitively derived with little stated criteria or procedure for assessment (Filsinger,

McAvoy, and Lewis, 1984; Synder, 1986). Nevertheless, empirically de-rived topologies have to be translated to become meaningful and workable within the context of therapeutic endeavour. Classifications which inte-grate the demands of both clinical practice and research, such as Olson's Circumplex model, can be very useful in stimulating discussion and think-ing, not only among professionals but also in the target clientele, the married people who wish to understand and review their marriages.

In clinical practice, classifications need to be relevant to both the spouses and to the counsellors. The marriage patterns derived from any classification system have to be familiar and they need to fall within the experience and observation of the spouses concerned in order to be meaningful. Moreover, marriage is a dynamic relationship and any classi-fication must allow for changes in the relationship, and take account of movement from one category to another over time. Care must be taken to avoid the danger of confining people to pure types. While recognizing the contribution of a classification system in organizing, linking and inte-grating information, we need also to take note of the risks in putting labels on people. Classification tends to be value laden, defining what may be considered the 'best' marriage, a perspective which is not only unrealistic but also irrelevant as each couple evolves a style unique to themselves and their preferences. Classification is by nature reductionistic, tends to lead to oversimplification, stereotyping, and to the possibility of prophesy fulfilling expectations. The greatest danger is misclassification and incorrect categorization and all the subsequent misinterpretations that can follow.

Nevertheless, the need to make some sense of complexity exists. Clas-sification systems guide the organization of data, permitting systematic assessment and informed intervention. To this end, clinicians and re-searchers attempt to identify patterns of marriages by designing a number of interesting and quite different classification systems. Many have been critically scrutinized and commended for their role in the development of the classification process; however, few have been adopted for active use (Fine, 1974; Fisher, 1976; Filsinger, McAvoy, and Lewis, 1984). This task still remains.

Chapter Five

Variations in the Marital Experience According to the Life Cycle

Apart from the differences between adjusted and non-adjusted groups and in the diverse types of marriages, variations in other aspects need also to be identified and critically examined. Analysis of the data reveals interesting patterns of change over different stages of the marital relationship. This chapter presents variations over time in the marital life cycle. Spouse scores from ENRICH are used for a cross-sectional analysis of life changes in marital satisfaction, cohesion, communication, conflict resolution, leisure activities, children and parenting, family and friends, personality issues, idealism, ethical orientation, financial management, sexual relations, egalitarian roles and adaptability.

The classification of marriages into patterns is a useful way of grouping together marriages with common characteristics. However, a group which shares some similarities may also have interesting variations in other aspects. Thus an analysis of the marriage of either adjusted and non-adjusted spouses at different points of the marital life cycle is likely to show that their experience at formation could differ substantially from their experience at a later stage. These variations need to be identified, as they indicate the points of stress and satisfaction during the various stages of spousal and family living.

Life Cycle Variations

The life cycle framework, which describes and examines family development in stage sequence, has been a very productive conceptual and
research tool (Glick, 1977; Nock, 1979). It has been used in theory building (Duvall, 1977; Hill and Rodgers 1964); in practice development (Carter
and McGoldrick, 1980; Falicov, 1988); and as the basis for designing a
life-span focus in family life education (Hennon and Arcus, 1993). Spanier
and Lewis's review (1980) of research in marital quality in the 1970s
identified life cycle studies and the effects of children on marriage as the
two topics that have received the greatest amount of attention. Glenn's
(1990) review of the 1980s also emphasized the concentration of continuing research in these areas.

Yet, despite prolific discussion and extensive research, even propo-
nents of the life cycle framework refer to its 'unfinished character'
(Mattessich and Hill, 1988) and to the approach as offering 'an incomplete explanation' (Rodgers, 1973). The main concern is that on its own
the life cycle theory has 'little empirical strength' though it is recognized
as offering a sound conceptual framework. Researchers point to the need
for further refinement. Nevertheless, the lively debate on the effectiveness and validity of the theory has served a useful purpose. Continuing
and close analysis of the stratification scheme for studying marital development has expanded our understanding of change and transformation
during various time periods of the life cycle.

The focus of interest has been on trends in the career of a marriage
and on types of change over different aspects and at different points of
time. A number of studies have confirmed the curvilinear patterns of a
drop in marital quality at the time of the arrival of children, rising again
during its later stages (Olson, 1983; Spanier, Lewis, and Cole, 1975).
Other research has shown variations in trends over different aspects of
marriage, such as love and affection, companionship, standards of living
(Rollins and Cannon, 1974), also changes at different stages in empathy
and self disclosure between spouses (Anderson, Russell, Schuum, 1983).

Changes in the form of different developmental demands and tasks
arise from changes in the composition of the family unit as the members
mature. These changes are generally predictive, in that they are normal
processes of marital and family living, such as the transition of the children through the school system, the wife taking on part time or full time
employment, the father's career progress. Research on these aspects has
focused on examining predictive changes and on identifying stressful
demands at various stages to ensure adequate preparation and increased
support at transition points.

In the Hong Kong study, variations over the life cycle in marital satisfaction, cohesion, communication, conflict resolution, leisure, children and parenting, family and friends, personality issues, idealism, ethical orientation, financial management, sexual relationships, egalitarian roles and adaptability will be analysed through the ENRICH scales. These will demonstrate:

1. Differences in trends over certain aspects of marriage.
2. Similarity in trends over certain aspects of marriage.
3. Differences in trends between adjusted and non-adjusted marriages.

The sample is examined in five stages on the basis of the age of the eldest child. Thus, the cycle progresses from:

couples with no children — *stage one*
couples with pre-school children(oldest child 0-5) — *stage two*
couples with school age children(oldest child 6-12)— *stage three*
couples with teenage children (oldest child 13-19) — *stage four*
couples with children ready to leave home (age 20+) — *stage five*

The findings show some interesting patterns of differences between adjusted spouses and non-adjusted spouses, and differences over the five life stages. However,it should be noted that cross-sectional analysis of such a small group of 204 spouses can but provide indicators of trends in this sample.

The W Pattern

Adjusted spouses in the Hong Kong sample show a W rather than a U pattern for satisfaction and cohesion over the five life stages. The graphs in Figure 5.1. illustrate a drop in satisfaction at the birth of the first child, rising at the stage of school age children, dropping again with teenage children, and rising slightly after the children leave home. The adjusted spouses **satisfaction** scores of around 60 according to ENRICH could indicate that the spouses are content about most aspects of their marriages throughout the five life stages.*

---

* Note: The ENRICH Computer Report explains the implications of high and low scores on the various scales. Individual percentage scores of 60 are considered high, indicating positive feelings in that aspect of the relationship. Scores of 30 are low, indicating tension and problems in that area of spousal transactions.

	No Children	Pre-School	Sch. Age	Teenage	Post-Parental
Stage	1	2	3	4	5
Adj. spouses (N)	26	22	48	12	6
Non-adj. spouses (N)	12	26	36	14	2
N = 204					

Trends for *non-adjusted spouses* follow a linear pattern. The arrival of a child increases satisfaction slightly, and continues to do so until the children leave home, then it drops drastically. It would seem that the presence of children contributes to marital satisfaction of parents in less adjusted relationships. A **satisfaction** score of around 30 according to ENRICH indicates that the spouses are unhappy and dissatisfied over certain aspects of their marriage.

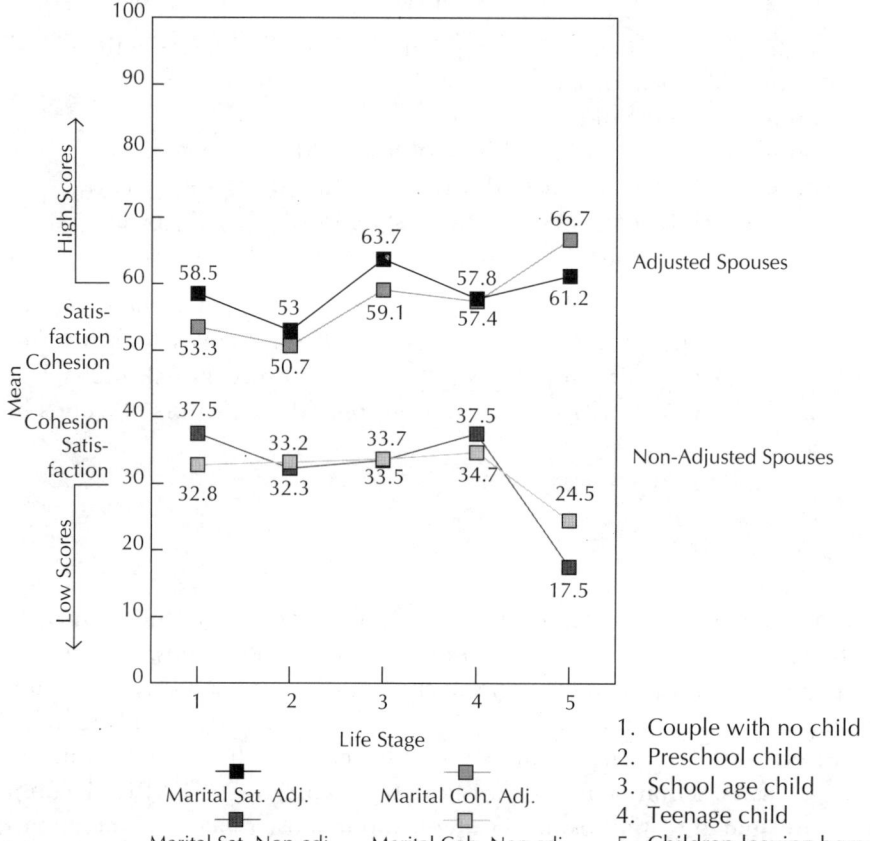

Figure 5.1   Life Cycle Variations in Marital Satisfaction & Cohesion

Cohesion for *adjusted spouses* records approximately the same scores and follows trends similar to those for satisfaction. Moderate cohesion scores of 30-70 in ENRICH reflect a balance of being able to share time together, decision making, mutual help, and closeness with each other. However, for the non-adjusted spouses, scores of around 30 indicate difficulties in these areas of marital sharing and closeness. The substantial drop in **cohesion** for *non-adjusted spouses* at the final stages certainly exposes the lack of emotional bonding between these spouses, and reveals the possible instability of these marriages.

The patterns for satisfaction and cohesion follow similar trends. This is not surprising as the correlation matrix between the satisfaction and the cohesion scales in ENRICH is $r = .65$, $p<.001$. Thus, the satisfaction scale is able to explain cohesion at .65 squared, that is 42%. Significance at .001 indicates that the chance factor is one in a thousand.

Most studies on marital satisfaction in the United States show a U curvilinear pattern (Olson, McCubbin, Barnes, Larsen, Muxem and Wilson, 1983; Rollins and Galligan, 1978). However, the Hong Kong sample of adjusted spouses presents a shallow W pattern over the life cycle. The drop in satisfaction among spouses with young children under five and with children at adolescence testifies to the stress and demands of child care and adolescence for parents in Hong Kong. However, the happy times for parents are when the children are between six and twelve. During this period, the parents' enjoyment of their role seem to increase, family communication become more active and there is more sharing of leisure activities as shown in Figure 5.2.

The Impact of Children

On the three dimensions of communication, conflict resolution and leisure activities there were two notable differences between the two groups of adjusted and non-adjusted spouses. First, they had very different trends and patterns. Second, the lowest score on any of the dimensions for the adjusted group is higher than the highest scores on any dimension for the non-adjusted group.

For *adjusted spouses*, communication, conflict resolution and leisure all drop when the children are in their pre-school years, then pick up as the child/children grow up, and drop again in later years. Leisure activities of adjusted spouses are particularly high when the children are at school age and at adolescence. According to ENRICH, high scores of 60 or more in **leisure activities** mean that the spouses share common interests, spend time together and do things separately.

Moderate scores of around 50 in **communication** for adjusted spouses could be interpreted as feeling reasonably understood by their partners and being moderately able to deal with differences and disagreements between them. Again, moderate scores on **conflict resolution** reflect that adjusted spouses feel able to discuss and resolve differences with their partners. Marital transactions in communication and conflict management seem to suffer some drawbacks with young children at the pre-school

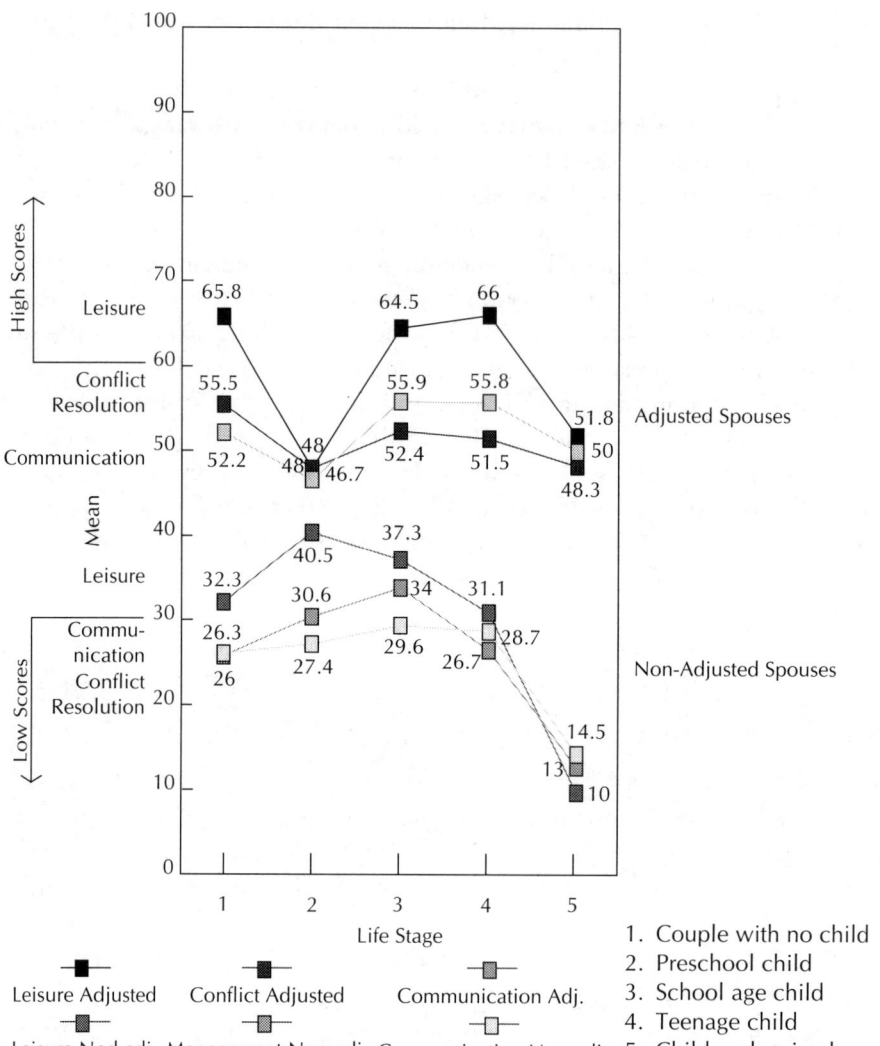

Figure 5.2   Life Cycle Variations in Communication, Conflict Management and Leisure

stage, but return to the previous early marriage level as the children grow, then dropping slightly as the children leave home.

Interestingly, while sharing leisure time activities and similar interests declined in adjusted marriages when the children are in their pre-school years, it increases in *non-adjusted marriages,* as though the child provides a common focus for sharing. Scores for **leisure activities** of around 40 for non-adjusted spouses imply that the spouses share some interests and time together when the children are in the pre-school and school age years. However, their scores of 30 or less before the arrival of the children, and when the children were in adolescence, and certainly after the children leave home, show that they prefer different interests, minimize time together, yet do not like activities on their own.

For the non-adjusted spouses, the presence of young children promotes communication and conflict resolution. This continues until the child reaches its teens, when there is a slight decline, followed by a noticeable decline in later years. Non-adjusted spouses with scores in the 30s in **communication** and **conflict resolution** feel disadvantaged in negotiations, and unable to express emotions congruently. They also feel that arguments are difficult to resolve, and that they have to avoid disagreement and give in to maintain harmony.

In Figure 5.2 the graphs for communication, conflict resolution and leisure follow a similar set of patterns for adjusted, and another set for non-adjusted spouses.

Fluctuating and Steady Trends

Different patterns in the life cycle for adjusted and non-adjusted couples over five aspects of the marriage can be observed. As defined in the ENRICH marital inventory, these are
- idealistic distortion
- children and parenting
- family and friends
- ethical orientation
- personality issues

The graphs for *adjusted spouses*, presented in Figure 5.3, show noticeable to modest variations over the life span in all the five areas. At the post-parental stage there are significant increases in idealistic distortion, family and friends, and in personality issues. **Idealistic distortion** scores in the 70s of adjusted spouses in the Hong Kong sample is very high. These high scores indicate that they are idealistic about their relationship and tend to minimize any problems. The consensus of the spouses over enjoyment in **parenting** is also high, and remains consistently high throughout the child care and post-parental years. Scores on **ethical orientation** around the 60s indicate that the sharing of common values and beliefs is important in the relationship. The particularly high scores when the children are adolescents seem to emphasize heightened consensus between the parents in maintaining their ethical convictions. The moderate scores for the **family and friends** scale seems to indicate that adjusted spouses have an average relationship with their parents and in-laws and middling ac-

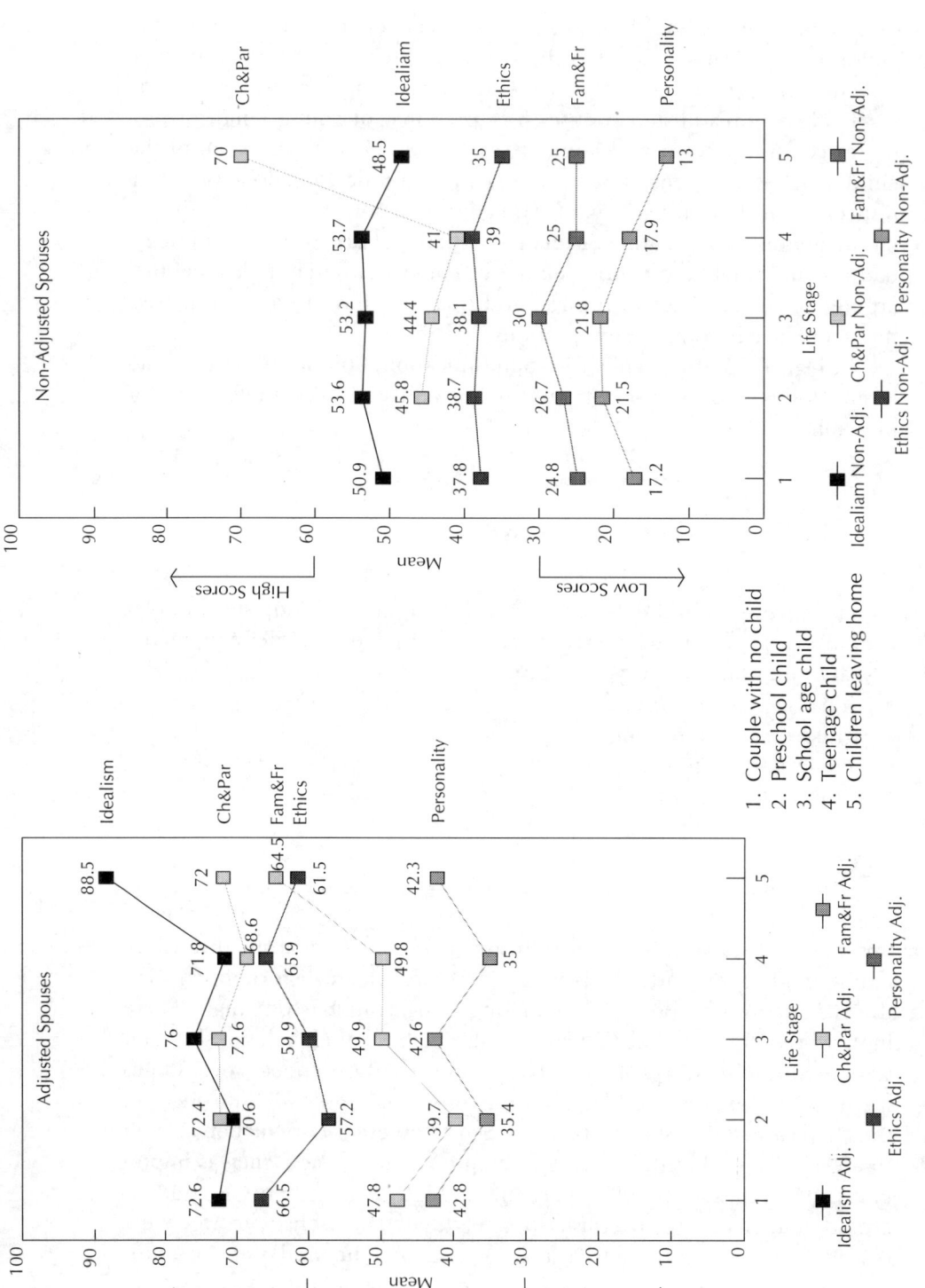

Figure 5.3   Life Cycle Trends in Idealistic Distortion, Children & Parenting, Family & Friends, Ethical Orientation, and Personality Issues

ceptance of their partner's time with friends. However, this improves at the later stages. Scores on the **personality issues** around the 30s show that the spouses are concerned about some of the personality traits, behaviour and habits of their partners. Acceptance of the partner is particularly low during the two stages when marital satisfaction is also low, that is, during the period when the children are young and when they are in their teens, which seem to be the particularly stressful years.

The graphs for the *non-adjusted spouses* show fairly stable and low trends, except for greater consensus on **children and parenting** when the children leave home. Overall, the spouses evaluation of their parenting experience is that they sometimes disagree over the importance of children in their marriage, and each other's responsibility and contribution in bringing up the children. Their scores for **idealistic distortion** is moderate. It would seem therefore that they are sometimes idealistic and sometimes open to admitting limitations in their relationship. Low scores for **ethical orientation** reflect lack of consensus or lack of awareness of the partner's values and beliefs. Low scores for **family and friends** reveal difficulties in relationships with parents, in-laws and friends. Finally, very low scores for **personality issues** suggest a lack of acceptance of certain personality traits, and the behaviourial patterns or habits of their partners.

The steady, flat patterns with little difference between one stage and another in the graphs for non-adjusted spouses, seem to illustrate the lack of change in troubled marriages. This may serve to explain the pervading sense of helplessness expressed by spouses who come for counselling and who dispiritedly comment that many aspects of their relationship have always been poor and will remain so. They do not expect change.

The trends on idealistic distortion are interesting in that the fairly high scores for both the adjusted and non-adjusted reflect the tendency of the spouses in this Hong Kong sample to answer ENRICH questions in a socially desirable manner. The much higher scores of the adjusted when compared with those of the non-adjusted spouses may suggest that a certain amount of idealistic distortion may be helpful in marriage relationships. Also of note is the upward swing in idealistic perception in the later years for adjusted spouses, and the downward drop for the non-adjusted as though they had given up on any further pretensions.

Declining Trends

It would not be surprising to find that certain aspects of marriage may show a steady decline from formation through the child caring years towards the later years of the marriage. In the Hong Kong study this decline can be seen in financial management, sexual relations, adaptability and equalitarian roles, as indicated by the mean scores on these ENRICH scales.

Financial management scores for *adjusted spouses* are very high at commencement of marriage when the couple's financial plans are realistic and they agree on budgeting and deployment of their resources. Though this drops drastically at the birth of the first child, their management of money matters still remains satisfactory. By the later years, financial disagreement and pressures are evident.

For the *non-adjusted spouses*, **financial** planning and management at the beginning of the marriage is moderately agreeable and realistic. With the arrival of children, the spouses are experiencing difficulties in deciding how to handle their finances and tension over finances becomes apparent. By the time the children leave home, the spouses have serious difficulties over financial matters.

Scores just below the 60s for **sexual relations** of *adjusted spouses* suggest that they feel fairly satisfied at being able to share affection, feelings and preferences over sexual issues and family planning. Adjusted marriages maintain a steady pattern of sharing in sexual issues and affection throughout four stages, declining in the last stage.

For the *non-adjusted spouses* there seems to be adequate sharing in **sexual relations** and affection at the beginning of marriage and in the couples' middle years when the children are in their teens. With the birth of a child and during the early child caring years tensions surface over sexual issues and preferences, over expressing affection, and over family planning. At the final stage sexual relations are problematic.

Attitudes towards **equalitarianism** seem to begin at the same level with spouses from both adjusted and non-adjusted marriages moderately wanting to equally share roles, decision making and household responsibilities. For the *adjusted spouses* this declines steadily and then more drastically, so that by the time the children are at school age, conventional husband-wife roles and areas of responsibility are adopted. Adjusted spouses scores are lower, perhaps reflecting more traditional role expectations.

During the child caring years *non-adjusted spouses* have a more equalitarian exchange, although this remains a tense balance. For older marriages, whether adjusted or otherwise, traditional expectations prevail.

Marital adaptability for *adjusted spouses* was high through the first three life stages, indicating a stable leadership pattern and flexibility in adaptation and change. Then gradually this declines with the children in adolescence and after they leave home, signifying less and less ability to adapt and change as people grow older.

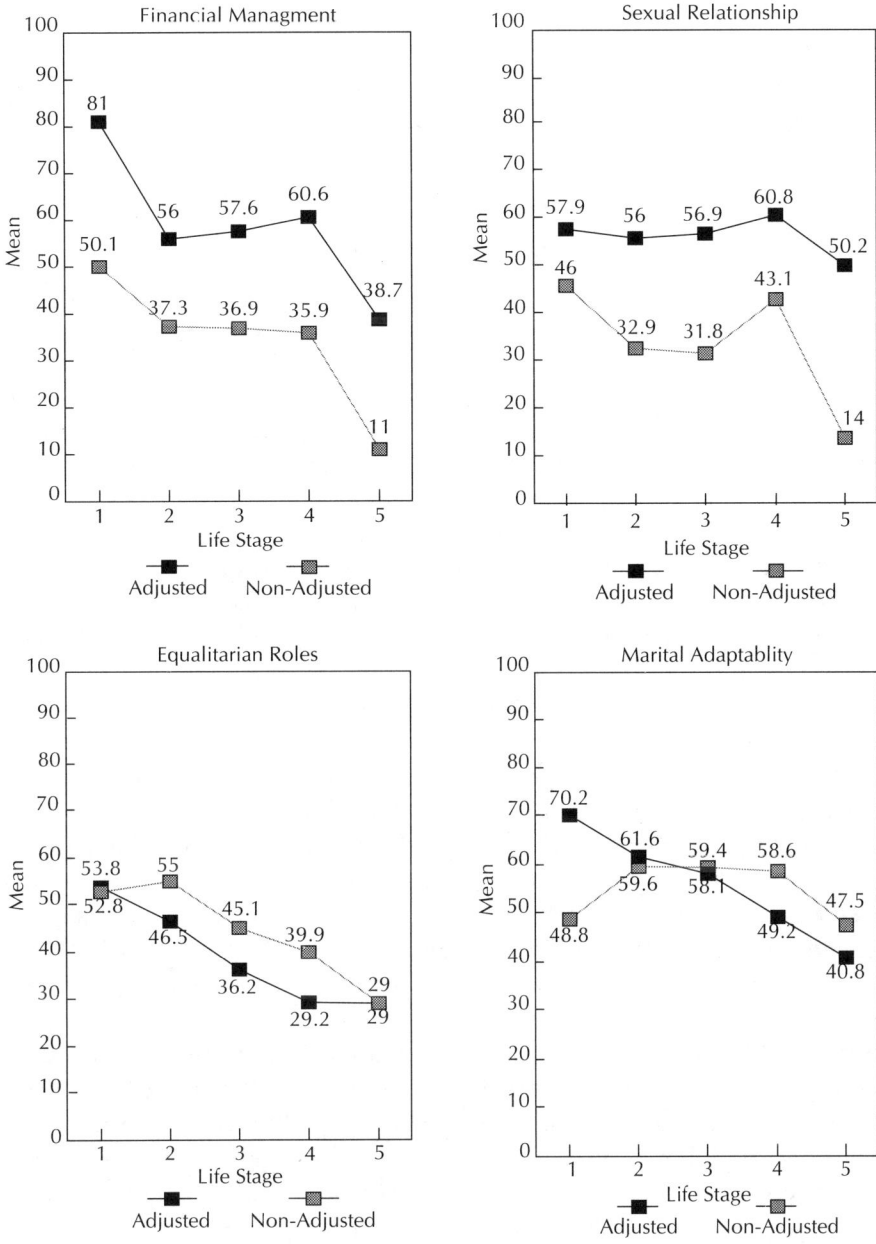

1. Couple with no child
2. Preschool child
3. School age child
4. Teenage child
5. Children leaving home

Figure 5.4   Downward Trends in Financial Management, Sexual Relations, Equalitarian Roles, Marital Adaptability

The **adaptability** pattern for *non-adjusted spouses* is an inverted U. These spouses' ability to adapt and change improves during child caring years, becoming and remaining higher than that of adjusted spouses, then it declines after the children leave home.

Impact of Children and Later Life Trends

Life cycle analysis of this sample reveals two findings of particular interest. The first indicates that children have different effects on marriages of different quality. The arrival of children detract from adjusted marriages in all 14 aspects to varying degrees. On the other hand, the presence of children results in improvements in non-adjusted marriages in satisfaction, communication, conflict resolution, levels of idealism, ethical orientation, relationship with family and friends, and in personality issues.

In this regard, the overall scores of adjusted spouses is still higher than those for the non-adjusted spouses. However, within their respective levels the effect of children appears to have a negative effect on adjusted marriages and a positive effect on non-adjusted marriages. All the findings in this study showed the spouses in this sample to be extremely child centred. It was clear from their attitudes that children were valued and crucial to the marriage. However, the effect of children on the spousal interaction was significant. In regard to the adjusted spouses it was clear that in concentrating on the children, their concentration on each other was reduced in areas such as communication, conflict management and sharing of leisure time together. In particular, children drastically affected the family's financial management.

It has been consistently documented that child care and child rearing put high demands on the parents' time, energy, emotional and economic resources, and that they affect marital companionship and satisfaction (Rollins and Feldman, 1970; Rollins and Galligan, 1978). The Hong Kong study bears this out. A study that reinforces our findings on the effect of children on marriages of different quality is Luckey and Bain's study of 40 married couples where the less satisfied couples reported that children were the only and greatest satisfaction in their relationship (Luckey and Bain, 1970).

The second interesting finding relates to the later life stage when the children leave home and the older couple gradually return to being a dyadic unit. At this stage, a number of aspects of marriage improve for adjusted spouses. These are marital satisfaction, cohesion, idealism, children and parenting, relationship with family and friends and personality issues. For non-adjusted spouses, tensions in their relationship get worse in all aspects except for relationships with family and friends.

The tendency for non-adjusted spouses to experience decline in the post-parental stage is observed in clinical work in Hong Kong. It would seem that neglect of the spousal relationship in the preceding years could lead to a point of no recovery at this stage. Increased time together, and changes in patterns of dependency associated with ill health and/ or retirement, put further strains on the relationship during the later life stage, when both personal and financial resources may be on the ebb.

The revitalisation of some marriages in the later years, as observed for adjusted spouses, has also been noted in other studies (Rollins and Cannon, 1974; Spanier,Lewis and Cole, 1975). Various explanations have been given as to why this occurs. Levinger (1979) considers that the basis for affectional bonds changes over time. Thus, while attraction, passion, and self disclosure promote the spousal relationship in the early stages, loyalty, familiarity and mutual interdependence sustain marriages at the later stages. Gilford and Bengston (1979) attribute this to the effects of positive interaction in later stages promoting an upward trend, and to a reduction of negative sentiments, such as sarcasm, disagreements, criticism and anger, leaving higher satisfaction in later life marriages. Spanier, Lewis and Cole (1975) propose that to be cognitively consistent, older couples put high value on the marriage to justify their years of investment. Studying commitment in long term marriages of retired couples, Swenson and Trahaug (1985) find that couples committed to each other as persons experience fewer problems and express more love, than couples committed to the institution of marriage. Each of these explanations may be relevant to particular couples in Hong Kong. The increasing proportion of older people in Hong Kong and a higher life expectancy calls for further in-depth research on the post parental marital life stage. The rather small number of spouses represented in this particular cohort may allow these findings to be questioned, and before any firm conclusions can be drawn further research is necessary.

This examination of ENRICH scores, utilizing the life cycle as an independent variable in cross-sectional analysis, is open to the various criticisms that have been levelled against cross-sectional research (Schram, 1979; Spanier and Lewis, 1980). These findings serve as indicators of possible trends of change in marriages at different stages. Further research is needed, particularly in regard to longitudinal studies specifically designed to study life cycle changes in Hong Kong which takes into account cultural and social changes as we merge with China. The patterns presented in this study alert us to changes and stability in different aspects of marriage at different times of family history, and provide the context for assessing events which occur and actions which are undertaken by marital partners at specific points of their lives together.

Chapter Six

Variations in the Marital Experience According to Gender and Generational Issues

Differences in spousal experience can be generated by the very nature of the marital system. Husbands and wives have varying experiences of their marriage, their difference in gender leads to distinct evaluations in many aspects of living. Family backgrounds and the formative years of the spouses have particular effects on their development of close relationships in later years. The nature of a couple's association with their parents affects the relationship which they build up together.

This chapter examines three areas of differences between husbands and wives for their effects on the development of the marital relationship. These refer to differences in gender, differences in early life experiences, and differences in the continuing relationship between the spouses and their paternal and maternal extended families.

Gender Differences in the Marital Experience

Bernard (1982) observed that there are two marriages in every marriage, his and hers. This is also discernible in some aspects of the Hong Kong study, where husbands generally considered their spousal relationship to be more adjusted and more satisfactory than did the wives. The husbands mean score of 106.3 on the DAS was significantly higher than the wives mean DAS at 99.9 (F=3.80, p=.05). Their sense of global satisfaction also differed significantly (F=4.61, p<.05). This trend is also noted in other research studies (Casas and Ortiz, 1985).

The husbands' perspective

From their responses, it would seem that the husbands generally considered themselves to be happy to very happy. They tended to be idealistic about their marriages and to minimize any problems. They believed that their marriage was forever, did not regret getting married and did not consider terminating the relationship. Even if allowances were made for the conventional nature of some of these responses or the desire of a husband to provide the appropriate answer, the replies consistently show the husbands to have a higher sense of permanency in the relationship and a feeling that they were getting a fair deal, hence they felt that it did not matter if they put more into the marriage. They reported little conflict and a high degree of consensus, in that they almost always agreed with their spouses on child rearing, sexual issues, recreation and major decisions. The majority (93.1%) said they were never too tired for sex. In stating their opinion of sex outside marriage, 73.4% agreed that sexual activity should be confined to marriage. This is an area of living where attitudes and behaviour do not necessarily coincide. In her review of sixty years of American research on marital and extramarital sexuality, Parkinson concludes that 'most people do not approve of extramarital sex whether they engage in it or not' (1991:90). The studies which Parkinson reviewed reported incidents of extramarital sex in married men ranging from 20% to 45%. Nevertheless, the General Social Survey of the National Opinion Center in the United States which interviews about 1400 respondents in person every year stated in 1993 that 21% of the men reported having an affair while married (Associated Press, October 1993).

The wives' perspective

On the other hand, the wives felt themselves to be happy to a little unhappy in their marriages. They rarely considered divorce, but occasionally regretted getting married. Their ambivalence could partly be associated with the concern that sometimes they felt that they had been taken advantage of and cheated in the marriage, even though they basically felt that it did not matter that they had put more into the relationship.

The wives reported more quarrelling, and admitted to a lower level of consensus in most areas of living. In particular, they said that they would like more leisure activities, more confiding, and more equalitarian sharing in day-to-day concerns. Most wives, 63.6%, answered that they did not refuse sex for reasons of being too tired. On the issue of extramarital sex, 83.7% of the wives considered that sexual activity should be confined to marriage (F=5.69, p<.05).

His and Her Marriages

In general, the picture seems to be that husbands experience more happiness, more cohesion, harmony, equity and more interest in sexual activities than their wives. A possible explanation is that the husbands tended to give more conventional answers from the perspective of what they considered to be socially acceptable. Nevertheless, these answers do reflect a difference in the position of husbands and wives. Bernard (1982), in drawing attention to discrepant responses to similar questions in a number of studies, concludes that these inconsistent replies do not arise from methodological inadequacies, but truly reflect differing perceptions of the two differing subjective realities of a couple's joint experience, arising from each spouse's needs, attitudes, beliefs, and backgrounds.

Since Bernard's observation was first made in 1972, there has been widespread interest in gender differences as experienced in marriage and family life (Cancian, 1986; Thompson and Walker, 1989; Wills, Weiss and Patterson, 1974). One of the explanations of differences in the experience of husbands and wives could be accounted for in gender disparity in defining pleasurable behaviour. In their study on the determinants of marital satisfaction, Wills, Weiss and Patterson (1974) found that males emphasize pleasurable instrumental behaviour, and women emphasize pleasurable affectional behaviour. Husbands consider being a responsible provider, doing practical things around the house, engaging in physical activities and sexual activities, as demonstrations of love, care and concern for their wives. Women desire emotional sharing, verbal disclosure, expressions of love, care and concern as demonstrations of intimacy. Each, therefore, uses different criteria for evaluating relationship transactions and events.

These preferences and differences are reinforced in Chinese society by practices and patterns which reflect patriarchal traditions. The term to get married in Chinese for a man is 娶, to acquire a woman. For a woman, it is 嫁, to build up a family and a home. Society assumes that a woman should marry for status, to obtain a setting for her adult life, hence for instrumental reasons. Traditionally and socially she is assigned the duty of orchestrating the emotional climate and affectional transactions in the marriage, family, home and kinship system. In Chinese society, therefore, women are inclined to derive their sense of satisfaction with marriage and with themselves from their appraisal of the adequacy of emotional sharing which they have engendered. They measure this from the feedback of others, and from the nature and extent of the involvement of their husbands as helpmates. On the other hand, men are socialized to be achievement oriented, outward looking, independent, unemotional, and to hide their vulnerability. They are inclined to use instrumental means in assessing marital and family well-being. Thus their wives are likely to experience less emotional sharing than they hope for. Moreover, expectations in marriage are often measured by husbands in terms of what they themselves do as providers. If they fulfil this responsibility they consider that expectations have been met. These differences are real, although they are not sufficiently marked to be statistically significant, except for expectations in confiding where the husbands were quite content while the wives would like more ($F=6.74$, $p<.01$). It is also of interest that differences in expectations of companionship and compatibility are near significance levels at $p<.06$.

The wives' responses on the ENRICH equalitarian roles indicate a wish for more sharing and greater participation in decision making, while the husbands' lower scores demonstrate a preference for traditional roles and responsibilities. Over the division of labour at home, both spouses subscribed to the cultural norm of role stereotypes, with the man focusing on matters outside the home, and the woman on what goes on inside. The husbands openly acknowledged their wives' greater competence in domestic tasks; and the wives accepted their care-taker role as this seemed to confirm their centrality and importance in the home. There was also agreement and acceptance by both sexes that the husbands' work is more important. However, a shift to more joint decision making was also discernible. The area of greatest tension emerged when wives worked outside the home. Husbands preferred the wives to work only if absolutely necessary, while many wives opted to work for self interest and self growth.

Aside from dissimilarities in expectations and preferences, the experiences of husbands and wives actually differed. Historically, women have been placed in a subordinate position in marriage, yet their well-being and their daily life experiences are intricately interwoven into and determined by the quality of their family lives. Women therefore have become conditioned to monitoring this relationship carefully, quickly becoming aware of any distress and deficits, and they are more reactive and active in putting things right. In this regard, a specific area of gender specialization is to be found in the parenting role imposed by most societies, where the wife as mother has the task and the responsibility for nurturing and caring for the young, while the man is in a supportive role. In child centred families, such as those in the Hong Kong sample, the burden of responsibility between the spouses over child-rearing tended to weigh heavily. The women, in striving to meet the exacting standards set by themselves and by society to be good wives and mothers, recorded lower contentment in these roles. Consequently, the husbands' mean score of 60.0 for children and parenting on ENRICH testifies to their sense of enjoyment and fulfilment in their children, while the wives' lower score at 48.6 reflects their concern and tension over child care ($F = 8.07$, $p<.01$).

Moreover, this difference in outlook as expressed by the wives may partly be explained by the fact that in Hong Kong as elsewhere, the woman's role is no longer to be found exclusively within the family. Whether through economic need, peer emulation, or personal fulfilment, women here now look or are forced to look beyond the home, with inevitable effects on the marital relationship on which the family is based. To an increasing extent the modern woman is faced with complex and often irreconcilable situations which defy her attempts to meet her own expectations, let alone the expectations of her spouse.

Differences in the Effects of Inter-generational Transmission

Descriptions of the parents' marriages

For each of us, our first and most intimate experience of marriage is of our parents' marriage. Each of us derives our sense of self from our growing experiences in childhood which are the formative years of our development as a person. The Hong Kong study therefore addressed the issue of the influence of the parents' marriage on a couple's marriage, and the influence of childhood experiences which affect what each husband and wife bring to the marriage. Each spouse was asked to describe their parents' marriage, and their childhood experiences.

Of the 204 spouses, 38.2% recalled their parents' marriage as conflictual, 30.9% as harmonious, 16.2% as traditional, and 13.7% reported one parent deceased. There was no statistical difference between adjusted and non-adjusted spouses in their recall of the nature of their parents' marriages. However, where the effects of their parents' marriage on them was recounted, there were significant differences between the perceptions of the adjusted and the non adjusted spouses as shown in Table 6.1.

Descriptions of childhood experiences

In describing their childhood, 51.5% of the sample recalled this as unhappy; 38.7 as happy; and 8.8% said they had no special feelings about this. About a quarter of them (27.3%) evaluated their growing years as smooth and ordinary, another quarter (26.8%) remembered feeling that they lacked love, and another quarter (24.2%) felt that their development had been affected by poverty. Although 38.2% of the spouses

Table 6.1   Perceived Effects of Parents' Marriage

	Adjusted N = 113	Non-Adjusted N = 87
	%	%
High expectations own marriage	41.6	37.9
Not repeat parents' experience	23.0	16.1
Lack confidence in own marriage	1.8	12.6
Nothing special	33.6	33.3

Chi-square =10.28, df3, p<.05

described their parents' marriage as conflictual, only 12.1% reported as having been directly affected by the strife. Rather they saw that the consequences of their parents' difficult marriage was that they had received less care, attention, support, and they sometimes experienced hardship through poverty as resources become unavailable. About one- tenth (9.6%) regarded their childhood years as demanding due to the high expectations of their parents. The reports of adjusted and non-adjusted spouses were very similar. However, where the effects of childhood experiences were concerned, the responses of the adjusted spouses demonstrated that they had developed self reliance to meet their own needs. The responses of the non-adjusted spouses also reflected efforts to become self reliant, but that they had also developed expectations that marriage and their spouse would meet their needs. These responses are presented in Table 6.2.

The spouses were open and quite ready to reminisce about their early childhood period. They described experiences both painful and joyful and referred to some memorable events which they would like to have foregone and some which they still held dear. They expressed little an-

Table 6.2   Perceived Effects of Childhood Experiences

	Adjusted %	Non-Adjusted %
High concern for own children	58.5	39.1
Learn independence	15.8	19.5
Work/study hard	14.9	11.5
More attention to own family	3.5	10.3
Low self esteem	6.1	8.0
Expect care/concern from spouse	0.9	11.5

Chi-square =18.62, df5, p<.01

ger: rather they emphasized the positive aspects of what they had learned from the experience of their parents' marriage and from their childhood, that had helped them to value and to make allowances in their own marriage. It is interesting to note that when describing the effects of certain experiences they were very solution oriented. They recalled how they had coped by 'reminding self not to repeat . . .', or, 'learned independence' and decided 'to work and study hard to do better' and 'to take responsibility by putting expectations on own life, own marriage'.

This review shows that negative childhood experiences and a conflictual parental marriage do not necessarily relate to difficulties in marital adjustment in adult life. Rather, it is the perception of how they are affected or are not affected, that impacts on marriage adjustment.

Early Life Experiences and Adult Development

A number of theoretical approaches emphasize the transmission of patterns and tendencies from one generation to the next (Boszormeny-Nagy and Spark, 1984; Bowen, 1978), and that early parent-child relationships impact on intimate relationships in later life (Hazan and Shaver,1987; Rutter, 1988). From this view, spouses repeat the harmony or the disharmony and the stability or instability of their parents' marriage in their own relationship. In clinical practice it can often be noted that aversive family and personal backgrounds can have detrimental effects on a marital situation. The questions that need to be addressed are the extent that generational transmission can be found among Chinese spouses; and whether these repetitive patterns are only to be found in troubled relationships. The findings of the Hong Kong Study show that there is no direct relationship between the troubled marriages of parents and those of their children: the spouses of adjusted as much as non-adjusted marriages could well have had their childhood in unhappy homes.

Although a direct link cannot be shown, it is undoubtedly true that there are indirect effects which can have a serious impact on the children even after they reach maturity, so that the quality of their lives is affected, including their marriages. These effects can be discerned in the way in which they shape their 'world view', from which they make interpretations and give meaning to what goes on in the world around them (Skinner, 1976). An example of this can be found in the Hong Kong study. One husband, whose father had died while he was in his infancy, recalled his shame at having to go to school in slippers instead of shoes and of having to go hungry, and he reaffirmed that however painful his relationship with his wife, he would remain in the marriage. He was

stepfather to a troubled and troublesome boy who had been father-
less at about the same age as himself. He was the nurturing person in this
particular family to both his stepson and his wife. The 'world view' that
he had formed out of his childhood experiences had clearly shaped his
determination, attitudes and feelings, to guide his actions and reactions
in the day-to-day transactions of his life.

Various studies have been conducted over the past few years on inter-
generational transmission, although the results have been somewhat
inconclusive. The most informative are those which examine long-term
outcomes for children growing up in intact and non-intact families
(Peterson and Zill, 1986; Wallerstein, 1988). In this regard, the studies by
Pope and Mueller (1976, 1977) ask some very pertinent questions, and
offer some interesting insights and propositions which have some bear-
ing on the Hong Kong study. Pope and Mueller set out to identify the
factors that contribute to the process of inter-generational transmission,
and to search out what may be the intervening variables that qualify this
process.

They begin by questioning whether the parents' broken marriages
make their children's marriages more susceptible to disruption, and
whether there is an inter-generational transmission of instability and dis-
organization. Their review of research and their own research lead them
to conclude that some degree of transmission exists but that this is not
strong. They then set out to find and test out some possible explanations
of transmission. Their research, based on five national samples, serves to
disprove the most commonly held rationale of the parental role *model*.
The parental role model of transmission postulates that children learn,
imitate and are socialized to the gender and marital role behaviours of
their two parents. Parents with conflictual or dissolved marriages would
have difficulty in providing the necessary experience or in serving as role
models for their children. Children who have not had the appropriate
experiences or appropriate role models are not adequately prepared for
the demands of marriage. Mueller and Pope (1977), using all five data
sets to make cross-race and cross-sex comparisons, conclude that their
findings do not confirm the role model explanation.

Rather, they find some evidence to support the possibility that what
may be transmitted are permissive attitudes of tolerance for dissolution.
They find that children whose parents' marriage has been dissolved are
more likely to voluntarily dissolve their own marriages than children from
intact marriages. Children from non intact families are also more vigilant
for signs of distress, more sensitive to tensions, and more likely to conclude that termination is an acceptable solution to disharmony. However,
this tendency is substantially reduced by the level of education attained at
the time of marriage.

On this line of enquiry, they proposed two explanations which they thought had some validity. Where parental separation through death or divorce resulted in financial hardship so that the child had to forego education and to find work or get married at an early age, then life instability associated with *low social economic* status resulted. They observed a pattern in which children from intact families formed higher status marriages, and children from broken families contracted earlier and limited education marriages. From this, they proposed mate selection as the causal link. They then concluded that the potential for marital instability may be found in the *restricted opportunities* forced on the disadvantaged child following loss of one parent.

Continuing research on the long-term effects of parental marriage on the adult adjustment of their children confirms that 'contrary to much of the literature and popular thought, these early experiences have, at most, a modest effect on adult development'(Kulka and Weingarten 1979: 50). These researchers also propose that this modest effect can be positive as well as negative. Children growing up with parental tension or loss may have learned to face and manage difficult crises and painful realities in childhood years which encourages coping and adaptation, providing them with a repertoire of behaviours different from those growing up in intact families (Bloom, Asher and White, 1978). Their fortitude and drive to make good is demonstrated by the number of successful men with very stressful childhood experiences. Difficult life experiences in the developmental years prime them to be more sensitive to discern undercurrents in their own marriages, and they show more willingness to admit to difficulties or inadequacies. Kulka and Weingarten's data also indicates that growing up in such homes affects their valuation of the major life roles of spouse and parents. In relation to their marital roles, the males display a weakened investment in the parent role and the females a greater investment in the parental role.

The findings from the Hong Kong Study indicate there are some aspects of inter-generational transmission which do affect the spouses' perceptions and therefore their behaviour. It has also been noted in a parallel study of marriage counselling cases in two Hong Kong agencies that wives with childhood difficulties are over involved in their mothering role, while husbands with childhood difficulties tend to put a high value on financial security and to be over careful about money matters (Young, 1993).

Using data from a four-generation study which began in Berkeley in 1928, Caspi and Elder examined the process by which behaviour is replicated across generations. They wanted to find out if 'problems beget problems'(1988:218). Their research focused more on inter-generational transmission of parenting behaviour rather than on spousal behaviour;

however, their findings are germane to close, caring relationships. They found that relational and behavioral styles developed in early years are recreated in adulthood under similar circumstances, and there is a tendency to transfer assumptions from previous relationships to new relationships. They also noted positive trends in that turning points do occur. This could come from the realization that certain courses of action lead in unrewarding directions, thus instigating attempts to find new paths and different outcomes. A wish frequently expressed by some spouses in the Hong Kong study was that they were determined to 'have a marriage different from their parents'. Spouses who perceived the constricting nature of their parents' traditional marriage aimed for a more open, equitable and equal relationship; those who had observed the disruptions of conflictual parental marriages aimed for a more nurturing and harmonious marriage for themselves.

In varying degrees, the lack of an appropriate role model, the existence of permissive attitudes to dissolution, disadvantages associated with poverty, restricted educational and marital opportunities, or the resurgence of early relational patterns all describe the circumstances of some of the marriages which seemed to be repeating patterns similar to those of previous generations. However, the awareness and the intention not to repeat parental patterns was also present. For some, past hardship and stressful conditions had enabled them to develop the adaptive skills and the will to have a marriage different from that of their parents. This is evident from the number of adjusted spouses whose parents had difficult marriages.

Inter-generational Relations With Extended Families

The concept of filial obligations between generations finds a natural place in the social ethos of Hong Kong. It is a value that has been upheld by an essentially Chinese population despite the widespread adoption of western practices and cosmopolitan styles of living. Since the ability to deal with in-law relationships can seriously affect the spouses' sense of satisfaction and harmony, the Hong Kong Marital Study examined the extent and nature of the exchange between spouses and their parents and, in particular, reciprocity between the spouses and the paternal and maternal families. As the largest proportion of the Hong Kong sample had children at school age, with husbands at the mean age of 37.4 and wives at the mean age of 34, their parents were likely to be still quite energetic and in their sixties.

Contact with extended families

Fifteen couples (14.7%) lived with family members other than the immediate nuclear family. Thirteen couples (12.7%) were in co-residence with
the husbands' parents and siblings, and 1.9% lived with the wives' parents.

Frequency of contact between the nuclear families in this sample and
the extended families on both sides is presented in Figure 6.1.

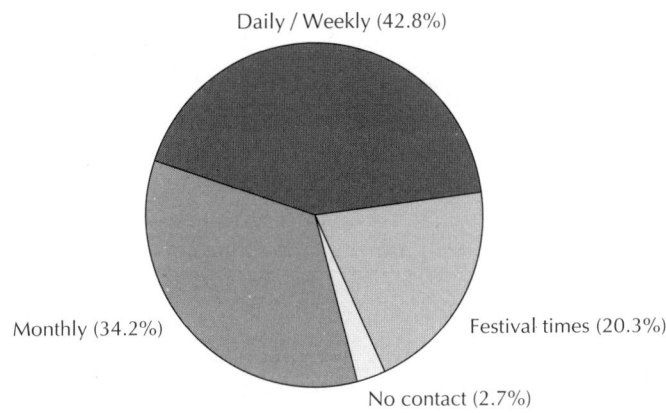

Figure 6.1   Frequency of Contact with Extended Families

The reciprocal exchange between the nuclear and the extended families

The giving and receiving of affection, advice, time, psychological support
and practical service were examined by asking each spouse to report on
these aspects in the exchange between them and their parents. Husbands
were requested to record whether they considered what they gave and
received from the paternal and the maternal families was too much,
enough, adequate, not enough, or none. Wives were independently asked
similar questions. Their perception of the reciprocity between themselves
and the extended families on both sides is given in Table 6.3.

In all these areas of exchange — time, affection, practical care, psychological support, finance and advice — the nuclear families maintained
an active reciprocity of giving and receiving with both the paternal or
maternal extended families although on balance they tended to give less
than they received. This may be due to the composition of this sample, in
which 18.6% of the couples were at the formation stage of marriage and

Table 6.3 Perception of the Reciprocal Exchange between the Nuclear and the Extended Families

| | Preception that the Nuclear Family | | | |
| | Give Enough To | Receive Enough From | Give Enough To | Receive Enough From |
	Paternal Extended Families		Maternal Extended Families	
	%	%	%	%
Time	54.1	61.7	62.4	66.5
Affection	63.3	76.0	76.2	83.3
Psych.support	57.6	68.0	71.1	78.7
Practical care	47.5	58.7	62.3	66.0
Finance	25.0	56.9	27.9	47.2
Advice	44.0	57.2	57.1	69.2

N = 204 nuclear families

were just in the process of separating from the family of origin to develop their own couple identity; 23.5% had pre-school age children, and 41.2% school age children. These families were at the stage when the need for general support and child rearing assistance, as well as financial expenditure, was very high. This pattern of bi-directional exchange of gifts and services in the form of contributions to rent, mortgage, remittance and financial supplements, goods in kind and care-giving between generations has also been described in Rosen's (1976) study of young middle-class couples in Hong Kong.

The figures reflect quite a high level of intergenerational connections between adult children and their parents. It should be noted that higher percentages of spouses recorded giving and receiving of time, affection, and psychological support, the emotional components of intergenerational exchange, than the giving and receiving of practical care, finance, and advice, the more instrumental components of exchange. Of particular interest is the affectional exchange reported by 63.3% to 83.3% of the husbands and wives. It would seem that for this sample their perception of reciprocity reflects affectional familism rather than utilitarianistic familism (Lau 1981).

It is interesting to note that finance is the one area where paternal families were considered to give more than the maternal family. One could speculate whether the Chinese patriarch tradition continues to function to retain resources within the male line.

Exchange with the paternal extended family

In the exchange of affection, time, advice and finance, the husbands reported levels of perceived reciprocity which were higher than those reported by the wives. It could be that the husbands do more with their own families than is known to the wives; or that their assessment is higher than that of the wives. On the other hand, some wives admitted they did not do enough in returning affection, psychological support, finance and advice to the paternal extended families.

The data was further analysed to differentiate adjusted and non-adjusted marriages.

In adjusted marriages compared to the non-adjusted, the husbands felt that they did not do enough for the paternal families in:

giving affection $\chi^2 = 11.64$, df4, p<.02
giving finance $\chi^2 = 9.87$, df3, p<.02

In non-adjusted marriages compared to adjusted, the husbands considered they did not

receive enough affection from the paternal families
$\chi^2 = 18.00$, df4, p<.001

The question arises as to whether contentment in marriage allows husbands to be more sensitive and concerned over the needs of their parents, while husbands experiencing marital stress feel the need for greater affectional support from their parents.

Exchange with the maternal extended family

The husbands' evaluation of the exchange with the maternal extended family is very similar to their wives responses. Except for affectional exchange with the maternal extended families, where the wives reported a significantly higher level than the husbands, chi square = 12.13, df 4, p<.02. In all other areas the difference in the reports of husbands and wives was not statistically significant.

As shown in Table 6.3, in the five areas of exchange, the reciprocity with the wives' families was higher, except for financial assistance from the paternal extended families to the nuclear families. It is interesting to note the high degree of affection and psychological support which the spouses perceived that they received from the maternal extended families. If this result is compared with the report of 55% of spouses who recalled unhappy childhood experiences, it would seem that these children in adulthood experience a more fulfilling relationship with their parents than when they were young.

Although it was not formally recorded, some interviewers observed that wives who were unable to fall back on the maternal extended family due to geographic distance, emotional cut-offs, or lack of resources or understanding, missed this extra support and reported more reliance or more tension with the in-law families.

These reports reflect some tensions in relationships between the nuclear families and the paternal extended families, and a more supportive relationship with the maternal extended families.

The Bidirectional Exchange of Affection, Gifts and Services

The frequency of contact between the married couples in the sample with their extended families is higher than that noted in other Hong Kong studies (Lau and Wan,1987; Lee, 1992). Many studies on kin support networks in Hong Kong report a high degree of contact and of active mutual assistance, particularly between parents and their children (Lee, 1992; Mitchell, 1972; Young, 1985). In a survey of social indicators in Hong Kong, Lee (1992) noted that 64.4% (N=343) reported that they rendered financial assistance to their parents, while 47.6% received financial assistance from their parents. In Lee's sample, 69.5% gave and 65.7% received advice from their parents. While respondents in Lee's study reported giving more than receiving assistance from their parents, the spouses in the Hong Kong Marital Study considered they received more than they gave. Since 44.1% of the husbands and wives in the marital sample were experiencing difficulties in marital adjustment, it could be that their energy and resources were taken up by their own problems and they were less able to provide for their parents. In the circumstances, they required extra assistance and support from the people around them.

A number of Hong Kong studies confirm a high level of economic cooperation within the kinship network (Lau, 1981; Mitchell, 1972; Rosen 1976). The recognition of financial obligations to parents is still very much a part of the tradition of filial responsibility among all ages in this community.

Mitchell (1972: 370) gives some interesting figures of financial support to parents amongst Chinese in Hong Kong, Singapore and Taipei:

Married people who give money to their parents

	Adult married sons	Adult married daughters
Hong Kong Chinese	65% (N = 805)	44% (N = 1264)
Singapore Chinese	67% (N = 270)	34% (N = 305)
Taipei Chinese	52% (N = 228)	27% (N = 309)

Findings from this Hong Kong Marital Study reveal a flow of resources from parents to their adult children which counters the myth of the financial autonomy of offspring after marriage. In this sample, 56.9% claimed that the paternal extended families gave adequate financial help to them; while 25% reported giving to the extended families. Overall, 47.2% reported receiving and 27.9% giving, financially to the maternal extended families. These figures are quite close to those reported in the Cleveland study quoted by Sussman (1965), where financial aid from the respondents to their parents was 14.6%, and from parents to the respondents 46.8%. Sussman from the 1950s drew attention to the active mutual reciprocity between generations and to the expectations of children that parents would continue to assist them through the early years of marriage, particularly in middle-class families in the United States.

Chinese sayings constantly reaffirm the paramount status and authority of the paternal family in determining the nature of the marital relationships of its members. In the traditional Chinese family, the wife as daughter-in-law is an outsider brought into the family to ensure continuity of lineage through having sons 不孝有三 ， 無後為大 . She complies with family rules, 入家門 ， 跟家規 and accepts and puts into operations her husband's decisions 出嫁從夫 . These sayings are still bandied around though their influence has waned and their sentiments may no longer be pertinent. Although wives may have been socialized to patriarchal values, their behaviour in adulthood demonstrates their natural affinity with their own mothers. While being the dutiful daughter-in-law, many wives also value their more comfortable alliance with their own families. Since they take the active role in maintaining kin relationships, it is therefore not surprising that it is with the maternal extended families that affiliations are stronger and the exchange is less tense. Table 6.3 shows that in time spent, affectional exchange, psychological support, practical care and advice giving, the spouses received and returned more on the maternal than on the paternal sides of the family. This stands true except in the area of financial assistance, where the exchange with the paternal extended family was more active.

The Interface Between the Areas of Differences

The four areas of differences — in life cycle changes, in the husbands' and wives' perspectives of their marriage, in the effects of parental models and early developmental experiences, and in their relations with the paternal and maternal extended families — have been separately presented for discussion purposes. There are, however, many aspects of rich interface between these differences. Systemically, all these areas of differences affect and are affected by each other as shown in Figure 6.2.

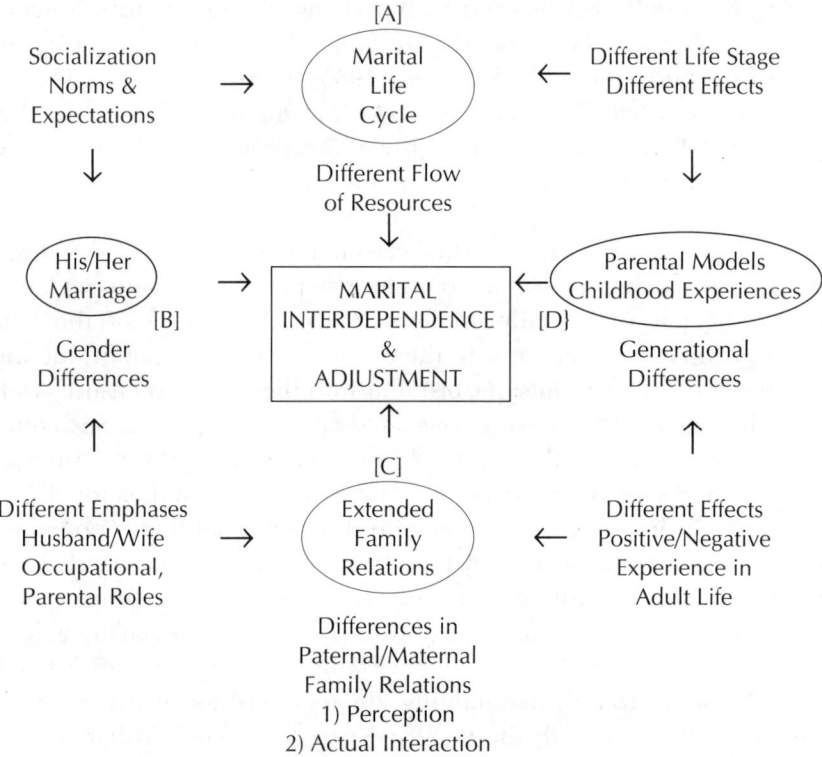

Fig. 6.2   Interface Between Areas of Differences

Relational and personal events have different meanings and repercussions according to their timing at different *life stages* [A]. Even as a couple go through the various life stages of their marriage together, they experience different subjective realities as husbands or wives, arising from cultural expectations, gender role requirements of their occupations inside and outside the home, and of dissimilar parenting demands as father or mother.

The socialization of male and female children to different norms and expectations of instrumental and expressive behaviour, paves the way for a number of variations that emerge in their later adult lives. In the Hong Kong study, this was discernible in the way the husbands and wives described their relationship [B], and in their relationships with their families of origin.

The quality and the extent of the connection with the extended families may depend on whether a couple evolves a segregated or a joint life style in their own relationship (Bott, 1974). The flow of goods and services between married persons and their parents varies over the life cycle and according to cultural norms (Sussman, 1965). At the same time, cultural and family norms shape the nature of their tasks and responsibilities in extra-familial exchanges [C], all of which contribute to their total experience within the marriage.

Early relationships and experiences [D], both positive and negative, from the family of origin could be transmitted and replicated in the intimacy of marital living.

All these important concerns testify to the complexities and multi-faceted nature of the marital interaction. Noting and taking into account the possible influences of these variations may enable us to evolve a fuller picture of the many ramifications of the marital interaction.

This review of differences serves to remind us of the complexities that need to be taken into account in assessing marriages. It also serves to remind us that marriages have a time in the past and a time in the future, as well as time in the present. Self rating scales provide a preliminary indication of the current status of the relationship. To acquire an holistic understanding of a marriage it is necessary to evaluate the nature of the interdependence and adjustment the couple have evolved now and in the context of their life course. Other systems that impinge on the dyadic exchange, the male and female socialization of each spouse and the sets of values, norms, expectations, personal style and propensies each brings to the relationship all contribute to shape each spouse's experience.

Part III

Marital Interdependence

Chapter Seven

The Transition From Traditional to Companionship Marriages

The convergence of Eastern and Western ideologies in Hong Kong necessarily impacts on marriage. An analysis of both the social trends of our society as well as the expressions and expectations of affection and sharing reported by the spouses in the study, suggests that in contemporary Hong Kong the trend is towards a companionship marriage based on familism.

Within the last generation, Hong Kong has undergone a series of social changes which have had a direct impact on marriage. In 1971, the Marriage Reform Ordinance restricted marriage to one husband and one wife, and formally abolished the traditional concubine, or *tsip sze*, status. In 1972, the no fault divorce was instituted. In 1990/1, the Law Reform Commission proposed the waiting period for divorce between two consenting parties to be reduced to separation after one year. Other social changes have also indirectly affected marriages. In 1978, compulsory education was instituted for all children up to the age of 15 and this provided opportunities for schooling for girls and their subsequent entry into the employment market. Participation in the labour force for women in the prime working age of 25 to 54 rose from 53.1% in 1981 to 61% in 1991. Family units have tended to become smaller, and average 3.5 persons per household, with 61.6% of the population living as one unextended nuclear family. Infant mortality, which is often used as an indicator of the general health of a community, is 6.4 per thousand live births, a figure somewhat better than that for Great Britain or the United States. The community has become economically affluent with a GDP per capita standing at HK$111,799 (1991 figures,Census and Statistics Department, 1993) leading to higher expectations in almost all areas of living. Politically, the community is faced with a major transition in 1997 which has initiated migratory patterns affecting marriage and family life.

In view of all these changes the question could well be asked as to where we are in Hong Kong in regard to our expectations in marriage.

Trends Towards Conjugalism

The experience of other societies shows that as industrialization and urbanization proceed, families change towards a conjugal model (Goode, 1963). Since the middle of this century Hong Kong has steadily developed as a manufacturing, then as a service centre. Initially invigorated by the influx of immigrants and capital which flowed from China after 1949, by the 1990s it has become a thriving cosmopolitan city open to multiple influences and idealogies. These changes have led to changes in patterns of family life.

Conjugalism emphasizes the centrality of the spousal relationship. A conjugal unit is represented by a nuclear family, with a couple and their children living in a separate household. Decisions are made through consultation and negotiation between the different sexes and different generations. Affection and care giving is shared, and loyalty is focused on the nuclear unit, which maintains contacts and exchanges mutual assistance with the extended families. In conjugal families the nature and degree of change in different aspects of interpersonal relationship vary. Change tends to occur at a faster pace in aspects related to choice of mate, relationships between the sexes, expressions of preferences and expectations of personal fulfilment. Aspects involving relationships with relatives of an older generation are likely to be maintained along more traditional lines.

Conjugalism reflects the way in which families respond and adjust to the particular requirements of industrialization. Such changes are difficult to gauge in precise terms and the extent of the change is likely to differ across the community. Families tend to retain valued aspects of their traditional outlook, modifying those that are restrictive but holding on to those that preserve useful connections and provide mutual assistance across the generations. However, despite a deeply rooted regard for traditional values, in broad terms it has to be recognized that the patterns of Asian family living are gradually being redefined and that this change has both direct and indirect effects on the nature of family living in Hong Kong and on the marital relationship.

One area where the direct impact of such change may undoubtedly be felt is in the way a nuclear family unit has to develop its own resources within a smaller household. The conjugal family needs to evolve new forms of spousal cooperation and communication different from when living in a larger extended family household. This is evident by the pressing needs for child care, particularly if both spouses are working outside the home. This cooperation can be displayed in minute ways, in the readiness of the spouses to share in domestic tasks. It can also be shown in the ability of the spouses to share in deciding important matters. In fact, spousal attitudes to male and female role models, which may be brought into focus with the shift from the extended to the nuclear family, can often be more easily examined through a couple's views on domesticity.

Over the past two decades, a number of sociologists in Hong Kong have examined the emergence of conjugalism from this perspective. In order to examine the extent to which modern industrialization may have affected the development of conjugalism in Hong Kong, Wong Fai Ming developed indices to measure family ideals, industrialization, and conjugalism (1972). He found the highest correlation between the family ideal index with the individual total index to be in the component — married for love r = .85. The highest correlation between conjugalism and the individual index were found in the three components — marriage as centre for advice and help r = .76, centre for emotional sustenance r = .72, and equalitarianism between mates r = .67.

Other studies in the 1970s on attitudes and values towards marriage do not demonstrate such a clear shift towards conjugalism. In their analysis of the views of young people on marriage, Chaney and Podmore (1974) found that 91% of the respondents agreed that love was the appropriate basis for marriage. However, 98% of their sample also agreed that the wife's first duty is to make a home for the husband; one-third agreed that the wife should obey the husband, and one-fifth considered that childless wives should allow their husbands to take another woman. With responses such as these it is difficult to share the researchers' conclusions that these views are more 'consonant with the Western conjugal family than the traditional Chinese family'. Nevertheless, such mixed responses are to be expected in a period of transition; other studies carried out at the same time have shown the steady decline of a traditional acceptance of male prerogatives and a more open recognition of the changing position of females in the family arising from women working outside the home (Rosen, 1976; Salaff, 1976).

By the 1980s, different patterns seemed to be emerging. In a study on the effects of maternal employment on the marital relationship, Wong reported that 80% of the fully employed mothers and 64% of the housewives in his sample enjoyed a 'mutually collaborative' marital relationship where

there is equalitarian sharing in decision making and in the division of labour. He also noted that 57.1% of the mothers in full employment and
43.5% of the housewives recorded that household tasks were equally shared
by husband and wife (Wong,1981). This is all the more surprising in that
his respondents were from a lower social economic section of the population where 90% of the mothers had less than six years of elementary
education. Other studies carried out in the same period do not present
such a favourable picture of task sharing in the home (Hong Kong YWCA,
1982; HKBGCA, 1984) Responses on this point all too often reflect an ideal
rather than the reality. When searching for social indicators for the sharing of domestic tasks between husband and wife, Lee Ming-kwan in the late
1980s recorded that 72.1% of his sample of close on 400 subjects indicated
that the wife was the actual person involved in the household chores, although in a preferred or `ideal' situation only 58.2% felt that this work
should be the responsibility of the wife (Lee, 1991). The Association for
the Advancement of Feminism in 1993 has produced even lower figures.

These studies, which examine different segments of the population at
different times and with different hypotheses, are not really comparable.
Nevertheless, in different ways they serve to illustrate the gradual dilution
of traditional values and practices based on the gender and age differen-
tials of the Chinese patriarchal family, and they do show a slow move
towards increasing conjugalism. In this process, the greatest leverage has
come from women engaging in gainful employment outside the home
requiring renegotiation and rearrangements in many areas of family living. Such change has been helped on by prevailing concepts of equality
and democracy and supported by increased opportunities in education
and employment in present day Hong Kong. The shifts in normative
patterns are more apparent in some aspects of marital living than others.
The sharing of decision making by husband and wife has proceeded
further and more satisfactorily than their sharing in household chores
(Lee, 1992). Wives socialized in the expressive role of care giving seem
ambivalent about surrendering this role. Husbands socialized to the instrumental role of provider consider the wives to be more competent in
domestic work.

However, whether husbands engage in household tasks or not seems
to be related to more than sex role perceptions. The findings in the
present marital study on this point show that with adjusted couples, 56%
of the husbands participated in household work, and 74% participated in
attending to the children, compared to 31% of husbands helping out in
the home and 26% sharing in child care in non-adjusted marriages. The
quality of the marital relationship appears to be a significant factor in
determining the nature of the conjugal relationship, including the sharing of household tasks. On the other hand, sex role perceptions do

contribute to determine behaviours and expectations within the spousal relationship, and in turn affects the quality of their marriage.

The Hong Kong Marital Study specifically addresses the affectional sharing and confiding components of a conjugal relationship. Aside from Wong's work on love and emotional sustenance (1981) and Lee's reference to the helping relationship, in which 27.3% replied that the spouse is the first person to turn to 'when one was upset and needed someone to talk to' (Lee, 1992) these aspects have received little attention in local studies.

A conjugal marriage is built on emotional bonding between spouses in a union formed from personal choice and attraction. Mate selection in the Hong Kong Marital Study shows that 42.6% of the sample married due to mutual attraction. A conjugal marriage is conserved by maintaining the spousal unit as the centre of advice, help and affection (Wong, 1972), such that the conjugal pair replaces the parent-child pair as the important relationship within the family. Certain findings from the study illustrate these emergent trends.

Valuing the Conjugal Relationship

For the Chinese, the emergence of conjugal marriages from the extended family system has involved a break with tradition greater than that in many other cultures. Three of the five cardinal relationships in the Confucian ethic — of father and son, husband and wife, and elder and younger brother — relate to kinship and uphold the concept of family ties which stretch through five generations, from an individual's ancestors back to the great-great-grandparents and descendants down to the great-great-grandchildren. It was an hierarchic system based on paternal authority, in which seniority across the generations was carefully observed, with a complex terminology of address to differentiate between paternal and maternal relatives (Reischauer and Fairbank, 1958). For centuries the Chinese child has been socialized to accept this hierarchy as appropriate and unchangeable, and so it has been. Francis Hsu, in comparing families in different cultures, observed that in Asian families the dominant dyad is the parent-child pair, while in the West a higher emphasis is reputedly placed on the conjugal dyad (Hsu, 1965).

Responses by the spouses in the Hong Kong Marital Study clearly indicate the shift away from the centrality of the filial relationship towards the conjugal bond. In determining the importance of various dyadic relationships in the family, 58.4% ranked the husband-wife relationship as primary, 38.6% ranked their relationship with their children first, only 4% ranked the relationship with elderly parents as primary. Spouses in adjusted and less adjusted marriages held very similar views. However, where satisfaction derived from these various relationships was concerned, the adjusted spouses ranked the spousal relationship as providing the greatest satisfaction, while for the non-adjusted spouses their relationship with their children provided the most satisfaction (F=22.14, p<.001).

The spouses in this sample had clearly shifted to conjugalism, with its emphasis on the centrality of the conjugal relationship and the nuclear family. The conjugal union is maintained on the basis of companionship, sharing and mutuality between the husband and the wife, and the provision of nurturance and the socialization of the children

The development of a companionship marriage could result from valuing the conjugal relationship and from valuing the gratifications which it offers.

Emerging Emphasis on Companionship

A fulfilling conjugal relationship takes on depth by becoming increasingly interdependent. In turn, this interdependence subtly affects the way the spouses respond to each other in building up a relationship based on companionship. A companionate relationship meets affiliative needs for association, intimacy in emotional and physical closeness, and empathic sharing of ideas and ideals. Some of these tendencies were expressed by the spouses in the study in their review of their relationships as described in Chapter 3.

The emergence of a companionship marriage based on 'mutual affection, intimate communication, and mutual acceptance of division of labour and procedures of decision-making' has been noted by Burgess, Locke and Thomes (1971: 9). According to their description, the companionship marriage emphasizes the emotional bond between the spouses, the quality and quantity of their time together, consensus in decision making, common interests and enjoyment of joint leisure, and the active sharing of family tasks and mutual concerns. The adjusted marriages in the study reflect many of these features. However, in their descriptions of their marital interaction, there are also many references to an active exchange with the larger family.

Companionship derived from marital benefits

The strength of a companionate relationship, and the way in which it differs from the institutional marriage, can be discerned by the nature of the benefits and gratification which the spouses enjoy from the relationship. About half of the sample (49.5%) specified love as the first or second most important benefit from marriage. This was followed by enjoyment of home life 39.2%, and sharing companionship 29.9%. Having children comes fourth in importance, 21.6%; followed by the benefits of having one's own flat, economic security, sharing common interests, and finally having a sexual partner.

To marry for love, or to seek interdependence by sharing one's life, or for companionship, all signify the desire for a companionate marriage. Having children to continue the family line, once the principal reason for marriage in the traditional family, has a lower priority in modern marriages. The benefits of having a home, economic security, having common interests and having a sexual partner, though gratifying in a stable marital state, are now also available to the non-married in contemporary Hong Kong. Modern marriages as illustrated by the Hong Kong spouses in this study are entered into primarily to meet the personal needs of the individual spouse.

Some differences in experience of benefits derived from marriage are reported in different types of marriages.

Ranking of benefits from marriage

Adjusted spouses	*Non-adjusted spouses*
1. Love	1. Home Life
2. Home Life	2. Love
3. Companionship	3. Children
4. Children	4. Companionship
5. Common Interest	5. Have own Home
6. Have own Home	6. Economic Security
7. Economic Security	7. Common Interest
8. Sexual Partner	8. Sexual Partner

More adjusted spouses ranked love first, and this was statistically significant, $F=11.09$, $p<.05$. More non-adjusted spouses considered having their own flat as important, $F=4.40$, $p<.05$. Wives ranked economic security more importantly than did the husbands, $F=9/82$, $p<.01$. Husbands ranked having a sexual partner higher, $F=27.18$, $p<.001$.

Companionship is not associated with equalitarianism

The trend towards more companionship and emotional sharing is not necessarily associated with more democratization in marriages in Hong

Kong. Wives still assume the responsibility for child care and household duties, though more companionable and caring husbands help out. However, whether husbands help out or not is influenced as much by the quality of the marriage as by gender attitudes. According to responses on equalitarian roles, it was clear that both husbands and wives subscribe to the expectations of clear gender division of labour.

The score on ENRICH equalitarian roles is outstanding as this is the one scale where non-adjusted wives score higher. Wives in non-adjusted marriages scored higher with a mean of 53.6 to a mean of 41.5 for wives in adjusted marriages, and this was significant $F(1/100) = 9.46$, $p \leq .003$. In Fowers and Olson's study (1989), dissatisfied wives also scored higher than satisfied wives. Taking the scores at their face value, it would seem that striving for egalitarianism does not contribute to marital adjustment and satisfaction in Hong Kong.

Evolving Social Norms — Companionship and Familism

In the changing socio-economic context of Hong Kong, even as spouses gradually build up companionate transactions within the privacy of their spousal boundaries they also consciously endeavour to maintain wider family connections.

The value of maintaining family ties in the Asian context offers the married person a sense of belonging to a more extensive unit, with mutual support, cooperation, and participation in the group's activities and resources. However, it also imposes obligations and the duty to promote the family's interests, prestige and continuity, sometimes requiring the subordination of individual needs to the common good. Chinese familism, which traditionally respects the authority of the elders and filial responsibility, has undergone redefinition over the decades. There is now an acknowledgement of the importance of the conjugal pair, mutual respect between different generations, and between members of different genders. In contemporary Hong Kong, modern ideas and ideals co-exist with traditional sentiments which continue to be valued and practised.

The familial marriage described in Chapter 4 incorporates spousal enjoyment of companionable interdependence with a joint approach in the nurturing and socialization of the young, as well as a caring exchange with the older generation. Many Chinese couples feel that being a part of a larger familial network strengthens their marriage. Extended family relationships and activities contribute to both marital quality and stability by strengthening barriers to dissolution. This can apply, whether relationships with the extended families are satisfactory or conflicting or, as is usual, both (Argyle and Furnham, 1983). Chinese literature and novels are replete with stories of family conflicts (Wolf, 1968). Yet, these associations continue, sometimes from necessity, but often from choice. Though many couples in the study experience in-law relationships to be sources of conflict, they commented that they nevertheless valued their parents' approval and are affected by their disapproval. Although filial duty may at times seem to be a burden, the adult married person is also likely to feel a real sense of personal relatedness to intimate kin. Transactions between them promotes a sense of personal worth, enjoyment in shared activities, and security in the connection. All of these can enrich other relationships, the marital, the parental and the grand-parental (Chu, 1992; Lam, 1992; Pun, 1992).

The Hong Kong Marital Study shows that many of the most outstanding marriages are companionate marriages with a familial orientation. In these marriages, the conjugal relationship is upheld as the dominant pair relationship. Interdependence is valued, and the emotional fulfilment of the partners is of primary concern. Their mutuality extends to their shared role as parents, and the care and love of their children are an integral part of their intimacy. At the same time, connections with their families of origin are maintained, and obligations and mutual benefits in their continuing association are acknowledged.

The term 'affective individualism' is often used to characterize modern marriages in the West. In the East, 'affective familism' could well be adopted to characterize contemporary marriages among the Chinese in Hong Kong. Familism can be defined as an orientation towards the family as the centre of loyalty and support, with members recognizing their mutual obligation to maintain the cohesion and integrity of the group. Affective familism emphasizes the dimension of affection in their transactions.

The profiles of the familial, the romantic, and the harmonious marriages described in Chapter 4 portray companionship marriages embedded in the supportive network of a larger family group. Each values the relationship with the other. Each functions to reinforce and promote the well-being and welfare of the other with affective familism.

Evolving Social Skills — for Companionship Marriages

Research on companionship tends to focus on behaviour related to doing things together. Miller (1976) suggests these include 'visited friends; gone to movie, entertainment; spent evening just chatting; entertained friends at home; had a good laugh, shared joke; eaten at restaurant; taken a drive or walk for fun; been warm, affectionate'. From the descriptions of the Hong Kong spouses, it would seem that they also see companionship as sharing affection, activities, feelings, thoughts, life events and mutual concerns. Companionship therefore refers to the affiliative component of joint participation in task and non-task activities. Companionate couples feel emotionally close to each other, share private thoughts, enjoy just being together.

Although both spouses may highly value companionship in their relationship they may vary in their perception of what constitutes companionable activities. Differences may arise from a dissimilar social outlook, varying needs for intimacy or independence, their skills in initiating and responding to expressive communication, and differences in gender expectations.

There is a tendency to regard expressive and instrumental behaviour as being distinct and disparate: to associate expressive behaviour as meeting feminine emotional needs; while instrumental behaviour meets the practical needs of the male. In fact, expressive and instrumental behaviour are both inherent aspects of marital interdependence and both are engaged in by the spouses as manifestations of affection and companionship. Wives in the study ranked love as most important, and companionship third in importance within a marriage. Husbands ranked love first and companionship fourth. While both sexes desired more love and companionship, their definition of what this entails was different. The women found affection and companionship in confiding, self-disclosure, the sharing of experiences and decision making, and in an explicit recognition of them and their contribution to family life. The men considered affectional and companionable expressions to be doing things for the partner, as in economic support and practical help, and in doing things with the partner either by just being together or in sexual activity. Thompson and Walker (1989), Cancian (1986), and Wills, Weiss and Patterson (1974) all suggest that wives need to use male socialization criteria and husbands to use female criteria to appreciate their spouses' expression of love and affection.

Attitudinal shifts in expressive behaviour may not come easily, especially for spouses schooled since childhood in the appropriate forms of social and personal response. The younger generations, however, have grown up in an atmosphere of encouragement rather than constraint, where it is acceptable to display rather than to hide one's feelings, and with their attitudes influenced by the emphasis that is placed on love and affection in personal relationships by television, films and novels. Moreover, the integrated nature of the nuclear family unit has encouraged informality and personalized the marital relationship, while the earning capacity of the modern wife has brought new meaning to the ideal of the marital partnership. Although perceptions of traditional role models between the sexes may never completely be abandoned, they have increasingly become less clear cut. Attitudes are changing, particularly in higher resourced marriages. If it is true that middle-class values are *avant garde* in a society (Rodman,1972), then the move towards more companionable marriages will steadily spread to all social classes in Hong Kong.

The Transition Towards Modern Marriages

The transition from the traditional to the modern marriage is a process which takes a long time. This transition occurs within the context of changes in the nature of the family unit, which both affects and reflects the patterns of marriage that the spouses may have. Overall, societal and cultural trends also have significant determining effects. The transitional process from the traditional through the complementary, the differentiated, the equal partnership of the modern marriages is diagrammatically represented in Figure 7.1. The shift towards conjugalism indicates that the transition from the [A] traditional patriarchal authority of the husband/father in charge, to the complementary marriage of the husband being central and wife supporting, to a differential partnership of the senior male partner and the junior female partner, to the modern marriage of an equal partnership, has been initiated in Hong Kong. In marriages based on patriarchal tradition, parent-child affection takes precedence over conjugal

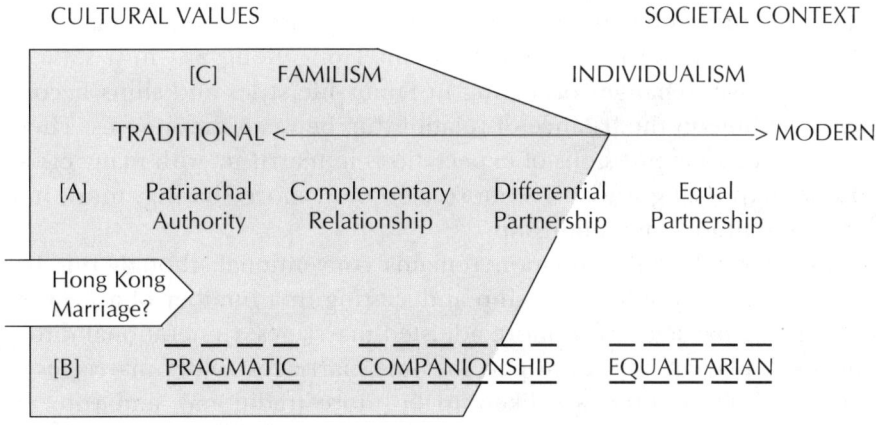

Generational and Social Class Differentiation

Figure 7.1   The Transition From Traditional to Modern Marriages

affection. In complementary marriages, the husband occupies the leadership and decision-making role while the wife reaffirms his position. In the
differential partnership the husband as senior partner is in charge, but
there is a clear division of labour and responsibility and the wife's contribution is acknowledged and upheld. The modern marriage is an equal
partnership of sharing tasks and responsibilities between peers, with each
participating in collaborative endeavours to build a life together.

Transitional changes in patterns of marriage parallel changes in expectations of marriage. People who marry to enter the institution of
marriage for the marital life style and to have children, feel bound by a
sense of duty and obligation to ensure that the pragmatic aspects of
married living are provided [B]. With the realization that marriage includes loving and sharing, the relationship shifts to a companionship
model. When expectations of sharing become equalitarian, the marriage
moves to a modern marriage of a democratic and equal partnership.

At the same time, it was clear that many of the spouses were still
clinging to certain traditional norms and ideals and that traditional pre-
cepts of appropriate behaviour still governed their relationship exchanges.
It seems that many people in Hong Kong still subscribe to traditional
values in marriage, perhaps arising from our cultural heritage of placing
a high value on familism rather than on individualism [C]. Similarly, our
expectations of personal satisfaction and fulfilment in life are derived
from a sense of belonging to a family unit, where reciprocity and mutuality promote the welfare of the family group.

In regard to the transitional process from the traditional to the modern, it would appear from the findings of this study that the general state
of the marital relationship in contemporary Hong Kong seems to lie
somewhere between a traditional-complementary arrangement and an
emerging differentiated partnership. The responses in the Hong Kong
Marital Study indicate that marriages in Hong Kong are in a state of
transition, with changes occurring in family life styles and shifts becoming noticeable in the balance of relationship between the spouses. There
were also open expressions of expectations in marriage, with many of the
spouses expressing a wish for more closeness, more sharing, more intimacy, and more companionship.

Gender role differentiation remains conventional, though this has
been softened by companionship and sharing in a number of aspects of
daily living, particularly in more adjusted marriages. Generational differences still play an important part in some marriages. Older marriages of
couples in their fifties are likely to be more traditional, and younger
marriages of couples in their twenties are likely to show more of a partnership pattern. There are also likely to be some social class variations, as
with many aspects of marriage.

To a real extent, patterns of family living and the types of marriage that make up these patterns, conform to the economic and social conditions of the society in which they are placed. When economic and societal conditions change, so do these patterns. This process of change is not quick, nor is it immediately discernible, even in the face of cataclysmic events, such as natural catastrophe or war, or of attempts at social engineering, as with China's one child policy. The process of change is lengthy and the manner in which it occurs is not immediately noticed by the people who are bringing it about. It may be forced on by emerging economic and social conditions but it is held back by concepts of loyalty and tradition. However, when viewed across the generations, the inexorable impact of this change can be seen.

Hong Kong now has the economic and societal structure associated with this form of change. It is an industrialized, technologically oriented urban society with a literate and socially mobile population which enjoys good educational and employment opportunities, a high life expectancy, and a stable government increasingly open to democratic ideals and the self expression of the individual. These are the elements of social change which cause traditional family systems to adapt and the nature of the marital relationship to be redefined.

Marriage and General Wellbeing

The social influences that have helped to transform modern marriages have not only had an effect on the form of the marriage relationship, they have also had a profound influence on the partners of the marriage, both in regard to their ability to adapt and to meet expectations arising from the relationship, and on them as individuals in terms of their personal development. The marriages of our grandparents were embedded in large complex family systems; with organizational structures that required hierarchial control and a clear-cut division of roles and responsibility. Smooth family relationships called for filial commitment and an emphasis on harmony. Individual self expression was as strong then as now, but it did not necessarily find its focus in the home. The contemporary Hong Kong marriage is evolving as a nuclear unit linked to an extended network of kin, some in the territory, some dispersed on the Mainland, some overseas. The conjugal unit is increasingly required to be the basis for adult life satisfaction, the major source of adult tension management and the springboard for development in adulthood. To fulfil these functions, spouses have to turn to each other to provide emotional support, mutual affirmation, the sharing of joys and problem solving based on interdependence within the spousal boundary. The underlying theme now becomes companionship as the basis of quality relationships.

For married persons the overall sense of well-being is highly affected by their marital experience. Glenn and Weaver (1981) examined the effect of marital happiness on global happiness using cumulative data from social surveys in the United States between 1973-1978. They found that for both husbands and wives, white, working full-time, and for the black married women, the perceived effect of marital happiness was greater than the combined effect of seven kinds of satisfaction. These include satisfaction from work, family life, financial situation, health, friendship, non-working activities, and the community.

The shift towards increasingly companionship marriages is double edged. As marital unions based on affection assume paramount importance, so could unions institutionalized by law and unions vested in family considerations lose their foundations. Thus, when affection fades or ceases to exist, and other bases for marriage lose their holding force, the likelihood of marital breakdown increases.

For many in Hong Kong, with the utilitarian aspects of living having been met in a thriving economy, the focus has shifted to social and personal fulfilment in the context of their marriage. Associated with this, to an increasing extent we now recognize that valued relationships need to be nurtured. This is accompanied by a widespread wish to understand and to work towards enhancing quality relationships. Married people are seeking to understand themselves more as persons, as spouses, and as parents. Research in intimate relationships can contribute to this trend.

Chapter Eight

Interdependence in Marital Relationships

The development and maintenance of the marital relationship is built on the interdependence that a couple gradually evolve through shared living.

The interpersonal processes of negotiating interdependence within the marital boundaries promote the development of bonds and the development of means of coping with conflicts and differences. These experiences may confirm an interdependence of commitment in long term reciprocity for mutual benefits. Or, uncertainty may result in an interdependence with an exchange orientation, based on a quid pro quo reciprocity of equitable returns for one's contribution to the marriage.

This theoretical framework has both guided the conduct of the study and been crystallized in the progress of the research. This chapter presents an overview of the conceptual foundation on which the design of the research has been based and from which the findings have been evaluated.

Social relations among the Chinese are governed by expectations of interdependence. Except for the parent-child relationship, which is one of commitment regardless of the nature of their transactions, interdependence in other relationships is based on various levels of reciprocity. This includes the relationship of marriage, in which husbands and wives contribute to and receive rights and obligations in complementary exchange. A conjugal relationship becomes increasing committed with the development of emotional interdependence, as with Leung Hung (梁鴻)

and Mung Kwong (孟光), characters in a frequently retold Chinese tale illustrative of conjugal love.

The Development and Maintenance of the Marital Relationship

Spouses build on their marriage through sharing more and more aspects of their daily lives. In practical terms, this may be a home to return to, a life style acceptable to both, perhaps a joint bank account and home ownership as well. Close association may lead to the development of mutual interests and the sharing of common concerns. Their joint network of kin, mutual friends, perhaps religious affiliations, may be steadily strengthened and extended. At a more personal level they share love, affection, sexual exchange, memories, some common values, beliefs and interests and, over time, children. In the ramifications of everyday living, mundane routines further cement family togetherness (Duck, 1988a: 89). These daily transactions in shared living contribute to the development of what Turner calls crescive bonds (1970: 80–87). He describes these as:

- incomplete actions in family life which are the unfinished actions, that keep members involved; examples are home decoration, vacation plans, even debts;
- shared experiences which contribute to the spouses constructing a common conception of reality, which increases their attachment;
- interlocking roles arising from a division of labour in handling daily chores, leading to increased reliance on each other;
- reduction of reserve which are the short cut transactions between family members which differentiate them from outsiders.

All these activities create an increasing interdependency which adds to the repertoire of gratifications that each spouse can offer the other, and to the development of mutual obligations, which further strengthen the relationship.

Marital Boundaries

Marital boundaries and the development of bonds

The gratifications and obligations which intimate partners build up over time constitute attractions which induce them to remain within the marital boundary. Levinger (1965) uses the phrase 'bonds and bars' to provide a vivid guideline of what needs to be done to maintain or enrich a marriage. Bonds are the positive forces holding partners within the boundary and bars the constraints against leaving.

From the systemic perspective, a functional marriage develops strong boundaries that allow the spouses to negotiate similar and disparate needs and interests in an atmosphere of flexible adaptability, free from intrusion and interference from other familial or extra-familial systems (Minuchin, 1979). Within the supportive environment of the spouse sub-system boundary, the couple need to achieve a balance in affection and sexual expression, distance regulation in the amount of intimacy or dependency or independency each can tolerate or allow, power balance as to who makes what decisions and how these decisions are negotiated.

Negotiations over these expressive areas contribute to the development of a couple identity, to satisfaction and to their bonding. These constitute the intrinsic rewards in interpersonal relations derived from valuing each other and valuing the relationship itself. Intimate partners find being together, doing something together and sharing the same experiences intrinsically gratifying, regardless of what they may be doing (Blau, 1964). Marriage also offers extrinsic rewards which are instrumental in achieving satisfaction in the more practical, utilitarian aspects of living.

Marital boundaries and the management of conflict

While the concept of marital boundaries provides the idea of a personal and private space within which spouses can negotiate the amount and manner of their interdependence, it is also the same space within which they negotiate to contain, regulate and manage conflict. Inherent in the development of inter-relatedness is the possibility of the development of conflict.

Haley (1963) sees negotiation between spouses as a struggle for power and control. This is particularly so at the formation of the marriage when the parties are contracting as to how to define their relationship. Foundations are laid in the first few years of marriage, though renegotiations continue for the entire course of the relationship. Many marital theorists and therapists see the mutual influence of spouses as a matter of reciprocal control, as each works to produce outcomes according to their own definitions (Haley, 1963; Madanes, 1981; Thibaut and Kelley, 1959). When two people join their lives in marriage, each gives the other power of control over the future. This being so, they must retain some means by which they can express and exercise personal choice. Outcomes over decisions regarding marital and familial issues depend on the choices made by each partner, further complicated by their particular life context. Each partner comes to the marriage with certain norms, expectations and propensities. Each attempts to influence the other in reciprocal control to their own perspectives. It is through this process of negotiation in sharing interests and intentions that they develop their unique relationship, 'a joint product of their interdependent actions' (Chadwick-Jones, 1976:8).

Research in the fields of social learning and behavioral perspectives indicates that adjusted marriages exercise positive control, using positive reinforcers to shape compliance, while distressed couples use negative, adversarial means towards coercive control (Jacobson and Margolin, 1979; Stuart, 1980). Nevertheless, research in general has confirmed the truism that conflict is an integral aspect of all close relationships including satisfactory close relationships (Argyle and Furnham, 1983; Birchler, Weiss, and Vincent, 1975; Braiken and Kelley, 1979).

Where there is affection, value consensus and attitudinal similarity, negotiations over differences and disappointments may be arrived at in a spirit of cooperation. Co-operation, according to Horowitz (1967:278) allows settlement 'in terms which make possible the continuation of differences and even fundamental disagreements'. Competing needs, divergent interests and intentions, different styles, opinions and values, can lead to conflict which, if not resolved, leads to discomfort and open aggression. These factors, and the anxiety over a possible deterioration of the relationship generated by the conflict, can motivate one or both partners to make adjustments, by accepting the other's perspective to arrive at a joint compromise. New norms and different expectations derived from this process deepen interdependency and commitment. Where spouses are unable to resolve their conflict harmoniously, they may reduce contact leading to disengagement, or they may adopt a habitual conflictual style of confrontation and coercion.

Marriage in contemporary Hong Kong not only has to cope with tensions arising from within the relationship. In the fast-paced style of life in an achievement oriented society, it has to cope also with stress and conflict arising from activities outside the relationship. Shift work, long work hours, separation due to work demands, children's academic demands, high mortgage payments and inflation all induce stress in personal relationships. Whether the marriage is able to withstand this stress and function as a source of adult tension management could be reflected in the satisfaction or otherwise to be found in the relationship.

Comparing marriage to eight other relationships in the family, in friendship and in the work place, Argyle and Furnham (1983) find the spousal relationship to be highest in satisfaction and in conflict, r = .57

p<.06, leading them to conclude that more satisfying relationships also tend to produce more conflict.

Satisfaction and conflict both contribute to and result from interdependence in marriage. However, while the increase in satisfaction and of bonds between partners strengthens the relationship, the increase of conflict leads to divergence, deterioration and disenchantment in the relationship.

The Interdependence of the Marital Pair

Interdependence is a multi-faceted concept. It is a value, a process and an outcome. It can be a value implying mutual care giving and care taking, and concern for the well-being of both self and other. It is a process of merging and sharing and developing crescive bonds. At the same time for married people, it is also a process of reciprocally influencing each other within their pair relationship. As an outcome, interdependence refers to the reliance of partners on each other for gratifications. It has a past, as early experiences of interdependence influence the shaping of current interdependence, which in turn continues to evolve towards anticipation of future interdependence. Each couple evolves the interdependence optimal to them at that point of time. This interdependence is constantly in process, dynamically changing to their varying maturation as adults and to the life circumstances they encounter. A couple can shift towards increasing attachment and personal dedication with increasing satisfaction and bonding, or through stress, conflict or indifference move towards an interdependence infused with resentment, hostility, and distancing leading to disengagement.

Kelley et al (1983: 32–36) consider that the task of analysing and describing a close relationship can be achieved through assessing the nature and extent of the interdependence on which it is built. He provides a comprehensive framework for defining this concept. He suggests that interdependence in a pair relationship can be understood by examining the intensity of a couple's interconnections, how strongly and how extensively they impact on each other in the course of daily living. The nature and range of activities shared could be far-reaching and prolonged, and the frequency of their interaction could be high as they help or hinder each other in their interactions. Overall the extent of the spouses' dependency on each other and the degree of their mutual influence provide indicators of the interdependence in a pair relationship.

Interdependence based on reciprocity

The nature of the interdependence between spouses is determined by the norms of reciprocity each spouse brings to the relationship, as well as by the actual reciprocal exchange between the couple throughout the development of their relationship, and in the here and now. Gouldner (1960) suggests that reciprocity is derived from learned moral norms that are instilled into men and women in terms of their rights and duties, and their appreciation of the rights and obligations of others in various roles. In Hong Kong society, men are considered to be socialized to instrumental task focused norms, and women to expressive person focused norms. The complementarity of these norms promotes an interdependence supported by social approval.

These learned internalized norms regarding the expectations of the rights and obligations of the Self and the Other form a part of the marital predispositions that spouses bring to their marriage (Lewis & Spanier, 1979). They both affect and are affected by the reciprocal exchanges in marriage, and result in either a commitment or an exchange orientation emerging in the relationship. Murstein and McDonald (1983) conducted a study with a non-probability purposive sample of 40 couples in order to test the hypothesis that commitment could be positively correlated and exchange negatively correlated with marital adjustment. They defined commitment as attachment to the spouse and to permanency in the relationship, and exchange as a balancing of input proportional to outcome, determined by the ratio of benefits and costs derived from the relationship. Their findings confirm the hypothesis. Commitment for both husbands and wives was significantly correlated with their adjustment in marriage, and an exchange orientation for husbands and wives negatively related to adjustment in marriage. Murstein, Cerreto and MacDonald (1977: 544) concluded that 'relationships in which individuals are strongly committed to each other, such as marriage, do not profit from exchange-oriented attitudes . . .'.

Interdependence leading to a commitment orientation

Mutual reciprocity, where one provides valued experiences, services and resources for another, engenders obligations which, when returned, initiate a continuing series of reciprocation, thus establishing commitment to the relationship.

Commitment in marriage could be a personal commitment to the spouse, or a social commitment to the institution of marriage (Johnson, 1982; Rosenblatt 1977). Hinde (1979) differentiates between endogenous commitment when both spouses work to promote mutual benefits to enhance their relationship, and exogenous commitment where the continuation of the relationship is based on external pressures. These differences could be reflected in the intrinsic marriage where, according to Cuber and Harroff (1974), the spouses marry and stay married because they value the uniqueness of the person of the spouse; or, in the instrumental marriage, where spouses marry and remain married for the marital life style in preference to being single. Turner (1970) suggests that when marital interdependence is based on a person bond, rather than on the function which the spouse fulfils, then he or she becomes irreplaceable. These person bond relationships are more enduring, there is less ambivalence regarding constraints of marriage, and less consideration of alternatives.

Debate on the conceptualization of commitment has been well documented (Kelley, 1983; Rusbult, 1980; Scanzoni, 1979). In this marital study, the focus has been on commitment as adherence to the continuity and stability of the relationship. This could be based on a personal attachment to the spouse, and to the relationship. On this perspective, commitment in marriage is built on the development of a number of marital qualities.

1. Attachment to the spouse,and adherence to the relationship. Increasing commitment leads to security in the relationship with further investment of confidence and trust, to 'progress towards greater intimacy' (Hinde, 1979:133).
2. Permanency and expectations of continuity and confidence in the future of the relationship.
3. Non-substitutability of the spouse and the relationship expressed in loyalty and preference, thus 'the exploration of alternatives is curtailed' (Cook and Emerson, 1978:728).

Commitment built on progressive interdependence becomes self generating and self maintaining. Commitment from one partner activates commitment in the other partner, so that giving becomes non-contingent, beyond reciprocity. It leads to the development of trust, a sense of confidence and reliance on the partner to provide expected gratifications and to look after one's well-being. This allows the partners of the relationship to forego immediate, short term returns for indefinite, long term mutuality. Trust permits risk taking, which may be considered bets on the future.

Commitment to the spouse and/or to the relationship implies investment and involvement with each other, leading to a collaborative set of joint endeavours for mutual benefits and corporate concerns. Committed couples will function to maximize positive joint outcomes as spouses consider their interests as being fairly met by the other.

Interdependence leading to an exchange orientation

Interdependence can also be built on an exchange orientation of short-term reciprocity in which 'what one party receives from the other requires some return, so that giving and receiving are mutually contingent' (Gouldner, 1960: 169). This individualistic position of balancing a rewards-costs ratio in relationships can be observed in clinical work with spouses expressing utilitarian expectations arising from negative experiences or conflict and from insecurity in the viability or continuation of the marriage.

Under such conditions, spouses will evaluate their relationship by balancing rewards and costs, to achieve optimal profits of the highest rewards with the lowest costs (Nye, 1982). Partners in an uncertain, hence vulnerable relationship need reassurance. They consider it is only prudent to collect on their exchange of advantages, goods and services immediately, in case the relationship does not continue for them to receive back what they contributed. They request fair play, just returns, equity in the exchange. If the relationship continues to be inequitable (experienced by them as not receiving just returns relative to their input of efforts) they may strive to restore equity by balancing rewards-costs; or consider terminating the relationship. Many people who seek marriage counselling are striving to restore equity in their marriage.

People in troubled marriages are conscious of thinking along the lines of 'what am I getting for what I am giving?' This is presented by Weiss (1978) as the 'Give ← → Get' behaviour exchange balance, a process by which couples institute changes in their relationship to accomplish beneficial, equitable parity.

Various aspects of the marital qualities which constitute commitment, namely attachment, permanency and non-substitutability, are retained in exchange relationships. However, they may become diluted and may be laced with conflict. Also, a tit-for-tat vigilance further exacerbates a difficult exchange. Such a situation allows for alternative means of satisfaction to become viable.

Differentiating commitment and exchange orientation

In summary, couples adjust to each other through negotiations over various facets of marital living to evolve and maintain an optimal interdependence in their partnership (Fig. 8.1). Their interdependence

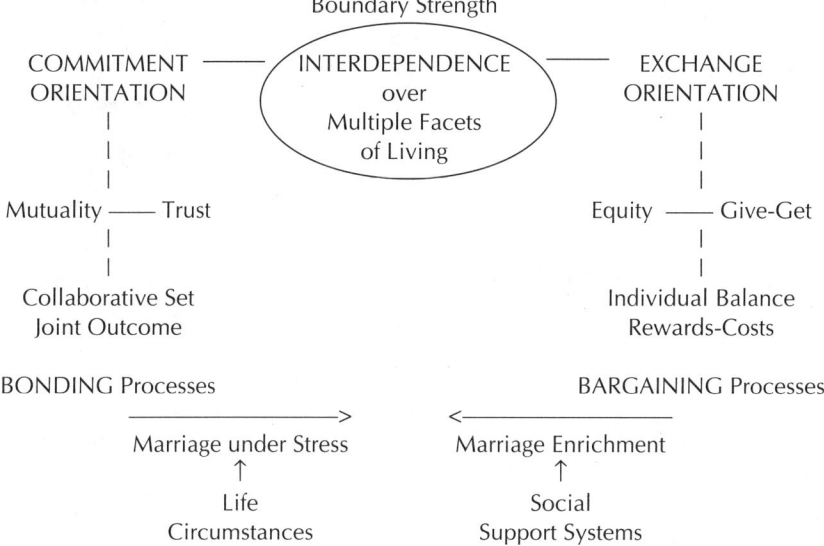

Figure 8.1   Differentiating Commitment and Exchange Orientation in Interdependence

could be one of a commitment orientation or an exchange orientation. It is postulated that spouses with commitment orientation are likely to experience mutuality and trust in their relationship and to function collaboratively to produce joint benefits. They are likely to adopt bonding processes and activities in their negotiation. Spouses with an exchange orientation are likely to focus on equity in their relationship to ensure a fair balance of rewards-costs for each other in return for their contributions. They are likely to use bargaining means in their negotiations to ensure that each person's interests are appropriate met.

The Interdependence Framework in Application

The Hong Kong Marital Study has been designed to examine the interdependence of the marital pair. In the development of their relationship, married people build up mutual reliance in the practical, social, familial and emotional areas of living. They evolve interdependence by adjusting to each other's personal characteristics, needs and interests, incorporating both positive and negative experiences in their daily transactions. If their subjective sense of shared living is enjoyable and enhances attachment, trust and security, the spouses are likely to increase their involvement and commitment to each other. Uncertainties in the relationship arising from conflict or questionable confidence in each other or the relation-

ship is likely to lead to vigilance and ambivalence over any further investment in interdependence. Instead, independence and self interest become
viable and even necessary.

Commitment, Equity and Exchange Orientations

The six items of the commitment scale and the ten items of the equity
scale from the Marital Comparison Level Index (MCLI) package were

Table 8.1   Factor Analysis of Commitment and Equity Scales of the MCLI Package

Factor I	*Exchange Orientation*	Factor loading
Equity 10	– feel cheated in relationship	.67
Equity 4	– feel taken advantage of	.66
Equity 1	– put in more into rel/ship than I get out	.66
Equity 7	– feel less powerful than spouse	.66
Equity 5	– partner less interested in rel/ship than I	.65
Equity 6	– often feel manipulated by partner	.65
Alpha .82		
Factor II	*Equity Orientation*	Factor loading
Equity 2	– equally dependent on each other	.73
Equity 8	– argue, usually reach fair solution	.70
Equity 9	– equally share power in our relationship	.70
Equity 3	– contribute equally to our relationship	.62
Commit 1	– feel very loyal to my partner	.44
Alpha .71		
Factor III	*Commitment Orientation*	Factor loading
Commit 6	– not like some behaviours,can live with them	.67
Commit 2	– boring to be committed to one partner	.63
Commit 3	– probably marry someone else	.58
Commit 7	– not matter that I do more	.52
Commit 4	– partner will sacrifice as I will	.50
Alpha .67		

Table 8.2   Commitment, Equity, Exchange and Adjustment Groups

	Adjusted group	Non-adjusted group	
Commitment group	28	2	15% – 30 Spouses
Equity group	73	30	51% – 100 Spouses
Exchange group	16	51	34% – 67 Spouses

X2 = 53.26 df2 p<.001

Table 8.3   Characteristic of the Commitment, Equity and Exchange Groups of Spouses

	Commitment oriented spouses 15% (N = 30)	Equity oriented spouses 51% (N = 100)	Exchange oriented spouses 34% (N = 67)	
Interdependence				F Value
Orientation	Mean	Mean	Mean	
Commitment (Max.score 25)	16.6	15.4	14.4	21.11
Equity (Max.score 25)	22.4	18.9	15.6	137.7
Exchange (Max.score 30)	9.9	13.4	18.8	122.26
Marital Adjustment				
Total DAS (Max.score 151)	123.6	110.9	84.3	61.04
– Affection (Max.score 12)	9.6	9.0	6.7	35.85
– Consensus (Max.score 65)	53.5	49.2	40.2	36.56
– Cohesion (Max.score 24)	18.7	15.7	10.9	22.57
– Satisfaction (Max.score 50)	41.9	37.0	26.6	71.17
Marital Expectations				
Expectations (Max.score 25)	20.2	17.0	13.4	53.83
Affectional (Max.score 25)	19.9	17.0	13.9	30.86
Sharing (Max.score 25)	19.8	17.2	14.4	30.55
Coping/Conflict (Max.score 25)	17.3	14.8	12.4	29.04
Global satisfaction in marriage according to ENRICH (Max.score 5)	4.0	3.2	2.4	30.78
Stability of the marriage according to considered divorce — ENRICH				
Yes, Considered Divorce	0	22%	52%	$x2=32.25$ df2

p<.001 on all scales and items.

combined to test differentiation between the various levels of interdependence of the spouses in the sample. Using principal component analysis with varimex rotation and selecting only those factors with eigenvalue greater than 1, produced a three factor solution which explained 50.5% of the total variance (Table 8.1).

These findings yield an interesting refinement in the study. Between commitment and exchange is a quality characterized by equitable considerations. Cluster analysis of the sample according to the three factors produced three distinct groups, with a commitment, an equity and an exchange orientation. When correlated with the adjustment scores, the scores of these groups were significant (Table 8.2).

Almost all the committed spouses were also adjusted. Approximately, two-thirds of the equity oriented spouses were adjusted, while two-thirds of the exchange oriented spouses, were not adjusted.

The characteristics of these three groups of couples are shown in Table 8.3, where the figures provide the data which addresses the hypotheses of this piece of research.

Hypotheses of the Hong Kong Marital Study

Hypothesis One.   Spouses evolve different orientations of interdependence in the course of the development of their relationship.

Hypothesis Two.   Different orientations in interdependence affect and are affected by the adjustment process, so that committed spouses are likely to report higher adjustment, higher satisfaction, and are not likely to think about divorce. Spouses with an equity orientation are likely to report moderate to high adjustment and satisfaction, and moderate to low consideration of divorce. Spouses with an exchange orientation are likely to report lower adjustment and satisfaction, and higher consideration of divorce.

Hypothesis Three.   The extent to which expectations are met within the marriage contribute to the development of marital adjustment and to the development of spousal interdependence.

These hypotheses are confirmed by the findings in this study.

It is therefore suggested that specific items with ability to discriminate between different orientations of interdependence could be used as the basis to construct a discreet set of measures suitable for assessment work in Hong Kong. These measures can be found by carefully selecting items from the DAS, ENRICH and MCLI package which have a particular significance for Hong Kong spouses.

A Marital Relationship Index for Application in Hong Kong

An assessment measure which could be described as a Marital Relationship Index is proposed for application with Hong Kong spouses. The Marital Relationship Index provides an overall view of the quality and stability of a marriage, through tapping the spouses' experience in the following four subscales:

1. The spouses' evaluation of *marital satisfaction.* This would provide a clear statement of their subjective evaluations of each other's experiences in the relationship at a specific point of time, and constitute an important baseline position to inform interventive efforts.
   [From ENRICH]

2. *Marital adjustment.* Eight items from the DAS correctly classified 96.1% of the adjusted spouses, and four items classified 82.3% of those who considered divorce. Ten items are selected from these two groups to assess adjustment and tensions in adjustment associated with consideration of divorce; two items which overlapped can be excluded.
   [From the Dyadic Adjustment Scale]

3. *Marital expectations.* Four items on expectations are of particular relevance to Hong Kong Spouses. These could provide indicators of the subjective experience of 'fit' in the marriage.
   Reliability using Cronbach's coefficient alpha is .79.
   [From MCLI Package]

4. *Interdependence orientation scale.* This 16 items inventory would yield scores to indicate whether the spouses' orientation is one of commitment, equity or exchange. Reliability using Cronbach's coefficient alpha is .67 for commitment items, .71 for equity items, and .82 for exchange.
   [From MCLI package]

The Chinese and English versions of the Marital Relationship Index, MRI, are presented in Appendix 4.

These 32 items of the Marital Relationship Index in combination provide indicators of global satisfaction, whether certain expectations are met or otherwise, dyadic adjustment, orientation in interdependence, and are related as shown in Table 8.4.

Table 8.4   Inter-correlation of the Subscales Factors in the Marital Relationship Index

	Equity	Exchange	Expectation	Adjust ment	Satis faction	Considered Divorce
Commitment	.48	−.60	.41	.54	.46	.43
Equity		−.46	.60	.66	.56	.41
Exchange			−.35	−.57	−.52	−.41
Expectations				.64	.59	.47
Adjustment					.72	.60
Satisfaction						.53

All at p<.001

The above scales in combination offer indications of the nature of the interdependence in the marriage. Spouses sharing an interdependence with a commitment, or an equity, or an exchange orientation, negotiate differently within their relationship. Spouses with a commitment orientation are likely to use predominantly bonding negotiations while spouses with an exchange orientation are likely to use bargaining negotiations. The next chapter examines the theoretical and the empirical evidence for this perspective on spousal negotiations.

Chapter Nine

Tuning Into Spousal Negotiations

This chapter discusses various negotiating processes, activities and strategies engaged in by spouses. It suggests that spouses negotiating from a cooperative stance are likely to be working towards joint benefits from a committed orientation in their relationship; while spouses negotiating predominantly from a competitive stance are working towards individualised interests and goals.

The Hong Kong Marital Study proposes two avenues to gain understanding of married people's experiences within their relationship: one through their responses on self report assessment measures, the other through listening to their descriptions of the negotiating processes they use in their daily transactions expressed during counselling sessions.

In their daily life, spouses regularly negotiate with each other over various issues of mutual concern. These exchanges may be overt or covert, active or passive, verbal or behavioral. They may be over small matters, or issues of serious concern. Communication is the life blood of any marriage, and in healthy marriages couples generally manage to establish channels satisfactory to both.

The process can break down in marriages where the confidence of the partners in each other is low, or when extraordinary situations occur within the marriage to threaten the marital balance. This is when the communicative strength of the relationship is tested and, if the communication channels are blocked, tensions increase as each partner experiences what he considers to be the other's lack of understanding.

When faced with extraordinary issues which they cannot resolve between themselves, spouses may turn to an outsider for help. This person, who may be a marriage counsellor, from listening to the couple's descriptions of events giving rise to the tension or the impasse, has to build up an understanding of the marital relationship and, at the same time, an appreciation of the nature of the negotiations that the spouses are engaging in, so that he can join in their negotiating processes in a meaningful and helpful manner.

Transactions in Close Relationships

In his analysis of social transactions Burns (1973) differentiates these as reflecting types of reciprocity spanning a spectrum from

Selflessness $\rightarrow$ to $\rightarrow$	Joint $\rightarrow$ to $\rightarrow$	Self $\rightarrow$ to $\rightarrow$	Hostility
for One	Self/Other	Interest	
Another	Interest		

Different constraints and incentives apply, and different strategies of negotiation are utilized along this spectrum. According to Burns, a tendency to establish goodwill is central to what he terms the social types of transaction, and equity to ensure fair and favourable outcomes the feature of economic types of transaction. Social types are defined as reflecting 'interlocking rights and obligations' between persons strongly attached to one another, and economic types of exchange as characterized by 'calculation and self interest'.

The Hong Kong Marital Study's presentation of interdependence along a range from commitment to equity to exchange orientation is similar to Burns' span of types of reciprocity, and Levinger's 'graduations of interpersonal relationships' (1974). At different times or under different circumstances of well-being or stress, marriages shift along this range towards commitment (higher levels of involvement), or equity (fair balance of self and spouses's involvement), or towards exchange (uncertain involvement).

Couples with different levels of interdependence use a mixture of different negotiation strategies (Burns, 1973; Fitzpatrick, 1988; McDonald, 1981). Couples committed to the relationship and to each other are likely to use more bonding strategies for negotiation (Johnson, 1986). Couples nearer an exchange orientation are likely to use more bargaining to achieve parity (Weiss, 1978). Both bonding and bargaining types of negotiation are resorted to at different times and over different issues.

Both can be effective forms of communication. A bargaining approach may signal areas of sensitivity and dissimilar preferences. Accordingly, where a couple is discussing activities concerning children they may use bonding means while in discussing activities with in-laws they may use a more quid pro quo approach.

The marriage counsellor participates in the negotiations between the spouses. Where they are negotiating from a cooperative stance and a commitment orientation, bonding communication is likely to be possible. Where they are negotiating from a competitive stance with an exchange orientation, bargaining communications may be necessary.

Negotiating From a Cooperative or a Competitive Stance

As spouses encounter issues of mutual concern in their daily lives, they may need to balance cooperative and competitive measures to achieve common as well as divergent goals. There has been a steady development in theory and research on cooperation and competition since Deutsch presented his seminal work in 1949. Cooperation generates more positive interpersonal relationships, while competition increases motivation and can lead to higher productivity. In testing out his theory on groups, Deutsch found that by adding interdependence as a factor, and requiring collective endeavour to produce a common output, the presence of cooperation facilitated group goals, while competition facilitated the achievement of individual goals (1949). In 1980, in a review of his work on conflict spanning fifty years, Deutsch points out that the participants' definition of their relationship determines the interactional process within that relationship. Thus a relationship perceived as cooperative and committed to the mutual benefit of both partners is likely to elicit cooperative interactional sequences and negotiations. A relationship perceived as competitive in which each partner safeguards his own advantage is likely to induce competitive interactional sequences and negotiations towards individual ends.

Whether spouses engage in cooperative or competitive negotiation is also affected by the very nature of reciprocity in social relationships. Escalation of anger evokes reciprocal anger, and conciliatory moves elicit conciliatory responses. Thus, a cooperative stance invites collaboration, and a competitive stance engenders contest. In marriage work the crux of the issue is to understand the balance of cooperation and competition in the relationship, and the conditions that would produce positive responses leading to a readiness to negotiate to achieve joint benefits.

The *cooperative stance* of spouses with a commitment orientation is founded on:
- attachment to the spouse and to the relationship;
- bonding communications towards increasing proximity and sharing;
- responsiveness to the needs of the partner.

The *competitive stance* of spouses with an exchange orientation is founded on:
- reciprocal balance of cost/benefits from the relationship;
- self protective communications and ambivalence regarding proximity and sharing;
- responsiveness contingent on obtaining approximate returns.

This implies:
- an internal state of security in the relationship;
- mutuality in caring and sharing;
- security in disclosure of affectional needs and vulnerability.

This implies;
- an internal state of lack of confidence in the relationship;
- anxiety about the giving and receiving fair returns;
- vigilance to strive for unilateral gains, ensuring self interests are protected.

From this interpersonal relationship base, bonding negotiations are likely to constitute the spouses' *modus operandi* in their daily transactions.

From this interpersonal relationship base, bargaining negotiations are likely to be the spouses' *modus operandi* in their daily transactions .

Committed spouses are likely to resolve issues arising from daily life through mainly cooperative and collaborative means of bonding negotiations. Over areas of disagreements, they may resort to bargaining means of persuasion. When stress lead to them to seek outside help, these spouses at that point of time would likely reflect an equity orientation.

Spouses with an *equity orientation* use a mixture of bonding & bargaining negotiations. Bargaining undertaken would be fairly concessional and facilitated by their basic attitudinal positivism.

Spouses with an *exchange orientation* would respond from their basic sense of vulnerability engaging in a give-get balance of what is fair exchange. Some bonding behaviours may be carefully included and can be negotiated as part of the bargaining process.

Bonding processes and activities

Bonding processes and activities refer to communications and negotiations that promote positive connections between spouses which are validating for both the one who makes the overture as well as the recipient. Bonding increases liking, affection, intimacy, goodwill, cooperation and attitudinal positiveness. Johnson (1986) suggests that the development of a bond with a preferred person in a secure relationship is the *sine qua non* of marriage. She sees this bond as evolving from the nurturance, the accessibility and the responsiveness of one spouse for the other. Spouses who are bonded seek proximity to each other, they enjoy being close physically, having sex, spending time together, doing things together.

In the Hong Kong Marital Study, the spouses considered emotional bonds in their relationship as manifested in confiding between the spouses, calmly discussing something, having time together, working on a project together, and tolerating the other's less likeable characteristics. These seem to be the significant indicators of love and concern for many Hong Kong couples, rather more than verbal expressions of affection.

Some research studies confirm the sharing of ideas and ideals, disclosure of experiences over daily events, or of feelings, opinions and judgement, as contributing to the spousal bond (Morton, 1978). The sharing of time together, interests and activities (Laurence, 1982; Yogev and Brett, 1985), emotional involvement of love and sexual affection (Kelley, 1983; L'Abate and Talmedge 1987), positivism and optimism in coping (Bowman, 1990; Sabournin, Laporte, Wright 1990), all could be considered bonding behaviours which enhance adjustment and interdependence.

Spouses who describe these process and activities as on-going in their marriage, are likely to find their relationship enjoyable and secure. This being so they would tend to adopt a cooperative stance in their negotiations, promoting further goodwill and positive attitudes in their interdependence.

Spouses who yearn for these processes and activities, who complain of deficiencies in relational exchange, or feel that they are unattainable, are likely to feel insecure in their relationship. In their disappointment at the least they may seek to acquire just returns for what they put in through bargaining.

Bargaining processes and activities

Bargaining refers to the negotiations between parties to settle what each shall give and receive in the transactions between them (Deutsch, 1973).

Each tries to arrange advantageous terms so that the benefits received outweigh or at least equal the balance of costs incurred. However, both may be willing to make concessions through the bargaining process on the basis that they could be better off or at least not worse off than if no agreement were reached. In a close relationship such as marriage, bargaining is engaged in when the partners share certain concordant interests with both desiring the same things while displaying divergent views, or they could be dealing with discordant interests, or discrepant goals. The stronger their cooperative interests, the easier to resolve their differences. The stronger the competitive interests, the more likely that they may be mutually obstructive.

An instance of bargaining where competitive interests prevail would be a highly disputed divorce settlement which leads the spouses to resort to the mediation of an impartial professional to help clarify issues and to identify options to arrive at a mutually acceptable and equitable settlement (Irving and Benjamin, 1987). In such a situation bargaining would be an inherent part of the negotiating process.

Contingency contracting, by definition, is a form of bargaining where partners agree to exchange adaptive behaviours in the expectation that the other would do likewise (Liberman, 1970). Agreements that rewards and benefits are contingent on performance of certain obligations and responsibilities serve the purpose of enabling each to express what they would like to give and receive from the other, thus formalizing expectations and wishes in specific terms. Where the giving and receiving between partners has been conflictual, or blocked, or reduced, contracting can re-initiate the flow of relational provisions on an equitable and secure basis.

However, bargaining is not necessarily or exclusively confrontive: it can lead into and strengthen the bonding process. This is illustrated in a beautifully designed technique in Stuart's 'Caring Days' (1980) to show how bonding may be facilitated through bargaining procedures. In faltering marriages where confidence in the spouse and in the relationship may be uncertain, each spouse offers the other small caring acts that are positively experienced by the other, often producing immediate beneficial effects. The exchange of a series of small positive concessions demonstrates that small gains are possible through give-get reciprocity. The beginning of good feelings about the other, and the build-up of mutual obligation, sets in motion other bonding communications.

Nevertheless, in evaluating various forms of negotiations, it is important to keep in mind a basic point made by Buckley (1967: 160) who views tension in complex systems as normal, ever present and dynamic. He reminds us that while attending to tension reduction processes it is necessary to also take into account the positive contributions of tension production processes. He suggests that tension in a relationship initiates a feedback exchange which requires the participants to elaborate, redefine and revise their expectations, motives and purposes, thus promoting change and new patterns of interaction.

Tuning Into Spousal Negotiations

Both bonding and bargaining negotiations are used by spouses over different issues,in different circumstances and at different times. Bonding tends to foster positive feelings of working as a team in handling both joyful and sad events in a marriage. Bargaining, if limited and controlled, can contribute to resolving controversial or sensitive issues. But if it is prolonged it can affect the relationship, leading to watchfulness over self interest.

At the interview for ENRICH, the couples' manner of utilizing the information from the computer report was noted by the social worker. Table 9.1 shows the different negotiating styles of spouses with different orientations.

Table 9.1   Bonding and Bargaining Negotiations in Responding to ENRICH Feedback

	Commitment orientation %	Equity orientation %	Exchange orientation %	Chi-square
– To share love and concern	33.3	26.0	10.6	8.19 p<.02
– To compliment each other	20.0	25.0	9.0	6.60 p<.04
– To deal with conflict	30.0	48.0	28.8	7.33 p<.03
– To raise sensitive issues	10.0	27.0	47.0	18.13 p<.001
– To complain about the other	20.0	25.0	53.0	16.95 p<.001
– To punish the other	–	–	6.1	8.04 p<.02

The box highlights the highest % score on that item.

The behavioral school of thought has consistently emphasized the point that spouses in satisfactory marriages use positive means in their negotiations while spouses in distressed marriages use adversive means to gain compliance.

Spouses experiencing high levels of satisfaction negotiate differently than spouses experiencing distress. It is possible to discern the nature of the marital relationship from the predominant negotiation strategies utilized by the spousal pair in their daily transactions.

In her research on communication in marriage Fitzpatrick found that negotiating styles in different types of marriages differ remarkably. She designed and applied her Relational Dimension Instrument based on three dimensions, ideological views, autonomy/interdependence, and conflict to derive four types of marriages according to the ideological orientation of the spouses. She describes the types as traditional, and independent marriages with high interdependence, separate marriages with low interdependence, and mixed marriages where spouses have different orientations. Fitzpatrick conducted a series of studies to find out how these types differ in the manner they negotiate to gain control, to manage conflict, to persuade, to disclose innermost thoughts, and to communicate non-verbally.

In particular, her findings on negotiations between spouses in conflict management and persuasion to gain compliance seem to be directly relevant to situations found in Hong Kong, and they could well be applied in clinical work here. In a marriage, when disagreement occurs spouses may use cooperative tactics in order to maintain the relationship. On the other hand, their concern for their own position may require them also to use assertive tactics. From these two components four strategies for coping with conflict become available, as shown diagrammatically below.

		Assertiveness	
		High	Low
High Cooperativeness		Collaboration	Accommodation
Low		Competition	Avoidance

Using **collaborative** strategies, spouses would be both assertive and cooperative in problem solving, in stating their positions, in validating each other, and in searching for solutions acceptable to each other to arrive at some settlement. **Accommodation** implies surrendering some of one's interests to maintain the relationship. While spouses may be willing to yield over casual issues, this may not be so over more important issues. **Avoidance** may be achieved through joking, silence, denial of the problem, or moves to withdraw from disputed issues. Avoidance may be a signal that the issue in dispute is extremely sensitive, imply indifference, or it may reflect a lack of confidence or a feeling that change or improvement may be impossible. It may also be adopted to avoid an escalation of conflict, or it may be a temporary measure to postpone discussion until a more appropriate time. **Competition** which is high on assertiveness and low on cooperation can be manifested in criticism, fault finding, hostile questions, or threats. In many marriages, contentious tactics are resorted to if the issue in dispute is important. However, in some marriages, the couple may report that they argue over trivial as well as serious concerns. Spouses employ all these strategies in coping with conflictual issues. However, different types of marriages may predominantly use more of one type than others. Fitzpatrick suggests that the degree of interdependence in the relationship affects the choice of strategies used. Where interdependence is high and the couple are concerned to promote common interests, more collaborative strategies are adopted. Where interdependence is low and the spouses push individual interests, competitive strategies would be in the forefront (Fitzpatrick, 1988; 138–145).

Couples also differ in the persuasive techniques they use to induce each other to their way of thinking or doing. Fitzpatrick and her associates propose three broad categories of compliance gaining strategies. One way to gain compliance is through reminding the partner of **expectancies and consequences** of action or non-action. These expectancies may allude to certain activities performed or not performed which would have negative or positive consequences. In emphasizing consequences of compliance or non-compliance, spouses would be asserting power to control or constrain the other. The second category refers to **invocations of the relationship**, accentuating 'US', the relational bond, sharing information about the issue, and making direct requests for compliance on the basis of its effect on the relationship. A third group of strategies makes **appeals to values and obligations** on the basis of the characteristics and contributions of ME, YOU, and external factors.

Fitzpatrick observed that spouses more interdependent on each other talk about their expectancies of compliance. They emphasize 'US', the value of the relationship and their identification with each other, to coax each other. Spouses with low levels of interdependence emphasize negative consequences of non-compliance, refer to 'You, Me' and external factors to demand acquiesence (Fitzpatrick, 1988: 159–163).

Tuning into Mr and Mrs Lee's negotiating processes

The prologue describes the outpourings of a couple in distress. Mr and Mrs Lee were talking about their attempts to cooperate and, at the same

time asserting their interests and needs. They were using more collaborative and accommodation strategies even though their goals were different
and seemingly irreconcilible. Even their complaints against the other
were couched in terms of appeals for the continuation of their mutual
interdependence, and their concern over the way that events were having
a negative effect on their marriage. Though ME and YOU messages were
exchanged, there were also many references to US. Each reminded the
other of their expectations and long-term plans which they had previously shared. Each seemed more concerned with persuading the other to
their point of view than to forcing compliance in a change of behaviour.
Listening to them reproach each other, my sense was that they were both
committed to the marriage and emotionally dependent. However, circumstances had unbalanced their relationship and begun to undermine
their interdependence, leaving each confused and insecure about their
future together. Both seem distressed at the possibiliy that they may
become increasingly polarized, so that each would be compelled to look
after their own separate interests. There was an urgent need to understand their marriage: to enable them to understand their marriage.

Counselling is talk therapy, in which the talking must be done by the
spouses not the counsellor. As spouses talk, they are effectively beginning
the process of renegotiation; and as the counsellor listens to the manner
in which spouses negotiate over various issues, the areas of common
ground on which they can begin to rebuild their future together may
gradually emerge.

Understanding Events in a Relationship Context

People in Hong Kong come for marriage counselling when some event
causes sufficient stress to trigger a decision to seek professional help. A
great deal of energy, emotion and attention is focused on the event,
which may be the latest disagreement with or about children, or in-laws,
verbal or physical abuse, loan shark threats over gambling debts, or the
revelation of an affair, to give but a few examples. While information
related to these events provides some indication of the quality of the
marriage, it is important to acquire as comprehensive and as balanced an
understanding of the relationship as possible. This provides the context
to see the issues in perspective, to appreciate the meaning and impact of
the event on the marriage, to identify the areas of disturbance and of
strength, and to recognize the bonding and bargaining processes adopted
by the couple in response to the event.

Huston and Robins (1982) propose a conceptual framework for understanding close relationships based on the interdependence that characterizes such relationships (Fig. 9.1). They note that in the course of their daily life, spouses encounter a series of events [A]. These could be overt or interpersonal events which are observable behaviours exerting a reciprocal influence upon the partners in the relationship, such as crying, arguing or comforting. Events could also be covert, subjective and not observable, but are influenced by others' feedback, such as feelings of self esteem. Spouses respond to events from their total experience of adjusting within the relationship. These experiences of events, past and present in aggregate constitute the relational properties [B] of their marriage which affect and are affected by continuing interaction within the

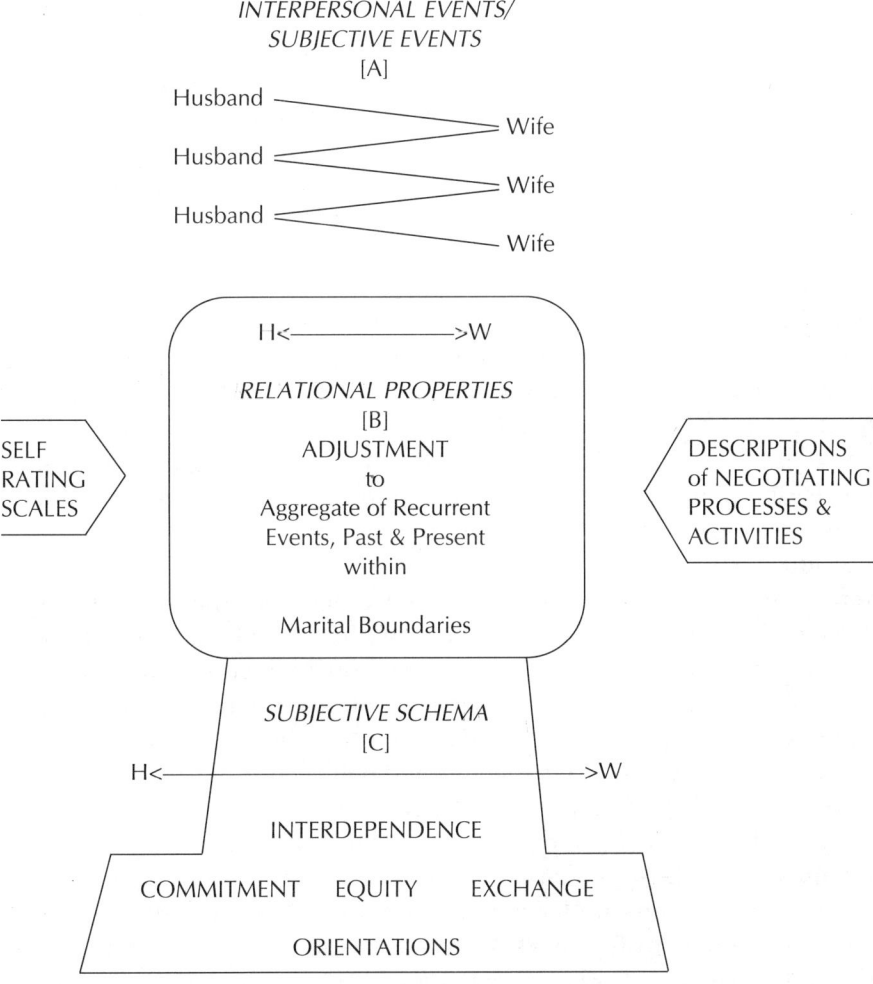

Figure 9.1   To Understand Events in a Relational Context

relationship. From this aggregate of experiences the couple evolve their personal subjective schema [C], which are the relatively stable attitudes, attributes and beliefs about each other and each other's intentions. This schema has been formed in part from experiences within their relationship, and in part from experiences of other relationships. The subjective schema once developed influence behaviour and influence the interpretation of events that arise in the course of the on-going marriage. Figure 9.1 presents the marital relationship focus of the Hong Kong Marital Study, which is a modified adaptation of Huston and Robins' diagrammatic representation.

Mr and Mrs Lee's interpretation and responses to the relational events confronting them — the decision on emigration, the purchase of a separate flat, running two households and teenage children increasingly becoming independent — have to be assessed in the context of their adjustment in a relationship spanning 18 years. Their lack of synchronization in the current context is contrary to their aggregate of experiences within their marriage. Their relational properties accumulated over the years have been built on mutuality and concern for each other's wellbeing. From this each has evolved a subjective schema of assumption about putting other's needs before one's own on the expectation that the other would do likewise. Their schema holds beliefs about sharing hopes, aspirations for the future, about working together to achieve these common goals, about sacrificing for each other and for the family.

Events confronting them have elicited responses inconsistent with their relational experiences and with their subjective schema. Hence their confusion and their turmoil. The Lees acknowledged and enjoyed their interdependence, but they were caught in a contradictory position that was tearing them apart. Both were trying to act cooperatively to maintain their interdependence and, at the same time, each was acting to protect individual self interests, and this was causing their distress. The couple were giving confusing messages to each other, and the confusion was reflected in their presentation of their positions to the marriage counsellor. Their ambivalence, whether to accommodate the other by conceding their self interest to restore the marriage, or to relinquish valued aspects of the relationship, was transmitted to the counsellor.

At that point, the need for another perspective, perhaps to be acquired through the precisely structured and focused assessment of self report scales, would have been most helpful to balance the emotional accounts of the distressed couple. At the early stages of marital work, the marriage counsellor's understanding could be facilitated with the availability of a number of avenues to gain access to the spouses' experience within the marriage. One essential avenue is understanding the meaning of what is happening from the spouses' accounts, the other could be to verify one's constantly developing perceptions with carefully designed self report measures.

Understanding Spousal Interdependence

In interview sessions, spouses explore interpersonal issues and events which have precipitated their distress. As they relate these events and describe their responses, they are sharing their experiences, their interpretation of the meaning of particular aspects for them, and recounting negotiating processes which they have already engaged in to deal with these issues confronting them.

The main aim in using self rating scales is to acquire information on the current status of a marital relationship, to enable the spouses and the counsellor to understand the 'events' in perspective. The Dyadic Adjustment Scale organizes the aggregate of events in the daily transactions of a marriage to give the spouses' insider view on their adjustment in affectional expression, cohesion, consensus and satisfaction. These events are examined for their descriptive aspects, and also to determine the spouses' experience of the processes of adjustment in response to these events. Events are recalled to examine their contribution to the development of the spouses' attitudinal structures regarding their marriage, which constitute their subjective schema. The commitment, equity and exchange scales furnish indices of the nature of their attitudinal orientation.

Assessment of adjustment and assessment of relational interdependence, whether one of commitment or equity or exchange orientation, in turn provide indicators of the negotiating responses utilized by the couple in their dealings with each other. It is possible to use information of the interdependence orientation of spouses obtained through self report measures and further explore the possible negotiating strategies they may adopt. It is also possible to form some idea of the interdependence orientations within a marriage from listening to the spouses' descriptions of events and negotiations which they predominantly use in their daily transactions. Understanding gleamed from interviews can be helpfully supplemented by information acquired through self report measures.

Marriage is a joint venture where partners build up an interdependence supportive of each other's growth within their pair relationship. Couples who seek help are searching for an understanding of the events that confront them. In this process, they are, at the same time, searching for an understanding of themselves, their partners, and their relationship. The marriage counsellor needs to assess these events in context, to be able to participate in the search for understanding of what is happening and to help the couple to work towards resolutions acceptable to both.

As the marriage counsellor prepares to join in the negotiating process of the spouses it is important to determine their current adjustment status, their attitudinal perspectives, and to gauge their readiness to participate in different negotiating processes. This essential information enables the outsider to join in the couple's negotiations in a manner conducive to generating cooperation in bonding transactions that promote mutuality, and to move gradually towards establishing or re-establishing a more fulfilling interdependence.

Appendices

The Measuring Instruments

Appendix 1a
The Dyadic Adjustment Scale (DAS)

丈夫/妻子   NO:＿＿＿＿＿＿

婚姻適應問卷

以下是您對您和配偶關係的看法，請於每題(✔)出自己之所屬程度:-

A. 您與配偶在以下事情上之一致性:-

	完全同意	幾乎完全同意	有時不同意	經常不同意	幾乎完全不同意	完全不同意
1. 家庭財政處理						
2. 康樂活動						
3. 宗教信仰						
4. 情感表達方式						
5. 結交朋友						
6. 性關係						
7. 傳統(正確合宜的行為)						
8. 人生哲學						
9. 與父母/姻親相處方式						
10. 認為重要的事情、目標						
11. 共同相處的時間多寡						
12. 作重要決定						
13. 家務安排						
14. 閒暇消遣方式						
15. 職業抉擇						

B. 您認為在您與配偶之間，以下項目發生的頻密程度:-

	任何時間	很多時	有時	間中	很少	從不
16. 考慮或討論離婚/分居/結束關係						
17. 配偶在打架/爭吵後離家而去						
18. 覺得與配偶關係進展良好						
19. 您信賴您的配偶						
20. 您可有後悔結婚/同居						
21. 與配偶爭吵						
22. 互相激怒對方						

	每天	差不多每天	間中	很少	從不
23. 親吻配偶					

	全部活動	大部份	部份	小部份	從不
24. 與配偶一起出外參加聚會/活動					

	從不	每月少於一次	每月一二次	每星期一二次	每天一次	經常
25. 有啟發性的意見交流						
26. 一起歡笑						
27. 一起冷靜地討論問題						
28. 共同合作進行一些事情/計劃						

在某些事情上，夫婦會意見一致或出現分歧，請指出在過去數星期內，下列事情有否導致大家出現不同的意見或使彼此之間出現問題:

	是	否
29. 對性方面感覺厭倦		
30. 沒有向對方表達愛意		

31. 您對現有婚姻關係的看法:

極不快樂	相當不快樂	少許不快樂	快樂	很快樂	極快樂	完美

32. 以下那句子能最貼切地形容您對您們關係的前景之看法?
- ☐ 我極渴望這段關係能能夠成功，為此我會竭盡所能
- ☐ 我很希望這段關係能能夠成功，我會盡量令它成功為此我會盡力而為
- ☐ 我很希望這段關係能能夠成功，為此我會做好我的本份
- ☐ 若這段關係能能夠成功當然最好，但我不能付出比現在更多去令它成功
- ☐ 若這段關係能能夠成功當然最好，但我拒絕付出比現在更多去維繫它
- ☐ 這段關係永不會成功，對其前景我亦覺得無能為力

© G.B. Spanier   香港大學社會工作及社會行政學系一譯

DAS (original questionnaire in English)

Within your marriage please indicate the extent you agree/disagree on these items:

	Always agree	Almost always agree	Occa- sionally disagree	Fre- quently disagree	Almost always disagree	Always disagree
1. Handling family finances						
2. Matters of recreation						
3. Religious matters						
4. Demonstrations of affection						
5. Friends						
6. Sex relations						
7. Conventionality (correct or proper behavior)						
8. Philosophy of life						
9. Ways of dealing with parents or in-laws						
10. Aims, goals, and things believed important						
11. Amount of time spent together						
12. Making major decisions						
13. Household tasks						
14. Leisure-time interests and activities						
15. Career decisions						

	All the time	Most of the time	More often than not	Occa- sionally	Rarely	Never
16. How often do you discuss or have you considered divorce, separation, or terminating your relationship?						
17. How often do you or your mate leave the house after a fight?						
18. In general, how often do you think that things between you and your partner are going well?						
19. Do you confide in your mate?						
20. Do you ever regret that you married (or live together)?						
21. How often do you and your partner quarrel?						
22. How often do you and your mate get on each other's nerves?						

© G.B. Spanier

	Every day	Almost every day	Occa- sionally	Rarely	Never
23. Do you kiss your mate?					

	All of them	Most of them	some of them	Very few of them	None of them
24. Do you and your mate engage in outside interests together?					

How often would you say the following occur between you and your mate:

	Never	Less than once a month	Once or twice a month	Once or twice a week	Once a day	More often
25. Have a stimulating exchange of ideas						
26. Laugh together						
27. Calmly discuss something						
28. Work together on a project						

There are some things about which couples agree and sometimes dis-agree. Indicate if either item below caused differences of opinions or were problems in your relationship during the past few weeks. (Check yes or no.)

	Yes	No
29. Being too tired for sex		
30. Not showing love		

31. The dots on the following line represents different degrees of happiness in your relationship. The point, "happy", represents the degree of happiness of most relationship. Please circle the dot that best describes the degree of happiness, all things considered, of your relationship

•   •   •   •   •   •   •

Extremely Unhappy	Fairly Unhappy	A Little Unhappy	Happy	Very Happy	Extremely Happy	Perfect

32. Which of the following statements best describes how you feel about the future of your relationship:
    5 I want desperately for my relationship to succeed and would go to almost any lengths to see that it does.
    4 I want very much for my relationship to succeed and will do all that I can to see that it does.
    3 I want very much for my relationship to succeed and will do my fair share to see that it does.
    2 It would be nice if my relationship succeeded, and I can't do much more than I am doing now to help it succeed.
    1 It would be nice if it succeeded, but I refuse to do any more than I am doing now to keep the relationship going.
    0 My relationship can never succeed, and there is no more that I can do to keep the relationship going.

Appendix 1b
ENRICH

豐盛

「豐盛」是一個根據科學發展而設計的測量表，以測試婚姻關係中14個重要的範疇，它們可分為以下各項：

理想偏差程度
婚姻滿意程度
性格問題
溝通
解決紛爭
財政管理
清閒活動
性關係
兒女和子女教養問題
家庭和朋友
平權角色
道德傾向
婚姻凝聚力
婚姻適應程度

每一個範疇得分越高，那麼婚姻關係就更為穩固，而伴侶之間也更為和諧、快樂。

如需要更多資料以完成 125 項 PREPARE / ENRICH 的測量表或是需要「豐盛」問卷的中文版本的資料，請寄信往以下地址申請：
PREPARE / ENRICH, P. O. Box 190, Minneapolis, MN55440-0190, U.S.A.

此測量方法是明尼蘇達大學，家庭社會科學院，
David H. Olson 教授研究而成，他亦是
PREPARE / ENRICH 組織主席

© 1992, David H. Olson
PREPARE/ENRICH
Life Innovations, Inc.

Sample Questions

The ENRICH inventory is a scientifically developed scale devised to assess 14 important areas of the couple relationship.

ENRICH — is designed for married couples who want to improve their marriage.

. PREPARE — is designed for premarital couples who are seriously dating and planning to marry.

This sample version of PREPARE and ENRICH provides an overview of some of the major areas included in the comprehensive inventories. The Sample is designed to encourage discussion between partners about important relationship issues. It is only a sample of the type of questions which are included in the PREPARE and ENRICH Inventories. It is not designed to be scientifically accurate or a predictor of a successful marriage.

PREPARE and ENRICH Sample Questions
by David H. Olson, Ph.D.

Realistic Expectations in PREPARE
(Idealistic Distortion in ENRICH)

Yes No 1. I expect some of our romatic love will fade after marriage.

Personality Issue

Yes No 2. My partner has some habits I dislike.

Communication

Yes No 3. I can easily share my positive and negative feelings with my partner.

Conflict Resolution

Yes No 4. We have some important disagreements that never seem to get resolved.

Financial Management

Yes No 5. We have decided how to handle our finances.

Leisure Activities

Yes No 6. At times I feel pressure to participate in activities my partner enjoys.

Sexual Relationship

Yes No 7. I am very satisfied with the amount of affection I receive from my partner.

Children and Marriage

Yes No 8. I have some concerns about how my partner will be as a parent.

Role Relationship
Yes   No   9. We have clearly decided how we will share household responsibilities.

Religion and Values
Yes   No   10. We sometimes disagree on how to practise our religious beliefs.

Scoring for Individuals
1. On the ODD numbers (1, 3, 5, 7 & 9)
    – count the number of YES responses _____
2. On the EVEN numbers (2, 4, 6, 8 & 10)
    – count the number of NO responses _____
3. Add the two categories together.
    Total Individual Score _____

Scoring for Couples
If you take this as a couple, you can count your level of couple agreement on these items. The greater the couple agreement, the more compatible and happy you will be as a couple.
1. On the ODD numbers (1, 3, 5, 7 & 9)
    – count the number of items where you *both* answered Yes _____
2. On the EVEN numbers (2, 4, 6, 8 & 10)
    – count the number of items where you *both* answered No _____
3. Add the two categories together.
    Total Couple Score _____

Interpreting Your Individual Score or Your Couple Agreement Score:
8 – 10   Mostly relationship strengths
6 – 7   Many relationship strengths, few growth areas
4 – 5   Few relationship strengths, many growth areas
0 – 3   Mostly growth areas

For more information about taking the complete 125-item PREPARE or ENRICH inventory, please apply to PREPARE/ENRICH, P.O. Box 190, Minneapolis, MN 55440–0190, USA.

Scales developed by David H. Olson, Ph.D.   © 1992, David H. Olson
Professor, Family Social Sciences,   PREPARE/ENRICH
Univearsity of Minnesota, and   Life Innovations, Inc.
President of PREPARE/ENRICH Inc.

Appendix 1c
The Marital Comparision Level Index (MCLI) Package

婚姻相處問卷

對婚姻的總期望: 請列出你的婚姻生活與期望的差距

若以 [0] 代表你對婚姻的感受與期望相同, 請以 ++ (更好); + (好), 或 - (差); -- (更差)來表示閣下現在的婚姻關係。

	與期望差距				
	更好 ++	好 +	等同 0	差 -	更差 --
1.你所感受被愛的程度	1.				
2.你與配偶的合適性	2.				
3.你們互相尊重的程度	3.				
4.期望能否實現	4.				
5.配偶展示的愛意	5.				
6.配偶的投入程度	6.				
7.配偶對性方面的興趣	7.				
8.婚姻中的伴侶關係	8.				
9.關係平等的程度	9.				
10.配偶的吸引力	10.				
11.夫妻間的坦誠	11.				
12.夫妻共處的時間	12.				
13.關於日常生活決定所產生的爭議	13.				
14.因瑣事而引起的爭論	14.				
15.性生活	15.				
16.因安排閒暇生活產生的矛盾	16.				
17.配偶作出的批評	17.				
18.夫妻對生活方式的同意程度	18.				
19.家務的分配	19.				
20.因應用金錢所產生的爭議	20.				

© R.M. Sabatelli and E.F. Cecil-Pigo, University of Connecticut

香港大學社會工作及社會行政學系—譯

請表示你贊成下列各句子的程度

II.　　　公平程度

	非常同意	同意	有時同意／不同意	不同意	非常不同意
1. 在我們的關係中，我常感到我付出的比我接受的為多					
2. 我與配偶同等倚靠對方					
3. 詳細考慮後，我與配偶對我們的關係都作出同等貢獻					
4. 我時常感到配偶利用我					
5. 我的配偶看來不如我那般對我們的關係感興趣					
6. 我常感到被配偶操縱					
7. 我覺得配偶比我較為有力					
8. 為一個決定而爭辯時，我們通常達致一個合理的解決方法					
9. 在我們的關係中，我與配偶享有同樣的權力					
10. 在我們的關係中，有時我會有被欺騙的感覺					

III.　　　關係投入感

	非常同意	同意	有時同意／不同意	不同意	非常不同意
1. 我對配偶非常忠誠					
2. 完全委身給一個人必然是一件非常沈悶的事					
3. 若要重新開始，我大概會娶/嫁給另外一個人					
4. 我願意為我的配偶作出犧牲					
5. 我能夠容忍配偶一些令我不悅的行為					
6. 我不介意我付出的比配偶多					

IV　　　婚姻的維持

	非常同意	同意	有時同意／不同意	不同意	非常不同意
1. 我深信婚姻是永恒的					
2. 若我們離婚，父母會感到不高興					
3. 若我放棄這段婚姻，我會損失良多					
4. 對未來的恐懼使我打消離婚的念頭					
5. 若我考慮離婚，他人的意見不會影響我的決定					
6. 兒女不會成為阻止我離婚最重要的考慮					

MCLI (original questionnaire in English)

Marital Expectations

Indicate with a _____ how your current experiences in your marriage compare with your expectations in the following aspects:

	Much Better than	Better than	About as	Worse than	Much Worse than
	. . . . Expected				
	++	+	0	−	− −
1. The amount of love you experience.					
2. The compatibility you experience.					
3. The mutual respect you experience.					
4. The degree expectations are met.					
5. The affection partner displays.					
6. The commitment from spouse.					
7. The interest in sex partner expresses.					
8. The companionship you experience.					
9. The relationship equality you experience.					
10. The physical attractiveness of your partner.					
11. The confiding between you and your spouse.					
12. The time you spend together.					
13. The amount of conflict over daily decisions.					
14. The amount of arguing over petty issues.					
15. The mount of sexual activities.					
16. The amount of conflict on leisure.					
17. The mount of criticism your partner expresses.					
18. The amount you agree on your life style.					
19. The amount of household tasks shared.					
20. The amount of conflict over money you experience.					

© R.M. Sabatelli and E.F. Cecil-Pigo, University of Connecticut

Indicate your degree of agreement with these statements.

	Strongly Agree	Agree	Sometimes Ag/Disag	Disagree	Strongly Disag

Equity Scale

1. I often feel I put more into our relationship than I get out.
2. My partner & I are equally dependent upon one another.
3. All things considered, my partner & I contribute equally to our rel.ship.
4. I often feel taken advantage of by my partner.
5. My parnter seems less interested in our relationship than I.
6. I often feel manipulated by my partner.
7. I feel less powerful than my partner.
8. When we argue about a decision we usually reach a fair solution.
9. My partner & I equally share power in our relationship.
10. There are times in our relationship when I have felt cheated.

Commitment Scale

1. I feel very loyal to my partner.
2. It must be boring to be committed to one person.
3. If I had to do it all over again I would probably marry someone else.
4. I am willing to sacrifice for my spouse.
5. I can live with them, though I do not like some of my partner's behaviour.
6. It does not matter that I do more for my partner than he/she for me.

Barriers to Dissolution

1. I strongly believe that marriage is forever.
2. My parents will be upset if we were to get divorce.
3. If I leave this marriage, I would loose a great deal.
4. My fear of the future will deter me from divorce.
5. The opinions of people will not affect my decision if I were considering divorce.
6. My children's needs will not be the most important consideration in deterring me from divorce.

Determining Criterion Groups

The couple score of 200 according to the Dyadic Adjustment Scale was adopted to determine criterion groups of adjusted and non-adjusted groups in the Hong Kong Marital Study. To confirm the appropriateness of this criteria, one-way analysis was conducted on other variables which could have served to determine criterion groups, with the DAS as the dependent variable.

Table A2.1   Univariate Analysis of Dyadic Adjustment Scale in Discriminating Perceived Marital Quality, Marital Satisfaction, and Considered Divorce

Criterion Groups		Mean DAS Score	ANOVA Results *
Perceived Marital Quality			
– Happy	N=113	115.6	F = 132.0
– Tense	N= 33	74.6	
Marital Satisfaction			
– High	N=131	114.0	F = 124.6
– Low	N= 73	83.5	
Considered Divorce			
– No	N=142	112.3	F = 108.4
– Yes	N= 62	82.0	

* p <.001 on all items

The three criteria to determine the discriminating validity of the DAS were:

1. The perceived quality of the marriage which was verbally stated by the spouses during the interview, as 'happy-satisfied' [113], or 'mixed, bit of both satisfaction and frustrations' [36], or 'tense-conflictual' [33].

2. Satisfaction with the marriage which was a global question asked in the ENRICH inventory with answers along a five point scale.
3. Ever considered Divorce, another question in ENRICH to which the answer is a 'yes' or 'no'.

Responses to these three items were organized into criterion groups. These refined criterion groups were treated as criterion variables and scores on the DAS were treated as the dependent variable in separate one-way analysis of variance. Results showed significant differences between mean scores for these criterion groups.

The Reliability and Validity of the Dyadic Assessment Scale

One way analysis of variance shows the difference between the mean scores of the DAS and the four DAS subscales are all statistically significant (Table A2.2).

Internal consistency reliability for the scale was assessed using Cronbach's coefficient alpha. The coefficient alpha of the Hong Kong sample is very similar to Spanier's sample of married persons in the Pennsylvania area (Table A2.3).

Table A2.2   One-way Analysis of Variance Results of DAS Subscales

	Adjusted (N = 114)	Non-Adjusted (N = 90)	F - Value *
Adjustment	119.7	82.1	330.18
Consensus	52.1	39.2	157.07
Cohesion	17.9	9.7	139.29
Satisfaction	40.1	26.5	277.24
Affection	9.5	6.7	112.68

* All scales $p < .001$

Table A2.3   Reliability (Cronbach Alpha) of the DAS

	Hong Kong Sample (N = 204)	Spanier's Sample (N = 218)
Dyadic Adjustment	.95	.96
Dyadic Consensus	.90	.90
Dyadic Cohesion	.85	.86
Dyadic Satisfaction	.90	.94
Affectional Expression	.73	.73

The intercorrelation matrix shows high to moderate correlation between the DAS subscales, demonstrating their convergent validity in measuring adjustment (Table A2.4).

Table A2.4   Intercorrelation of DAS Subscales

	Affection	Cohesion	Satisfaction	Consensus
Affection		.56	.72	.69
Cohesion			.66	.54
Satisfaction				.71

p<.001 on all subscales

Logistic regression to find the discriminant capacity of the DAS subscales shows that three scales, measuring the dimensions satisfaction, cohesion, and consensus correctly predicted 93.14% overall of the groups (Table A2.5). These subscales demonstrate high sensitivity in classifying 93.86% (107) of the adjusted spouses, and 92.22% (83) of the non-adjusted spouses, with false positives of seven adjusted and false negatives of seven non-adjusted spouses misclassified.

Table A2.5   Logistic Regression Analysis in Discriminating Adjustment by DAS Subscales

	Predicted		% Correct
	ADJUSTED GROUP	NON-ADJUSTED GROUP	
Observed			
ADJUSTED GROUP	107	7	93.86%
NONADJUSTED GROUP	7	83	92.22%
		Overall	93.14%

Variable	B	S.E.	Sig.	Exp(B)
DASCONSENSUS	-.1363	.0406	.0008	.8726
DASCOHESION	-.2137	.0663	.0013	.8076
DASSATISFACTION	-.3396	.0663	.0000	.7121
Constant	20.6719	3.1622	.0000	

Logistic regression shows that eight DAS items correctly classified 96.08% of the adjusted group membership (Table A2.6). This demonstrated that the number of items of the questionnaire could be further reduced and still maintain its discriminant capacity.

Table A2.6 Logistic Regression Analysis in Discriminating Adjustment by DAS Items

	Predicted		% Correct
	ADJUSTED GROUP	NONADJUSTED GROUP	
Observed			
ADJUSTED GROUP	109	5	95.61%
NONADJUSTED GROUP	3	87	96.67%
		Overall	96.08%

Variable	B	S.E.	Sig.	Exp(B)
DAS1	−1.0584	.4392	.0160	.3470
DAS14	−1.0127	.4120	.0140	.3632
DAS16	−1.6979	.4566	.0002	.1831
DAS17	− .8780	.4163	.0349	.4156
DAS19	−1.2476	.5558	.0248	.2872
DAS26	− .7345	.3476	.0346	.4797
DAS28	− .6610	.3253	.0421	.5163
DAS31	− .8333	.3572	.0196	.4346
Constant	29.5120	6.0572	.0000	

Logistic regression identifies four DAS items as being able to predict 82.27% of those spouses who have or have not considered divorce (Table A2.7). These items are less sensitive in discriminating those who had considered divorce, correctly classifying 64.52%, and more able to correctly classify 90.07% of those who have not considered divorce.

Table A2.7 Logistic Regression Analysis in Discriminating Considered Divorce by DAS Items

		Predicted		
		Yes	No	Percent Correct
Observed:	Yes	40	22	64.52%
	No	14	127	90.07%
			Overall	82.27%

Variable	B	SE	Sig	Exp(B)
DAS 8	.5281	.2340	.0240	1.6957
DAS16	.9502	.2027	.0000	2.5863
DAS20	.4758	.1899	.0122	1.6094
DAS27	.3114	.1404	.0266	1.3653
Constant	-6.62421	.1026	.0000	

Reliability and Validity of ENRICH

One-way Analysis of Variance

Table A2.8   Individual Mean Scores on ENRICH Scales

	Adjusted Group (N =114)	Non-Adjusted Group (N =90)	F-Value
Idealistic Distortion	74.42	52.98	106.91 ***
Marital Satisfaction	59.67	33.38	150.88 ***
Personality Issues	40.45	20.30	74.12 ***
Communication	52.96	28.07	139.85 ***
Conflict Resolution	51.94	30.36	100.66 ***
Financial Management	61.94	38.04	41.17 ***
Leisure Activities	61.11	36.01	47.10 ***
Sexual Relationship	57.03	36.39	86.59 ***
Children & Parenting	63.21	42.89	28.01 ***
Family & Friends	48.23	27.17	55.06 ***
Equalitarian Roles	41.09	47.82	5.52 *
Ethical Orientation	61.58	38.29	114.54 ***
Marital Adaptability	59.69	57.66	0.74 ns
Marital Cohesion	56.4	33.95	77.73 ***

* p<.05 *** p<.001

Table A2.9   Positive Couple Agreement Mean Scores on ENRICH Scales

Scales	Adjusted couples N = 57	Non-adjusted couples N = 45	F value
Marital Satisfaction	57.4	16.0	85.41 ***
Personality Issues	22.8	6.2	32.00 ***
Communication	37.0	8.4	70.83 ***
Conflict Resolution	34.9	13.3	39.80 ***
Financial Management	50.9	25.8	32.76 ***
Leisure Activities	46,5	25.8	31.19 ***
Sexual Relations	58.8	27.3	48.08 ***
Children & Parenting	49.1	24.0	23.50 ***
Family & Friends	46.0	22.9	34.97 ***
Equalitarian Roles	70.9	60.0	11.60 **
Ethical Orientation	70.9	42.0	77.74 ***
Marital Adaptability	68.8	61.3	2.34 ns
Marital Cohesion	77.5	77.3	0.0034 ns

** p<.01 *** p<.001

The adaptability scale showed no significant difference between adjusted and non-adjusted groups for both the Individual Mean Scores (Table A2.8) and for the Positive Couple Agreement Scores (Table A2.9). The cohesion scale is significant at p<.001 according to individual mean scores but not for the two groups on PCA scores.

Table A2.10   Reliability (Cronbach Alpha) of ENRICH

	Hong Kong Study (N = 102 couples)	Olson's Study (N = 7261 couples)
Marital Satisfaction	.84	.86
Idealistic Distortion	.66	.83
Personality Issues	.76	.82
Communication	.72	.82
Conflict Management	.68	.84
Financial Management	.76	.82
Leisure Activities	.50	.72
Sexual Relationship	.75	.85
Children & Parenting	.76	.78
Family & Friends	.64	.79
Equalitarian Roles	.32	.68
Ethical Orientation	.67	.84

The reliability of the ENRICH scales applied to the Hong Kong sample using Cronbach coefficient alpha is generally lower than for Olson's sample (Table A2.10). Leisure Activities with an alpha of .50 and Equalitarian Roles with an alpha of .32 show low internal consistency and require review of the appropriateness of some of the items for Hong Kong marriages.

The marital satisfaction scale reflects moderate to high correlation with most of the other ENRICH scales except equalitarian Roles and adaptability (Table A2.11). These two scales have the lowest correlation with the other scales. The highest correlation is between communication and conflict management scales.

Logistic regression carried out to determine the predictive capacity of the PCA scores indicates that two scales, communication and ethical orientation are able to predict 84.31% of an adjusted group membership (Table A2.12). Ethical orientation has also been identified as significant in predicting adjustment using individual scores, and as seen in the following table, is significant in discriminating spouses who have considered divorce.

Four scales — sexual relations, children and parenting, equalitarian roles and ethical orientation — can correctly predict 82.84% group membership of spouses who consider divorce (Table A2.13).

Table A2.11   Intercorrelation of ENRICH Scales

(N=204)

	MS	PI	CO	CR	FM	LA	SR	CP	FF	ER	EO	ADA	COH
MS	-	.56***	.76***	.68***	.53***	.51***	.68***	.57***	.58***	-.14	.64***	.10	.65***
PI		-	.67***	.67***	.42***	.48***	.51***	.28***	.54***	.04	.42***	.09	.38***
CO			-	.77***	.46***	.56***	.60***	.36***	.56***	-.14*	.53***	-.01	.64***
CR				-	.44***	.56***	.57***	.32***	.53***	-.04	.54***	.06	.52***
FM					-	.41***	.52***	.25***	.47***	.16*	.49***	.21**	.38***
LA						-	.45***	.25***	.51***	.002	.45***	.02	.49***
SR							-	.37***	.50***	-.04	.55***	.17*	.54***
CP								-	.37***	-.13	.36***	.04	.39
FF									-	-.04	.47***	.10	.51***
ER										-	-.01	.18*	-.17*
EO											-	.01	.49***
ADA												-	-.002
COH													-

* P <.05   ** P<.01   *** P<.001

MS	=	Marital Satisfaction
PI	=	Personality Issue
CO	=	Communication
CR	=	Conflict Resolution
FM	=	Financial Management
LA	=	Leisure Activities
SR	=	Sexual Relations
CP	=	Children & Parenting
FF	=	Family & Friends
ER	=	Equalitarian Roles
EO	=	Ethical Orientation
ADA	=	Adaptability
COH	=	Cohesion

Table A2.12   Logistic Regression Analysis in Discriminating Adjustment by ENRICH PCA Scores

	Predicted		
Observed	Adjusted group	Non-adjusted goup	Percent correct
Adjusted Group	48	9	84.21%
Non-Adj Group	7	38	84.44%
		Overall	84.31%

Variable	B	S.E.	Sig	Exp(B)
Communication	-.0881	.0246	.0003	.9157
Ethical Orient.	-.0714	.0203	.0004	.9311

Table A2.13   Logistic Regression Analysis for Discriminating Considered Divorce by ENRICH Scales

		Predicted			
		Yes	No		Percent Correct
Observed:	Yes	43	19		69.35%
	No	16	126		88.73%
				Overall	82.84%

Variable	B	S.E.	Sig.	Exp(B)
Sexual Relations	.0323	.0119	.0068	1.0238
Children/Parenting	.0162	.0071	.0226	1.0163
Equalitarian Roles	−.0196	.0092	.0326	.9806
Ethical Orientation	.0536	.0133	.0001	1.0551

The Reliability and Validity of the MCLI Package of Scales

Table A2.14   Oneway Analysis of Variance of the MCLI Package-Scores on Expectations, Equity, Commitment, and Barriers to Dissolution Scales

Scale	Adjusted spouses (N = 114)		Non-adjusted spouses (N = 82)		F Value
MCLI –	Mean	% Score	Mean	% Score	
Expectation	70.9	(70.9%)	54.0	(54%)	112.85 ***
Equity	38.3	(76.6%)	31.5	(63%)	82.42 ***
Commitment	24.1	(80%)	20.46	(68.3%)	76.28 ***
Barriers	20	(66.7%)	19.1	(63.3%)	4.05 *

* p<.05 *** p<.001

All the four scales are able to differentiate between adjusted and non-adjusted groups, though the barriers scale has a lower significance (Table A2.14).

Table A2.15   Reliability (Cronbach Alpha) of MCLI Equity,Commitment,Barriers Scales

		Hong Kong Sample (N = 204)	Sabatelli's Sample (N = 301)
MCLI –	Expectations	.95	.93
	Equity	.75	.85
	Commitment	.67	.82
	Barriers	.33	.74

The coefficient alpha of the equity and the commitment scales in the Hong Kong Marital Study are not as high as in Sabatelli's study (Table A2.15). However, the alpha of the expectation scale is higher, while that of the barriers scale is unacceptably lower.

Table A2.16   Intercorrelation of MCLI Package Scales

		Equity	Commitment	Barriers
MCLI -	Expectation	.78	.74	.62
	Equity		.84	.61
	Commitment			.66

p<.001 on all scales

The correlation between the commitment and the equity scales is very high, indicating some overlap between these two scales (Table A2.16).

Table A2.17   Logistic Regression Analysis in Discriminating Adjustment by MCLI Package Items

		Predicted		
		Adjusted Group	Non-Adjusted Group	
				Percent Correct
Observed:	Adjusted Group	99	14	87.61%
	Non-Adj. Group	12	70	85.37%
			Overall	86.67%

Variable	B	S.E.	Sig	Exp(B)
MAEXP6	-1.2568	.4023	.0018	.2846
MAEXP11	.6897	.3130	.0276	1.9932
MAEXP12	-1.0745	.2947	.0003	.3415
MAEXP15	.9322	.3350	.0054	.3937
MAEQU6	-.6948	.2653	.0088	.4992
MAEQU8	-1.1131	.3096	.0003	.3285
MACOM2	-1.0033	.3127	.0013	.3667
MACOM4	-.9488	.3249	.0035	.3872
Constant	20.2556	2.9983	.0000	

Discriminant analysis through logistic regression of the 42 items in the MCLI package identified eight items as significant in discriminating adjusted or non-adjusted groups. These items correctly classified 86.67% of adjusted membership (Table A2.17).

Table A2.18   Logistic Regression Analysis in Discriminating Considered Divorce by Items from the MCLI Package

		Predicted			
		Yes	No		Percent Correct
Observed:	Yes	36	21		63.16%
	No	14	124		89.86%
				Overall	82.05%

Variable	B	S.E.	Sig	Exp(B)
MAEXP4	1.0476	.2525	.0000	2.8509
MAEQU4	.0217	.2263	.0003	2.2744
MACOM3	.6397	.2266	.0048	1.8960
MASTE3	.5358	.1901	.0048	1.7088
MASTE6	−.3860	.1928	.0453	.6798
Constant	−7.9549	1.6175	.0000	

Of the 42 items from the MCLI package, five were significant predictors of instability, being able to discriminate 82.05% of spouses who had considered divorce (Table A2.18). As with the DAS items, and the ENRICH scales, the MCLI package items are more sensitive in discriminating spouses who had not considered divorce.

Statistical Tests Applied in the Study

Reliability of a scale refers to its consistency of performance internally, item by item, which should not fluctuate as a result of random error or chance factors. Reliabilities above .60 are acceptable.

ANOVA is a short term for analysis of variance, a test which assesses significant differences when more than one comparison is made. Variance is the sum of standard deviation squared and provides information on the spread of the scores. The F test compares the spread of different distributions (for example adjusted and non-adjusted spouses) to determine whether the two differ significantly on particular variables.

Correlation matrix measures specifically the extend of association between variables. The DAS subscale affectional expression correlates with consensus subscale at .69 p<.001. Thus scores from affectional expression is able to explain consensus at .69 squared = 48%. Significance at p<.001 indicate that the role of chance factors is one in a thousand.

Regressive equation estimates or predicts the score on a variable from, a known score of another variable. Logistic regression analysis demonstrate the extent scores on a particular item, or subscale or scale can estimate or predict the group membership of spouses who are adjusted or who have considered divorce.

Thus in Table A2.4, the three DAS subscales — consensus, cohesion and satisfaction — are able to correctly classify 107, and misclassify 7 of the adjusted spouses, and correctly classify 83, and misclassify 7 of the non-adjusted spouses. The overall percentage of spouses correctly classified is 93.14%.

Chi-square (χ^2) is a measure of differences in frequency or association. The higher the value of χ^2, the more likely the distribution differs.

The degree of freedom, df, indicates the number of cells free to vary in frequency.

Factor analysis clusters items with certain properties (i.e. homogeneity) into factor groups which reflects particular constructs. Factor loading denotes the correlation between the item and the construct. The higher the factor loading, the higher its power to explain that construct.

Variance indicates the percentage the total variance (total individual differences) explained by the factors extracted.

The Marital Relationship Index — MRI

丈夫/妻子

No: _____

婚姻關係問卷

這婚姻關係指標是特地為了幫助你檢討你婚姻中一些環節而設計。
按你的看法去回答全部問題:

Ｉ． 婚姻滿意程度

您對您的婚姻滿意程度?

您認為您的配偶對您們的婚姻的滿意程度?

極為滿意	⑤⑤
很滿意	④④
滿意	③③
有些不滿意	②②
不滿意	①①

ＩＩ． 婚姻適應

您與配偶對以下事情之一致性:-

	非常同意	同意	有時同不意/	不同意	非常不同意
1. 家庭財政處理	□	□	□	□	□
2. 人生哲學	□	□	□	□	□
3. 閒暇消遣方式	□	□	□	□	□

	很多時	有時	間中	很少	從不
4. 考慮或討論分居/結束關係	□	□	□	□	□
5. 配偶在打架/爭吵後離家而去	□	□	□	□	□
6. 您可有後悔結婚/同居	□	□	□	□	□
7. 一起歡笑	□	□	□	□	□
8. 一起冷靜地討論問題	□	□	□	□	□
9. 共同合作進行一些事情/計劃	□	□	□	□	□

10. 你對現有婚姻關係的看法:

很不快樂	少許不快樂	快樂	很快樂	極快樂
□	□	□	□	□

III. 婚姻期望

請列出你對婚姻所感受與及期望的差距

若以[0]代表你對婚姻的感受及期望相同，請以(更好)；+(好)；或-(差)；--(更差)
來表示閣下現在的婚姻關係:-

與期望差距

	更好 ++	好 +	等同 0	差 -	更差 --
1. 從配偶身上感受的投入程度	☐	☐	☐	☐	☐
2. 夫妻共處的時間	☐	☐	☐	☐	☐
3. 性生活	☐	☐	☐	☐	☐
4. 夫妻間的信賴程度	☐	☐	☐	☐	☐

IV. 互倚性量表

請表示你贊成下列各句子的程度:

	非常同意	同意	有時同意/有時不同意	不同意	非常不同意
1. 我對配偶非常忠誠	☐	☐	☐	☐	☐
2. 我能夠容忍配偶一些令我不悅的行為	☐	☐	☐	☐	☐
3. 我的配偶看來不如我那般對我們的關係感興趣	☐	☐	☐	☐	☐
4. 我與配偶同等倚靠對方	☐	☐	☐	☐	☐
5. 完全委身給一個人必然是一件非常沈悶的事	☐	☐	☐	☐	☐
6. 我時常感到配偶利用我	☐	☐	☐	☐	☐
7. 為一個決定而爭辯時，我們通常都能達致一個合理的解決方法	☐	☐	☐	☐	☐
8. 若要重新開始，我大概會娶/嫁給另外一個人	☐	☐	☐	☐	☐
9. 在我們的關係中，有時我會有被欺騙的感覺	☐	☐	☐	☐	☐
10. 在我們的關係中，我與配偶享有同樣的權力	☐	☐	☐	☐	☐
11. 我不介意我付出的比配偶多	☐	☐	☐	☐	☐
12. 我常感到被配偶操縱	☐	☐	☐	☐	☐
13. 詳細考慮後，我與配偶對我們的關係都作出同等頁獻	☐	☐	☐	☐	☐
14. 我很有信心我與配偶會為對方作出犧牲	☐	☐	☐	☐	☐
15. 我覺得配偶比我更為有力	☐	☐	☐	☐	☐
16. 在我們的關係中，我常感到我的付出比我接受的為多	☐	☐	☐	☐	☐

The Marital Relationship Index

I. Marital Satisfaction — Adopted from ENRICH

How satisfied are you with your   How satisfied do you think your
marriage?   partner is with your marriage?

[ ]	[ ]	Extremely satisfied
[ ]	[ ]	Very satisfied
[ ]	[ ]	Satisfied
[ ]	[ ]	Somewhat dissatisfied
[ ]	[ ]	Dissatisfied

II. Marital Adjustment — Adopted from DAS

How often do you and your partner agree on:

	Always Agree [ ]	Almost Always Agree [ ]	Occasion-ally Disagree [ ]	Frequently Disagree [ ]	Almost Always Disagree [ ]
1. Handling family finances.					
2. Philosophy of life.					
3. Leisure time interests & activities					

	All the Time [ ]	Most of the Time [ ]	More Often than Not [ ]	Occassion-ally [ ]	Never [ ]
4. How often do you discuss or considered separation/terminating your relationship?					
5. How often do you or your partner leave the house after a fight?					
6. Do you ever regret that you married?					

How often would this occur between you and your partner.

	Never	Less than Once a Month	Once or Twice a Month	Once a Week	Once a Day
7. Laugh together.					
8. Calmly discuss something.					
9. Work together on a project.					

10. Please indicate the degree of happiness, all things considered, in your relationship:

Extremely Happy	Very Happy	Happy	Fairly Unhappy	Extremely Unhappy

III. Marital Expectations — Adopted from MCLI Package

Please indicate how your current experience in your marriage compare with your expectations, in the following aspects:-

	Much Better than	Better than	About as Expected	Worse than	Much Worse than
1. The commitment of your spouse.					
2. The time you spend together.					
3. The amount of sexual activities.					
4. The amount of confiding between you.					

IV. Interdependence Orientation Scale

	Strongly Agree	Agree	Sometimes Agree	Disagree	Strongly Disagree
1. I feel very loyal to my partner.					
2. Though I do not like some of my partner's behaviours I can live with them.					
3. My partner seems less interested in our relationship than I.					
4. My partner and I are equally dependent upon one another.					
5. It must be boring to be committed to one person.					
6. I often feel taken advantage of by my partner.					
7. When we argue about a decision, we usually reach a fair solution.					
8. If I had to do it all over again, I would probably marry someone else.					
9. There are times in our relationship when I feel cheated.					
10. My partner and I usually share power in our relationship.					
11. It does not matter that I do more for my partner than he/she does for me.					
12. I often feel manipulated by my partner.					

	Strongly Agree	Agree	Sometimes Agree	Disagree	Strongly Disagree
13. All things considered, my partner and I contribute equally to our relationship.					
14. I am confident my partner will sacrifice for me.					
15. I feel less powerful than my spouse.					
16. I often feel I put in more into our relationship than I get out.					

Bibliography

(Abbreviation: *JMF* stands for *Journal of Marriage and the Family.*)

Anderson S., Russell C.S. and Schuum W.R. (1983) Perceived quality and family life cycle categories: a further analysis. *JMF* 45:127–139.

Argyle M. and Furnham A. (1983) Source of satisfaction and conflict in long-term relationships. *JMF* 45:481–493.

Association for the Advancement of Feminism (1993) *The Hong Kong Women's File.*

Barker R. (1988) *Treating couples in crisis.* Free Press.

Baucom D.H. and Epstein N. (1990) *Cognitive-behavioral marital therapy.* Brunner/Mazel.

Beavers W.R. and Voeller M.N. (1984) Family Models. Comparing and contrasting the Olson Circumplex Model and the Beavers System Model. In D. Olson and B. Miller (Eds) *Families studies review yearbook.*

Berado F. (1990) Trends and directions in family research in the 1980's. *JMF* 52:809–817.

Bernard J. (1982) *The future of marriage.* (Rev. Ed) Yale University Press.

Birchler G.R., Weiss R.L. and Vincent J.P. (1975) Multimethod analysis of social reinforcement exchange between maritally distressed & non-distressed spouse & stranger dyads. *Journal of Personality & Social Psychology* 31:349–366.

Blau P.M. (1964) *Exchange and power in social life.* Wiley.

Bloom B.L., Asher L. and White S.W. (1978) Marital disruption as stressor: a review and analysis. *Psychological Bulletin* 85(4):867–894.

Booth A. and Edwards J. (1987) Marital instability scale. 155–157. In N. Fredman and R. Sherman, *Handbook of measurement for marriage and family therapy.* New York: Brunner-Mazel.

Boszormeny-Nagy I. and Spark G.M. (1984) *Invisible loyalities. Reciprocity in intergenerational family therapy*. New York: Brunner-Mazel. p 83, p 97

Bott E. (1974) *Family & social network*. 5th Ed. Tavistock.

Bowen M. (1978) *Family therapy in clinical practice*. Aronson.

Bowman M.L. (1990) Coping efforts and marital satisfaction: measuring marital coping and its correlates. *JMF* 52:463–474.

Braiken H.B. and Kelley H.H. (1979) Conflict in the development of close relationships. In R.L. Burgess and T.L. Huston (Eds) *Social exchange in developing relationships*. Academic Press.

Buckley W. (1967) *Sociology and modern systems theory*. Prentice Hall.

Burgess E.W., Locke H.J. and Thomes M. (1971) 4th Edition. *The family: from traditional to companionship*. Van Nostrand Reinhold.

Burns T. (1973) A structural theory of social exchange. *Acta Sociologica*. 16(3):188–208.

Cancian F. (1986) The feminization of love. *Signs* 11:692–708.

Carter E. and McGoldrick M. (1980) Eds. *The family life cycle. A framework for family therapy*. Gardner.

Casas J.M. and Ortiz S. (1985) Exploring the applicability of the DAS for assessing levels of marital adjustment in Mexican Americans. *JMF* 47:1023–1027.

Caspi A. and Elder G.H. (1988) Emergent family patterns; The intergenerational construction of problem behaviour and relationships. In R.A. Hinde and J. Stevenson-Hinde (Eds) *Relationships within families*. Oxford: Oxford Science Publications.

Chadwick-Jones J.K. (1976) *Social exchange theory*. Academic Press.

Chaney D. and Podmore D. (1973) *Young adults in Hong Kong: Attitudes in a modernizing society*. University of Hong Kong, Centre of Asian Studies.

Chu Mai Lee Christine (1992) Mother-in-law and daughter-in-law relationships. MSW dissertation, University of Hong Kong.

Cook K.S. and Emerson R.A. (1978) Power, equity and commitment in exchange networks *American Sociological Review* 43(5):721–739.

Crowe M, Ridley J. (1990) *Therapy with couples*. Oxford: Blackwell Scientific Publications.

Cuber J.F. and Harroff P.B. (1974) Five kinds of relationships. In M.B. Sussman (Ed) *Sourcebook of marriage and the family*. 4th Edition. Boston: Houghton Mifflin Company.

Davidson B., Balswick J. and Halverson C. (1983) Affective self-disclosure & marital adjustment. A test of equity theory. *JMF* 45:93–102.

Deutsch M. (1980) Fifty years of conflict. In L. Festinger (Ed) *Four decades of social psychology*. New York: Oxford University Press.

Deutsch M. (1973) *The resolution of conflict*. Yale University Press.

Deutsch M. (1949) An experimental study of the effects of cooperation and competion upon group process. *Human Relations* 2: 199–231.

Duck S. (1988) *Relating to others.* Open University Press.

Duvall E.M. (1977) *Family development.* 5th Edn. Lippincourt.

Epstein N.B., Bishop D.S. and Baldwin L.M. (1984) McMaster model of family functioning. In D.Olson and B. Miller (Eds) *Family studies review yearbook.*

Falicov C.J. (1988) Ed. *Family transitions. Continuity and change over the life cycle.* Guilford.

Filsinger E., McAvoy P. and Lewis R.A. (1984) Empirical typology of dyadic formation. In D.H. Olson and B.C Miller (Eds.) *Family Studies Review Yearbook.* V.2. Sage.

Fincham F. and Bradbury T.N. (1987) The assessment of marital quality. *JMF* 49:797–809.

Fine S (1974) Troubled families. Parameters for diagnosis and strategies for change. *Comprehensive Psychiatry* 15:73–77.

Fisher L. (1976) Dimensions of family assessment. A critical review. *Journal of Marriage & Family Counselling* (2–4):376–382.

Fitzpatrick M.A. (1988) *Between husbands and wives. Communication in marriage.* Sage.

Floyd F.J. and Markman H.J. (1983) Observational biases in spouse observation: towards a cognitive-behavioral model of marriage. *Journal of Consulting & Clinical Psychology* 51(3):450–457.

Fournier D.G., Olson D.H., Druckman J.M. (1983) Assessing marital and premarital relationships: The PREPARE — ENRICH Inventories. In E.E. Filsinger (Ed) *Marriage & family assessment.* C.A.: Sage.

Fowers B.J. and Olson D.H. (1989) *ENRICH* Marital Inventory: a discriminant validity and cross-validation assessment. *Journal of Marriage and Family Therapy* 15:65–79.

Fredman N. and Sherman R. (1987) *Handbook of measurements to marriage and family therapy.* Brunner-Mazel

Galligan R.J. (1982) Innovative techniques: siren or rose. *JMF* 44: 875–886.

Gilford R. and Bengston V.L. (1979) Measuring marital satisfaction in three generations: positive and negative dimensions. *JMF* 41: 387–398.

Glenn N.D. (1990) Quantitative research on marital quality in the 1980's. A critical review. *JMF* 52:818–831.

Glenn N.D. and Weaver C.N. (1981) The contribution of marital happiness to global happiness. *JMF* 43:161–168.

Glick P.L. (1977) Updating the life cycle of the family. *JMF* 39:5–13.

Goode W.J (1963) *World revolution and family patterns.* Free Press.

Gouldner A.V. (1960) The norm of reciprocity: a preliminary statement. *American Sociological Review* 25:161–178.

Guerin P. (1987) *The evaluation and treatment of marital conflict.* Basic Books.

Gurman A.S. (1978) Contemporary marital therapies: A criticque and comparative analysis of psychoanalytic, behavioral and system theory approaches. In T. Paolino and B. McCrady (Eds) *Marriage and marital therapy.* New York: Brunner/Mazel.

Haley J. (1963) Marriage therapy. *Archives of General Psychiatry* 8:213–234.

Hamilton G.A. (1929) *Research in marriage.* New York: Boni.

Harvey J.H., Christensen A. and McClintock E. (1983) Research methods. In H.H. Kelley, E. Bershceid, A. Christensen, J.H. Harvey, T.L. Huston, G. Levinger, E. McClintock, L.A. Peplau and D.R. Peterson. *Close relationships.* W.H. Freeman.

Hazan C. and Shaver P. (1987) Romantic love conceptualized as an attachment process. *Journal of Personality and Social Psychology.* 52(3):511–524.

Hennon C.B. and Arcus M. (1993) Life-Span Family Life Education. In T. Brubaker (Ed) *Family relations. Challenges for the future.* Sage.

Hicks M. and Platt M. (1970) Marital happiness and stability: a review of the research in the sixties. *JMF* 32:553–574.

Hinde R. (1979) *Understanding relationships.* Academic Press.

Hill R. and Rogers R. (1964) The developmental approach. In Christensen H. (Ed) *Handbook of marriage and the family.* Rand McNally.

Homans G.C. (1974) *Social behaviour: its elementary forms.* Harcourt, Brace Jovanorich.

Hong Kong Boys and Girls Club Association (1984) *Fatherhood in Hong Kong.*

Hong Kong Council of Social Services (1991) *Clientele information system for family counselling and casework services, 1988–1990.* Unpublished Report.

Hong Kong Census & Statistical Department (1993) *Social and Economic Trends 1982–1992.* Hong Kong Government.

Hong Kong Census & Statistical Department (1991) *Population Census, Summary Results.* Hong Kong Government.

Hong Kong Government (1992) *Annual Report.*

Hong Kong Social Welfare Department (1990–91) *Annual Report.* Hong Kong Government.

Hong Kong Young Women Christian Association (1982) *Report on working mothers in family functioning.*

Horowitz I.L. (1967) Consensus, conflict and cooperation. In N.J. Demerath and R.A. Peterson (Eds) *Systems, change and conflict.* Free Press.

Hsu F.L.K. (1965) The effect of dominant kinship relationships on kin and non-kin beliefs: an hypothesis. *American Anthropologist* 67(3):638–661.

Huston T.L. and Robins E. (1982) Conceptual and methodological issues in studying close relationships. *JMF* 44:901–925.

Irving H. and Benjamin M. (1987) *Family mediation. Theory and practice of dispute resolution.* Carswell.

Jacobson N. and Margolin G. (1979) *Marital therapy. Strategies based on social learning and behaviour exchange principles.* Brunner-Mazel.

Johnson M.P. (1982) S*ocial and cognitive features of the dissolution of commitment to relationships* In S.W. Duck (Ed) *Personal relationships. 4 Dissolving personal relationships.* Academic Press.

Johnson S. (1986) Bonds or bargains: relationship paradigms and their significance for marital therapy. *Journal of Marriage and Family Therapy* 12(3):259–267.

Kelley H.H. (1983) Love and commitment. In H.H. Kelley, R. Berscheid, A. Christensen, J.H. Harvey, T.L. Huston, G. Levinger, D. McClintock, L.A. Pepau and D.R. Peterson (Eds) *Close relationships.* W.H. Freeman

Kelley H.H., Berscheid R., Christensen A., Harvey J.H., Huston T.L., Levinger G., McClintock D., Pepau L.A. and Peterson D.R. (1983) Analysing close relationships. In H.H. Kelley et al (Eds) Close *relatipnships.* W.H. Freeman.

Kelley H.H. and Thibaut J.W. (1978) *Interpersonal relations: a theory of interdependence.* Wiley-Interscience.

Knox A.B. (1977) *Adult development and learning.* Jossey-Bass.

Kulka R.A. and Weingarten H. (1979) The long-term effects of parental divorce in childhood on adult adjustment. *Journal of Social Issues* 35(4):50–78.

L'Abate L. and Talmadge W. (1987) Love, intimacy and sex. In G. Weeks and L. Hof (Eds) *Integrating sex and marital therapy: a clinical guide.* Brunner-Mazel.

Lam Chan Wai Kuen, Catherine (1992) *Child rearing in three-generation families.* MSW dissertation, University of Hong Kong.

Lau S.K. and Wan P.S. (1987) *Research on social indicators in Hong Kong. A preliminary report.* Social Research Centre, The Chinese University of Hong Kong [in Chinese].

Lau S.K. (1981) Chinese familism in an urban-industrial setting: the case of Hong Kong. *JMF* 43:977–992.

Laurence L. (1982) *Couple constancy. Conversations with to-day's happily married people.* UMI Research Press.

Lederer W.J. and Jackson D.D. (1968) *The mirages of marriage.* Norton.

Lee, M.K. (1992) Family and gender issues. In S.K. Lau et. al. (Eds) *Indicators of Social Development: Hong Kong 1990.* Hong Kong: Hong Kong Institute of Asia-Pacific Studies, the Chinese University of Hong Kong.

Lee, M.K. (1991) Family and social life. In S.K. Lau et. al. (Eds) *Indicators of Social Development: Hong Kong 1988.* Hong Kong: Hong Kong Institute of Asia-Pacific Studies, Chinese University of Hong Kong.

Levinger G. (1974) A three level approach to attraction: Towards an understanding of pair relatedness. In T.L. Huston (Ed) *Foundations of interpersonal attraction.* Academic Press.

Levinger G. (1965) Marital cohesiveness and dissolution. An integrative view. *JMF* 27:19–28.

Lewis R.A. and Spanier G.B. (1979) Theorizing about the quality and stability of marriage. In I. Burr, R. Hill, I. Nye and I. Reiss (Eds) *Contemporary theories about the family*. Free Press.

Liberman R.P. (1970) Behavioral approaches to family and couple therapy. *American Journal of Orthopsychiatry* 40:106–118.

Locke H.J. and Wallace K.M. (1959) Short marital-adjustment tests: their reliability and validity. *Marriage and Family Living* 21:251–255.

Luckey E.B. and Bain J.K. (1970) Children: a factor in marital satisfaction. *JMF* 32:43–44.

Madanes C. (1981) *Strategic family therapy*. Jossey-Bass.

McDonald G.W. (1981) Structural exchange and marital interaction. *JMF* 43:825–839.

Mattessich P. and Hill R. (1988) Life cycle and family development. In H.B. Sussman and S.K. Steinmetz (Eds) *Handbook of marriage and the family*. Plenum Press.

Meissner W.W. (1978) The conceptualization of marriage and family dynamics from a psychoanalytic perspective. In T. Paolino and B. McCrady (Eds) *Marriage and marital therapy*. New York: Brunner/Mazel.

Miller B.C. (1976) A multivariate developmental model of marital satisfaction. *JMF* 39:653–657.

Miller R.S. and Lefcourt H.M. (1982) The assessment of social intimacy. *Journal of Personality Assessment* 46:514–518.

Minuchin S. (1979) Families and family therapy. London: Tavistock Publications.

Mitchell R.E. (1972) *Family life in Hong Kong. Vols.I & II*. Orient Cultural Service.

Morton T. (1978) Intimacy and reciprocity of exchange. A comparison of spouses and strangers. *Journal of Personality and Social Psychology* 36:72–81.

Mueller C.W. and Pope H. (1977) Marital instability: a study of its transmission between generations. *JMF* 39:83–93.

Murstein B.I. and MacDonald M.G. (1983) The relationship of exchange orientation and commitment scales to marital adjustment. *International Journal of Psychology*. 18:297–311.

Murstein B., Cerreto M. and MacDonald M.G. (1977) A theory and investigation of the effect of exchange orientation on marriage and friendship. *JMF* 39:543–548.

Nadelson C.C. (1978) Marital therapy from the psychoanalytic perspective. In T. Paolino and B. McCrady (Eds) *Marriage and marital therapy*. New York: Brunner/Mazel.

Nock S. (1979) Family Life Cycle. Empirical or Conceptual Tool. *JMF* 41:15–26.

Norton R. (1983) Measuring marital quality. A critical look at the dependent variable. *JMF* 45:141–152.

Nye F.I. (1982) The basic theory. In F.I. Nye (Ed) *Family relationships. Rewards and costs.* Sage.

Olson D.H., Fournier D.G. and Druckman J.M. (1987) *PREPARE/ENRICH counsellor's manual.* (Rev Ed) PREPARE-ENRICH Inc.

Olson D.H., McCubbin H., Barnes A., Larsen A., Muxen M. and Wilson M. (1983) *Families: what makes them work.* Sage.

Olson D.H. (1977) Insider's and outsider's views of relationships. In G. Levinger and H.L. Raush (Eds) *Close relationships, perspectives on the meaning of intimacy.* University of Massachusetts Press.

Parkinson A. (1991) Marital and extramarital sexuality. 65–96. In S.J. Bahr (Ed) *Family research. A sixty year review, 1930–1990.* Lexington Books.

Peterson J.L. and Zill N. (1986) Marital disruption, parent child relationships and behavior problems in children. *JMF* 48:295–307.

Pope H. and Mueller C.W. (1976) The intergenerational transmission of marital instability: comparisons by race and sex. *Journal of Social Issues* 32(1):49–66.

Prosky P.P. and Prosky P. (1980) Thoughts on family life: a developmental model of intimate relationships. Parts 1 & 2. *Social Worker* 48:1–2

Pun Wai Yi, Helena (1992) Aging mother-adult daughter relationships. MSW dissertation, University of Hong Kong.

Reischauer E.O. and Fairbank J.K. (1958) *East Asia: the great tradition.* Houghton Mifflin.

Rodgers R.H. (1973) *Family interaction and transaction. A development approach.* Prentice-Hall.

Rodman H. (1972) Marital power and the theory of resource in cultural context. *Journal of Comparative Family Studies* 3:50–69.

Rollins B. and Galligan R. (1978) The developing child and marital satisfaction of parents. In R.K. Lerner and G.B. Spanier (Eds) *Child influences on marital and family interaction.* Academic Press.

Rollins B. and Cannon D. (1974) Marital satisfaction over the family life cycle: a re-evaluation. *JMF* 36:20–28.

Rollins B. and Feldman H. (1970) Marital satisfaction over the family life cycle. *JMF* 32:30–38.

Rosen S. (1976) *Mei Foo Sun Chuen: middle-class Chinese families in transition.* Orient Cultural Service.

Rosenblatt P.C. (1977) Needed research on commitment in marriage. In G. Levinger and H.L. Raush (Eds) *Close relationships: perspectives on the meaning of intimacy.* University of Massachusetts Press.

Rusbult C.E. (1980) Commitment and satisfaction in romantic association: a test of the investment model. *Journal of Experimental and Social Psychology* 16:172–186.

Rutter M. (1988) Functions and consequences of relationships; Some psychopathological considerations. In R.A. Hinde and J. Stevenson-Hinde (Eds) *Relationships within families*. Oxford; Oxford Science Publications.

Sabatelli R.M. (1988) Measurement issues in marital research: a review and critique of contemporary survey instruments. *JMF* 50:891–915.

Sabatelli R.M. (1984) The Marital Comparison Level Index: a measure for assessing outcomes relative to expectations. *JMF* 46:651–661.

Sabatelli R.M. and Cecil-Pigo E.F. (1985) Relational interdependence and commitment in marriage. *JMF* 47:931–937.

Sabournin S., Laporte L. and Wright J. (1990) Problem solving self-appraisal and coping efforts in distressed and non-distressed couples *Journal of Marital and Family Therapy* 16(1):89–97.

Sager C.J. (1977) A typology of intimate relationships. *Journal of Sex & Marital Therapy* 3:83–112.

Salaff J. (1976) Working daughters in the Hong Kong Chinese family. *JMF* 38:439–465.

Scanzoni J. (1979) Social exchange and behavioral interdependence. In T. Huston and R. Burgess (Eds) *Social exchange in developing relationships*. Academic Press.

Schram R.W. (1979) Marital satisfaction over the family life cycle: a critique and proposal. *JMF* 41:7–12.

Schumm W.R. and Bugaighis (1986) Marital quality over the marital career: alternative explanations. *JMF* 48:165–168.

Schwartz R. and Breulin O. (1983) Why clinicians should bother with research. *The Family Therapy Networker* 7(4):22–27.

Skinner R. (1976) *One flesh, separate persons*. London: Constable.

Sharpley C.F. and Cross D.G. (1982) A psychometric evaluation of the Spanier Dyadic Adjustment Scale. *JMF* 44:739–742.

Spanier G.B. (1988) Assessing the strengths of the Dyadic Adjustment Scale. *Journal of Family Psychology* 2 (1) 92–94.

Spanier G.B. and Thompson L. (1982) A confirmatory analysis of the Dyadic Adjustment Scales. *JMF* 44:731–738.

Spanier G.B. and Lewis R.A. (1980) Marital quality: a review of the seventies. *JMF* 42:825–839.

Spanier G.B. (1976) Measuring dyadic adjustment. New scales for assessing the quality of marriage and similar dyads. *JMF* 38: 15–28.

Spanier G.B. and Cole C.L. (1976) Towards clarification and investigation of marital adjustment. *International Journal of Sociology of the Family* 6:121–146.

Spanier G.B., Lewis R.A. and Cole C.L. (1975) Marital adjustment over the family life cycle. The issue of curvilinearity. *JMF* 37:263–275.

Strachan I. (1993) Strachan' family action plan. *Hong Kong South China Morning Post*. 21 May.

Strauss M.A. (1979) Measuring intrafamily conflict and violence. The conflect tacts (CT) scales. *JMF* 41 : 75–85.

Stuart R.B. (1980) *Helping couples change.* Guilford.

Sussman M.B. (1965) Relationship of adult children with their parents. In E. Shanas and G. Streib (Eds) *Social structure and family generational relations.* Prentice-Hall.

Swenson C. and Trahaug G. (1985) Commitment and long-term marriage relationships *JMF* 47:939–945.

Synder D.K. and Smith G.T. (1986) Classification of marital relationships: an empirical approach. *JMF* 48:137–146.

Synder D.K. (1979) Multidimensional assessment of marital satisfaction. *JMF* 41:813–823.

Taylor R.M. and Morrison L.P., (1984) *Taylor-Johnson Temperament Analysis Manual.* Psychological Publication Inc.

Terman L. (1938) *Psychological factors in marital happiness.* New York: McGraw-Hill.

Thibaut J.W. and Kelley H.H. (1959) *The social psychology of groups.* Wiley.

Thompson L. and Walker A.J. (1989) Gender in families. women and men in marriage, work and parenthood. *JMF* 51:845–872.

Thompson L. and Walker A.J. (1982) The dyad as the unit of analysis: conceptual and methodological issues. *JMF* 44:889–900.

Turner R. (1970) *Family interaction.* Wiley.

Wallerstein J.S. (1988) Children of divorce: a ten year study. In E.M. Hetherington and J. Arasteh (Eds) *The impact of divorce, single parenting and step-parenting on children.* Hillsdale, NJ: Erlbaum.

Ward J.H. (1963) Hierarchial groupings to optimize an objective function. *Journal of the Statistical Association* 58:236–244.

Weeks G. and Hof L. (1989) *Integrating sexual and marital therapy.* Brunner-Mazel.

Weiss R.L. and Cerreto M.C. (1980) The marital status inventory. Development of a measure of dissolution potential. *American Journal of Family Therapy.* 8; 80–85.

Weiss R.L. (1978) The conceptualization of marriage from a behavioral perspective. In T. Paolino and B. McCrady (Eds) *Marriage and marital therapy.* New York: Brunner/Mazel.

Wills T.A., Weiss R.L. and Patterson G.R. (1974) A behavioral analysis of the determinants of marital satisfaction. *Journal of Consulting and Clinical Psychology* 42(6):802–811.

Wolf M. (1968) *The House of Lim.* Appleton Century Crofts.

Wong F.M. (1981) Effects of the employment of mothers on marital role and power differentiation in Hong Kong. In A.Y.C. King and R. Lee (Eds) *Social life and development in Hong Kong.* Hong Kong: Chinese University Press.

Wong F. M. (1972) Modern ideology, industrialization, and conjugalism: The case of Hong Kong. *International Journal of Sociology of the Family.* 2: 139–150.

Wynne L. (1988) An epigenetic model of family processes. In Falicov C. (Ed) *Family transitions.* Guilford.

Yogev S. and Brett J. (1985) Perceptions of the division of housework and child care and marital satisfaction. *JMF* 47:609–618.

Young K. (1993) Marriages under stress. *A report on marriage counselling cases at the Hong Kong Family Welfare Society and the Hong Kong Catholic Marriage Advisory Council.* Department of Social Work, University of Hong Kong. Resource Paper Series. No. 20.

Young K. (1985) *A report on single parent families in Hong Kong.* Department of Social Work, University of Hong Kong. Resource Paper Series. No. 9.

Author Index

Subject Index